A TREASURY OF HOME BUSINESS OPPORTUNITIES

by

Russ von Hoelscher

Published by

George Sterne
PROFIT IDEAS
8361 Vickers, Suite 304
San Diego, CA 92111

THE ENCYCLOPEDIA OF WEALTH BUILDING OPPORTUNITIES

MONEY MANUAL NO. 1—REAL ESTATE WEALTH BUILDING OPPORTUNITIES
How To Buy And Sell Real Estate
For Maximum Profits

MONEY MANUAL NO 2—INVESTMENT OPPORTUNITIES FOR THE 1980'S
Wealth Building Strategies In The Stock Market,
Gold, Silver, Diamonds...

MONEY MANUAL NO. 3—SECRETS OF THE MILLIONAIRES
How The Rich Made It Big

MONEY MANUAL NO. 4—THE DYNAMICS OF PERSONAL FINANCIAL PLANNING
How To Save, Invest, And Multiply Your Money.

MONEY MANUAL NO. 5—HOW TO START MAKING MONEY IN A BUSINESS OF YOUR OWN
A Guide To Money Making Opportunities

MONEY MANUAL NO. 6—A TREASURY OF HOME BUSINESS OPPORTUNITIES
How to Make Money Without Leaving Home.

MONEY MANUAL NO. 7—HOW TO ACHIEVE TOTAL SUCCESS
How To Use The Power Of Creative Thought

A TREASURY OF HOME BUSINESS OPPORTUNITIES
by Russ von Hoelscher
©1984 by George Sterne, PROFIT IDEAS

First Edition manufacturered in the United States of America.
For information write to: Profit Ideas, 8361 Vickers, Suite 304,
San Diego, California 92111
ISBN 0-940398-08-7

i

A TREASURY OF HOME BUSINESS OPPORTUNITIES

Section One—Home Business Opportunities

Section Two—Home Writing/Self-Publishing Opportunities

Section Three—Home Mailorder Opportunities

SECTION ONE
TABLE OF CONTENTS
A TREASURY OF HOME BUSINESS OPPORTUNITIES

iv

SECTION TWO
TABLE OF CONTENTS
SELLING WORDS
How to Make Money As A Writer And/Or Self-Publisher

SECTION THREE
TABLE OF CONTENTS
MAIL-ORDER OPPORTUNITIES

How To Stay Home And Make Money In the World's Most Popular And Exciting Home Business.

PREFACE: A TON OF OPPORTUNITY
FOR ANYONE WITH
AN OUNCE OF CREATIVITY

The best of times, the worst of times; a good description of economic conditions in America and most of the *Free World* during the mid-1980s.

For some the decade of the 80s has turned into a grim battle for financial survival. Recurring bouts with inflation and recession have taken their toll. Each recession is deeper and more painful and every new inflation spiral is wilder and more unpredictable. What can the average person do to reach financial freedom, or at least obtain and maintain a decent standard of living? In three words, *make more money!* Easier said than done? Perhaps, but there are many ways to dramatically increase your earning power today.

This book is about making money, substantial sums of money. It is filled with both new and proven ideas, plans, concepts and strategies to help you become wealthy, or at least comfortable.

It is unique because all the business, writing/publishing and mail order plans found within can be operated from your own home or apartment. No commercial office or retail space is required.

History does seem to be repeating itself. Although we have entered the hi-tech age of information and automation, we seem to be, at the moment, reverting back to a "cottage industry society" which was prominent over 100 years ago. Estimates vary, and exact data is not available but there are probably ten million people working in their homes in 1984. Some sources will put that number in the fifteen to twenty million range. The majority are part timers but the ranks of the full time entrepreneurs are rapidly increasing.

In addition to offering you a rich buffet of home money-making opportunities, I have included only those wealth-building opportunities that can be launched with little or no start-up capital. This is a book loaded with high profit plans that do not require huge investments.

If you have an ounce of creativity, and a pound of burning desire for success, you can still make a ton of money regardless of prevailing economic conditions. And this book will help!

A TREASURY OF
HOME BUSINESS OPPORTUNITIES

Can I make money without leaving my home...is it really possible? The answer is an unqualified YES! Within the pages of this remarkable book you are to discover hundreds of unique ways to earn a sparetime or full-time income within the walls of your own home or apartment.

Several hundreds of thousands of people are earning part or all of their income from home-based businesses and services and the number is rapidly expanding each year. Futurist Alvin Toffler, best selling author of "The Third wave" and "Future Shock" believes nearly half of all Americans will work at home by the year 2000. The trend is unquestionably pointing in that direction.

The advantages of making money while remaining at home are many-fold. Time and money are saved by not driving to and from work. There is no space that must be rented and no parking problems. Meals in your home will usually be both cheaper and better than restaurant dining. These and other considerations make home-based money-making activities very desirable.

The disadvantages to working at home seem to be limited, but there are a few. For example, some people have trouble "getting busy" at the task at hand. If you have always thought of your home as only a place of recreation and relaxation, you would need to overcome this perception in order to run productive in-house money-making activities. Another potential drawback is operating any business that requires a lot of face-to-face selling of goods or services, since some people have developed the idea that a conventional store or attractive business office is the best place to go to obtain merchandise and services.

Overall, I believe, in most cases, the advantages greatly outweigh the disadvantages, making the home a great place to do business in.

This book has been divided into three sections:

(1) A TREASURY OF HOME BUSINESS OPPORTUN-ITIES—A complete buffet of many different ways to stay home and make money.
(2) WRITING AND SELF-PUBLISHING OPPORTUN-ITIES—How to sell "Words" for rich profits. A great home-based moneymaking activity.
(3) MAIL ORDER OPPORTUNITIES—How to stay home and make money in the world's most popular home business.

In all three areas you'll find cottage industry plans that offer great potential to the enterprising individual, and require little investment. An excellent way to go into business for yourself! Why not go for it?!

HOME TYPING

While our *Treasury of Home Business Opportunities* is not listed in any specific order, I feel it is quite appropriate to kick-off this section with the most popular home business of them all—typing at home! Your only equipment and supplies are a good quality machine and a supply of paper and related accessories. Profits are not spectacular but they can be steady.

Home typing can include a huge assortment of typing-for-pay activities. Here we list a few of the more profitable plans:

(1) General Typing: This includes letters, forms and circulars for small businessmen, attorneys, etc. The market is any and all owners of small businesses, or professionals who either (a) do not have enough work for a full-time secretary or (b) have too much for their current secretary. To solicit business, small ads can be run in local newspapers, notices placed on bulletin boards in various retail stores and laundries, and/or circulars and flyers circulated to ALL (Remember: Almost any retail business or wholesale business or professional office is a potential customer) possible clients. Printing shops can be a great source of business.

(2) Resume Typing: This can be an ideal typing home business all by itself or combined with other typing activities. The job market has become more competitive during the early 1980s and those people seeking the better jobs must submit attractive resumes. If you're not familiar with resume layout and typing (clients will furnish details about their past education and employment history, but you will have to put things in order, layout each resume and type it in logical order),

1

there are several excellent books available at your local library. Business can be obtained from small ads in newspapers. Also, place ads in college papers and on campus bulletin boards. Prior to graduation, students can be an excellent source of business. Also, send details of your services to any professional organizations in your area. Professional people make more job changes than the average worker and have great need of professional resume services.

(3) Typing information for State, Federal and County Courts: All courts employ reporters who use shorthand (at speeds of 200+ words per minute) to record their proceedings. Once a shorthand record is made, these court recorders either type up this information themselves or dictate their notes into tapes and have someone else transcribe them.

Rates vary from city to city, state to state, but are usually in the 50¢ to 75¢ per page range.

How fast you type does not matter here (at least not to the courts since they are paying per page—not per hour) except to earn decent money ($600+ per month) you will need speed. What is critically important is accuracy and good vocabulary. Misspelled words or poor grammar are not tolerated here.

To obtain business, go to your local courthouses (city, county, state, and/or federal) and see as many court reporters as possible. You state's "Legal Directory," available at most libraries, can also be a rich source of contacts.

Although doing legal typing for lawyers is not exactly the

same as doing business with the courts, it can be a related source of extra profits. Attorney offices are a vast source of typing business.

The above forms of home typing represent only a tiny fraction of the huge volume of typing available. Just remember: Any type of business or profession is a potential customer. Another great thing about running a home typing business is you can get started very cheaply (less than one hundred dollars will rent a good typewriter and supplies), and you're able to work as few or as many hours per week as you choose. Of course, your profits will depend on how many hours you devote to your home business as well as how fast you can accurately type. Forty or fifty words per minute may be okay for starters, but to make your home business really profitable, you should raise your speed to eighty words per minute, or more.

Profit Range: Can range from $40 or $50 to $300 or more per week, depending on your ability to solicit business and put in the time to turn out the work. Again I say, not the best of the lot, but a popular business to start with.

HOTLINE: TELEPHONE PROFITS

Direct marketing (mail order, direct mail, direct response radio and television, etc.) is booming in America today. Americans always have loved to shop at home and the trend is increasing.

Although most folks still send in their orders or inquiries by mail, an increasing number of people are shopping by phone. We have all seen the TV commercials that tell you to call this 800 number to order your records, books, gadgets, or whatever! When you're in the order and inquiry taking phone business, it is your phone number flashing on the screen or being given by the announcer or appearing on printed matter.

This booming industry offers anyone a great home-operated business (although many of the larger firms do rent office space). Burgeoning entrepreneurs are making substantial profits. Start-up cost can be initially limited to the installation of two WATS lines from Ma Bell to handle calls from the state you live in and one to take calls from the rest of the nation.

AD CLIPPINGS

Here's an offshoot of the newspaper clipping service that you can operate with hometown merchants. Merchants need good new advertising and merchandising ideas for their stores, and it doesn't really matter what kind of business they are engaged in—cocktail lounge, furniture store, bookstore, jewelry store, etc.

Here's the plan: Your own Ad Clipping Bureau furnishes local merchants with ads used by merchants in similar trades.

Your source of supply is all available advertising—in papers, magazines, etc. You then separate them by type and bring or mail them to your subscribers.

Payment: You should receive at least $1 per ad you supply.

This can be a great little part time endeavor or the perfect complement to your news clipping activities.

IMPORTANT DATES

A housewife in Akron, Ohio, earns "an extra $40 to $45 per week" using this little number.

Half the population has poor memories when it comes to important dates in their lives (birthdays, anniversaries, engagements, etc.)

The plan is simple: A small classified ad in daily papers lets people know that for a small fee a postcard will remind them in advance (usually one week in advance) of important dates. A supply of postcards plus a handy file index plus a few dollars puts one in business.

Opinion: You won't get rich fast with this one but the small profits come pretty easy and you can "get into business" for $25 or less. A good tie-in with a telephone service.

FANCY WRITING FOR FANCY PROFITS

Mary Ellen Johnson of Milwaukee, Wisconsin, made over $50,000 last year doing ornate lettering for publishers, restaurant owners (menus), sales awards, educational diplomas, etc.—fifty grand a year with only a couple hundred dollars worth of supplies working out of her own home. Initially, she invested a little money in advertising. Now she has more business than she can handle via word-of-mouth. Over

90¢ on every dollar she earns is net before tax profit!

Originally a dental receptionist, Mary Ellen learned her craft during two years of both night school and private lesson calligraphy classes. Her advice to others interested in making money through ornate writing, "if you already write and print clearly, you can learn calligraphy." Old English is probably the most in-demand form of scribe writing. No, it is not simple, but it can be mastered.

At $50,000 per year, it is a skill worth looking into.

QUESTIONS AND ANSWERS BUREAU

We all seem to have questions that we would like answers to. Many of these questions require research that not everyone has time for, or at least, thinks he or she doesn't have time for. A Phoenix, Arizona student has turned people's quesons into super parttime profits. Ed placed an ad in both the daily paper and his college weekly, advertising that he would research questions at a rate of $2 per question and up. Response was greater than anticipated. Within a few weeks, profits of $200 to $250 were obtained on a sparetime basis!

Startup capital is practically nil ($20 or $50 to place a few small ads). Most research is done at the local public library, although Ed says he tries to check out reference material whenever possible so as to keep his business in his apartment. His claim of $10 (average) per hour of research makes this an attractive home enterprise.

CASH FOR CARTOONS

Even if you think you have no art calling or drawing ability, you still could learn this highly-specialized calling.

You don't have to have great artistic talent to learn cartooning. What is more important is a sense of humor and an outrageous outlook on life. Sure, the ability to draw a tree that looks like a tree (not a lollipop!) and your males and females should be distinguishable, but really, imagination and creativity are your greatest assets.

Leaf through current magazines and newspapers. Clip out all the cartoons you find (and you will find many). Decide (A) which type (political, social, slapstick, etc.) you like best or (B) which type you think you can do best.

The tools of the cartoon trade: Supplies include ordinary pencils, sketch pads (a good grade 20 to 25 pound with 20% rag content is desirable), some brushes, ink and a drawing table (these can be rather expensive, especially a "lighted table," but you could build your own). Lots of famous cartoonists, and many more not so famous, started out with only a breadboard or a simple chunk of plywood.

Desire: As is the case with the writer, you are not going to be a cartoonist unless you have a burning desire to do so.

Money to be Made: The real pros earn up to a thousand a week (many without leaving their home), but the vast majority of cartoonists do something else to earn their main income and delight in occasional sales to various print markets.

You should be able to find several good books on the subject at your local library.

SELL A CARTOON COURSE

Once you master the art of cartooning, or even if you never do, you can make money selling a cartooning course. Here's how Debbie of Dallas, Texas did it.

Debbie's friend Joel was a very talented artist who also was a first-class cartoonist (the two do not always go together). Joel in turn had a buddy, Rob, who could write well. The two fellows had talent but little promotional ability, and that's where Debbie made her mark. Debbie knew many people were interested in cartooning, so she formed a three-way partnership with Rob and Joel to put together a course.

Her plan involved putting together a 180-page course (oversized, 8½ x 11 format). Ads are placed in local newspapers and college newspapers. A 500 press run cost our trio $1,950 (or $650 each). Within 90 days they sold all 500 manuals (called "courses" for effect) at $24.95. That's $12,475 less $1,950 printing and $1,800 advertising, which left $10,725 to be split three ways.

Obviously, anyone with all three talents, (1) promotion, (2) cartooning and (3) writing and a couple thousand for printing could do it all and reap all the profits, provided that they were as creative as Debbie.

ENTERTAINMENT BUREAU

If you live in or near a good-sized city (one hundred thousand plus), you may be able to earn great fulltime or parttime money by establishing an Entertainment Bureau.

To work this plan, you must contact as many musicians, dancers, comedians, ventriloquists, hypnotists, etc. as you can find. You then audition them to be certain you're dealing with people with some talents. Once you have gathered several "acts" who agree to give you 10% to 15% (go for 15% if you can get it!) for representing them.

To line up booking you must have printed letterheads and envelopes, circulars or brochures advertising the group and rate cards. Send these to nightclubs, social clubs, churches and charitable organizations soliciting engagements.

A little-known technique that can work wonders: Put special emphasis on social and fraternal clubs, churches and other non-profitable organizations. Work to line up dates with these rich sources of tailor-made (through their membership) audiences in which they will receive a split (usually 50-50) on all revenue that comes in. These groups will often be very pleased to produce a large turnout when they realize a good hunk of the proceeds will come to them.

We know of two partners in St. Louis, Missouri who started out from scratch in 1979 and in just two years grossed $250,000 with their talent agency. The profits are out there for anyone who has a flair for promotion and who is willing to work with and for various artists who, at times, are somewhat temperamental.

Successful Entertainment Bureau promoters soon may find themselves working closely with big stars. We know of one San Diego agency who started small and who now is engaged in booking dates for country stars such as Willie Nelson and Anne Murray. You must walk before you trot and trot before you run. However, in this entertaining business, you can rise to the top fast if you possess real promotional ability and enjoy working with creative people.

This kind of operation could be listed under "spare time business" as well as "home business." It is usually wise to get started on a parttime basis.

INVENTORS REP

In every city and hamlet in our nation, many local inventors are eager to market their brainchildren. If you have real promotional skills, you can earn lucrative profits by representing these inventors and assisting them in their marketing desires.

You can, without spending a lot of money, establish an inventors' bureau; publicize the inventions and act as an "inventors agent" in marketing. Inserting a small advertisement in your local paper announcing your services will secure you a list of inventors. They generally seek such assistance. You can also be of invaluable marketing assistance by studying the invention, determining who would most likely desire to buy it and then contacting these sources, either by mail or in person.

Similar services normally charge up to five hundred dollars and more for invention "evaluation" plus 10% to 15% of all proceeds that result from your marketing contacts. You will have no problem obtaining many creative clients if you launch this home business by offering substantially lower rates. We have recently heard of a Los Angeles, California man who got started from scratch and earned $30,000 net profits in his first (1980) year with his own Inventors Bureau.

VOCATIONAL COUNSELLING

People nowadays are constantly switching jobs and vocations. This has created a potentially lucrative, fulltime or sparetime business that can be operated out of a home office.

Mary Jane of Seattle, Washington started a vocational counseling service in Seattle a few years ago on a parttime basis and has seen it develop into a $25,000 plus per year business.

She first performed this service among her friends and subsequently advertised in publications of mass appeal. She offered to give complete vocational analysis for a low fee. Upon receiving the application, she would submit a questionnaire, requesting data on the applicant's age, schooling, present job, etc. This data enabled her to gauge the qualifications of the writer and to offer suitable vocational advice. Consultation of various psychology books yielded much information concerning questionnaires, vocational adaptability and other necessary subjects that aid her in her booming profession. She charges twenty dollars for each analysis and now has a waiting list of new clients and has even had to hire a retired school teacher to work parttime to assist her.

Our analysis indicates this business is tailor-made to the changing job market of the 1980s.

Following is a group of home businesses that concern themselves with arts and crafts, gardening, food and cooking...

BRAID RUGS

Americans have been indicating new interest in handmade rugs. Rug-braiding is not difficult and can be learned as easily as knitting. The materials are quite reasonable and there is an expanding market for them. Once you learn to produce braided rugs in a reasonable amount of time, you could expand into doormats, knit purses, potholders, chairpads, etc., all of which are less time-consuming than rugs.

There are several fine firms that will be happy to supply you with materials and instructions.

Write:

Barclay
170-30 Jamaica Avenue
Jamaica, New York 11432

Adams & Swett
380 Dorchester Avenue
Boston, Massachusetts 02127

Heirloom
38 Harlem Street
Rumford, Rhode Island 01916

Your markets include department stores, hobby and craft shops, boutiques, rug shops and related outlets. You can also mail-order your wares through ads in craft magazines. "Needlepoint" is the leading magazine in this field.

Potential profits are good as you often can mark-up your rugs and other accessories four or five times your raw cost for materials. Even by allowing a 50% discount to retail stores, your profits can be substantial.

DESIGN HATS

Custom millinery—hat-making—is an ancient art practiced from the time of the Egyptians to the present date. For the man or woman who enjoys sewing, likes working with her/his hands and who keeps up with fashion, this creative art can earn attractive profits.

To get started, save all fabrics, feathers, beads, material, blocks, ribbons, bows and nets—you can use them all. Books on hat-making can be found in libraries and bookstores, and once you have read up on techniques you can, if you wish, begin. If you want to study millinery, inquire at the local millinery shop about courses given or learn from a friend. Study the hats at the boutiques and see if you can duplicate them. Study at home can also be arranged. For information write:

Academy of Millinery Design
1500 Cardinal Drive
Little Falls, New Jersey 07424

The Academy supplies you with the tools and materials necessary to begin.

Where to sell your hats? At the millinery shops, ladies' clothing shops, special orders for weddings or for women's clubs, crafts shops, theatrical-costume shops. You can also consider giving courses yourself once you are a master of the hat universe and teach others this little-known art. As this is being written, the current hat craze in America continues to be western headgear. Sharp designers are getting up to $100 and more for their one-of-a-kind western hats.

FURNITURE UPHOLSTERING

Homemakers, offices, hotels and motels all use the services of upholsterers. This can be the ideal work out of your home business, parttime or fulltime.

How to begin? First, be certain that upholstery is your scene. It requires certain tastes and certain talents. You must like fabric and the tactile sensations; you must have a feeling for furniture; you must have a color sense; you must enjoy seeing your hands at work. If all these check out, go to it. Upholstery is not limited to simple recovering—you may be called to hang drapes and sew them, make slipcovers or pillows, do automobile upholstery and basic furniture repair and the like. If you decide to learn upholstery at home, contact:

Modern Upholstery Institute
Orange, California

If you plan to work at home, a good idea is to upholster your own living room and use it as a showcase for your work. The Modern Upholstery Institute will also help you—they provide advertising for you and a kit that includes business invitation letters, a mailing-list guide, business stationery and forms and a business advisory service. One nice thing about this trade is that it allows a husband and wife to work together at home as a team.

Amount You Must Spend? The course from the Upholstery Institute costs $238 ($215 if the full sum for tuition is paid at once). The course includes many of the basic tools, but the rest must be purchased separately.

Amount You Can Make? Working parttime can still bring in as much as $150 a week. To reupholster one couch takes two or three days, and you can charge from $75 to $100 for the work.

ART AND CRAFT BROKERAGE

Steve and Shannon of Newport Beach, California live in a beautiful seacoast village that has become a colony of artists and creative craft workers. While most of these people are high on talent, they generally are not so blessed with business knowledge. Enter Steve and Shannon!

Steve and Shannon had been party-plan sales people for years but were looking for a new, profitable and stimulating enterprise. They found they could relate well to the artists and craft people in this seaside village, and they outlined a marketing plan that suited many of the creative people.

Shannon and Steve load up their VW van once per week with the crafts, sculptures and art and head down the freeway to selective shops, stores and boutiques in the Los Angeles area. Special emphasis is given to the posh shops in wealthy Beverly Hills.

Steve and Shannon operate a "cash on delivery" business with their established network of retailers.

They keep 25% of all sales as their commission. "We were lucky to make $50 or $60 a week when we got started last year," Steve informed us, "but now we often earn $400 to $500 per week. Not bad for less than ten hours of work per week." We call it great!

Not bad at all. Anyone living near an arts and crafts center or near almost any big city could organize a similar distribution setup.

GROW ORGANIC VEGETABLES

The natural food movement that got into full swing in the 60s and 70s is definitely going to continue and increase during the 1980s. Today people are more aware than ever of the dangers certain sprays, colorings, dyes, refining and preservatives present. The health-food market is experiencing record growth. If you have some land (even ⅓ acre can produce a vast harvest using modern growing techniques) and a green thumb, you can turn your green thumb into long green cash.

How to Begin? If you have done any gardening, there is

really little that must be learned or changed in order to grow organic vegetables. Seeds taken from organic vegetables are considered to be organic seeds. Start from there. When your vegetables start to grow, you treat them with natural sprays and fertilizers that protect the produce completely and at the same time leave them untainted by any poison or artificial chemical. Today you will have little trouble selling your organic foods once they mature. People drive miles to obtain them, and the only thing you need to do is spread the word. If you've sold vegetables in the past, so much the better. You can sell from roadside stands, at your house, to the local markets or on consignment. For information on basic organic gardening, write for the book list from:

Rodale Press
33 East Minor Street
Emmaus, Pennsylvania 18049

To obtain the names of the various suppliers of organic materials, look at a copy of Rodale's magazine Organic Gardening, which costs $1 on the newsstand. Two other good suppliers of organic materials are:

National Development Co.
Bainbridge, Pennsylvania 17502

Vita Green Farms
P.O. Box 878
Vista, California 92083

While profits will vary depending on the yield of your ground and your ability to produce a bountiful harvest, we have heard of folks earning up to $7,000 per acre of land.

FLOWER POWER PROFITS

A green thumb plus a salesman's license is all you need to enter this home business. And don't despair if you live in a house or apartment with no room for a flower garden. If you can sell this blooming product, local suppliers will be available to you.

There are many ways to peddle beautiful flowers (roses and carnations are two of the most popular varieties, but several others qualify also for fast sales). Any good, busy street cor-ner (with or without a wooden flower cart) can yield a gross of $100 or more per day selling your flowers in $2 to $5 bunches.

Here's another technique that is red hot. We have heard of a flower peddler in Houston, Texas who earns up to $1,000 net per week with this little jewel. This entrepreneur hires attractive young women to sell his roses (he buys them at wholesale since he is not a grower) in popular restaurants, bars and clubs in the Houston area. We are told he splits the profits with his pretty salesgirls, but with a group of six to eight attractive "flower girls," his profits soar. You may want to look into this. Even if you're not a grower, a $5 "bunch" of flowers will probably cost you $1.50 or less, leaving you an excellent mark-up, even if you hire others to help you make sales. Caution: Flowers do perish quickly. Do not buy or grow more than you realistically believe you can sell. If you're buying wholesale from a grower, it's often wise to buy a fresh batch daily rather than to purchase several days supply. Nobody buys cut flowers that have wilted.

KITCHEN CANDY PROFITS

Bess Peterson of Duluth, Minnesota makes the best fudge east of the Mississippi River. Ask any of her relatives or friends who receive "fudge baskets" as birthday or Christmas gifts. Only a few years ago did she take her "heavenly fudge" public. A niece who opened her own restaurant finally talked Bess into placing some of her fudge in neatly wrapped packages at the counter of her breakfast and lunch diner. Her fudge was an instant sensation. Soon other establishments were clamoring for her fudge. Bess went into business, but only to the extent that she could remain in her kitchen (thank goodness, Uncle Bob enlarged it by another 300 square feet!).

Now, in addition to fudge, Bess also makes her delicious brownies available to the good folks in the Duluth-Superior area. She could double or triple her business if she wanted to. A candy and cookie distributor wanted her to increase her business and give him an exclusive on the Minneapolis-St. Paul market. But Bess refused. She is already "earning more money than Uncle Bob and I need, and we don't want to work longer hours. If folks in the twin cities want my brownies and fudge, they'll have to drive 100 miles to Duluth."

Well, so much for Aunt Bess. She has as large a share of the "kitchen market" as she wants. God bless her.

Many old family recipes can launch a super home business. Some of the greatest tasty food items never make it to the marketplace. As important as good food items are, the ability to promote them is just as vital. Since the great cook is not always the great entrepreneur, often times a partnership is called for.

If you have an Aunt Bess in your family who has a great food dish, or a mother or grandma who has a "secret recipe," why not get busy forming a kitchen partnership that can make mucho money for you both. Good food items can become an overnight success when strong marketing strategies are employed.

It is often smart to begin your technique by "test marketing" your food item at a handful of selected stores or restaurants. Then, based on these results, you can plan a more ambitious advertising and marketing campaign.

An Important Tip: Try to keep control of your product during the early going. If it proves to have national appeal and you don't have the capital to launch a national marketing campaign, you can arrange to sell out at a profit. First prove its appeal; then decide if you want to maintain control or whether you (and your famous cook) will take your profit and let someone else carry the ball.

MULTI-LEVEL MARKETING OPPORTUNITIES

The fabulous success of Amway and other pioneers in multi-level marketing has spawned thousands of imitators. In recent years the mails and magazines have been full of three, four, five, and more-level-multi-marketing propositions. Companies involved range from multi-national firms with millions in assets to shoestring entrepreneurs. The products and services offered on multi-level propositions cover a wide gamut, from books to brushes and from home computers to herbs and vitamins. Almost any type of product or service can be marketed on a multi-level basis.

Several multi-marketing setups do offer good potential profits; however, it is important that you do not get involved in a chain-marketing or chain-letter scheme that is illegal. While we cannot offer any legal opinion here, a key point seems to be that a bonafide product or service must be involved. Sending money back and forth to people, when no real products or services are received for payment rendered, is usually characteristic of an illegal "chain" operation.

Big success in multi-level marketing is more often the result of establishing dealerships than the actual product or service involved. By setting up a long line of dealers, you share in their success and receive commissions on their sales. However, the product should also have real merit and be in demand.

THE MULTI—LEVEL CONCEPT

Regardless of the product or service offered, the concept behind multi-level selling is hooked into the recruiting of as many new distributors as possible to continue to sell the product or service.

Let's say you get in early on a five (5) level multi-level marketing deal. As an example, let's say you're promoting Aloe Vera juice (very much in demand today!) and your basic selling unit is 4 quarts (one gallon) for twenty dollars. And let's suppose you are allowed to keep $5.00 out of every $20.00 sale you make. This is level one. Now let's say that you will be allowed $1.00 on every order your distributors make on levels two through five.

21

Here is an example of the amount of money you could make if you signed up only four distributors, who in turn duplicated your efforts. Using the hypothetical figures outlined above ($5.00 profit per original sale and $1.00 commission on the next four levels):

Level #1 you acquire 4, and receive $5.00 each $20.00
Level #2 your 4 acquire 4 each $16.00
Level #3 these 16 acquire 4 each $64.00
Level #4 these 64 acquire 4 each $256.00
Level #5 these 256 acquire 4 each $1,024.00
TOTAL $1,380.00

Within a very short time, with only four people duplicating your sales production, you could earn $1,380.00 from a very minimal effort of only four sales.

Sounds great doesn't it? And sometimes it even works that well—but not always. It is unlikely that a minimum effort of only four sales with distributor setups would hold up so well through five levels. Multi-level marketing experts tell me that you have to set up ten distributorships, on the average, to get one outstanding "go getter" who will prove to be an outstanding source of "downline" commissions.

Sign up two hundred or more active distributorships and you may actually get rich, or at least receive nice, steady monthly checks from your multi-level headquarters.

Multi-level selling originally centered around household products sold in person house-to-house or through party plan selling, but now it has entered the world of mail order too. Books, booklets, reports and other "printed matter" are probably the most popular multi-level mail order items, but many other products (survival food stuffs, vitamins, health juices, jewelry, exercise equipment, novelties, etc.) are also available.

IS MULTI-LEVEL FOR YOU?

Maybe yes. Maybe no. The decision is strictly yours. There are many pros and there are many cons. On the "pro" side are (1) the opportunity to make good money quickly if you can produce sales and set up dealers, and (2) the chance to make money from the efforts of others (your dealers). The two major potential negatives are (1) to earn long-range profits, you must be working with a parent company (the primary source) that is sound and likely to be in business a long time and (2) the "quality" of the service or product being sold must be good, to assure continued sales and likelihood of establishing more dealerships.

Another major consideration for you, if you intend to get into multi-level selling, is the legality of your product. It is wise to shy away from companies which are making outlandish claims regarding their goods. If it all sounds too good to be true, it probably is. Be extremely wary of products which make exaggerated "health cure claims." The Food and Drug Administration and the postal service tend to take a dim view of such operations. Although you would probably come under the heading of "Independent Contractor," and not be considered an employee of the company's headquarters, you still could be subject to harrassment or even prosecution if you are distributing (in person or through the mails) products or information that are deemed to be harmful or dangerous

23

or grossly misleading in nature.

If the proposition in question troubles you, stay away from it. If it seems just too good to pass up, consult an attorney for a legal opinion.

GET THE FACTS AND FIGURES FROM "THE HORSE'S MOUTH"

If you are anxious to learn more about the kind of services and products plus commissions available in multi-level selling, the following partial list of main distributors and/or prime sources of multi-level marketing organizations can furnish you, without obligation, full information on the merits of their programs. Write to several or all of them; look over the wide range of products, services and specials available; compare the various marketing plans (mail order, in-house party selling, etc.) and "projected earning schedules" before making your decision. Give special consideration to the plans and the products.

When writing any of these firms simply ask that they send you details on their multi-level marketing program.

The following firms offer a wide variety of products and services sold via various multi-marketing plans. They are listed here as sources of information only. While we hope that they all offer marketing plans that are sound, legal and beneficial, we cannot guarantee this to be true. The reader is acting on his or her own risk solely in dealing with any individual or firm listed here.

24

PARTIAL LISTING OF
MULTI-LEVEL COMPANIES

J & R SUNSHINE AND CHEER CO., J & R Plaza, Bridgewater, IA 50837 "Coupon Shoppers Club"

MULTI-LEVEL ASTROLOGER, 24228-B Hawthorne Blvd., Torrance, CA 90505. "Astrology for Fun and Profit"

MERWIN K and JERI E. STOUTT, 3067 West Ave., Fresno, CA 93707. "Tel-A-Call Long-distance Phone Service:.

HAWAII DIET PLAN, INC. 737 Bishop St., Suite 2990, Honolulu, HI 96813. Phone: 800/367-5216. "Weight Loss Plan with Delicious Flavors"

THE SUNRIDER GROUP, P.O. Box 2020, Provo, UT 84603. "Personal Health-Care"

ZENITH ADVANCED HEALTH SYSTEMS, Box 1739, Corvallis, OR 97339. "Advanced Health-care Products"

JIM SWEENEY, SYNERGETIC PUBLISHING CO., 5513 Twin Knolls Rd., Suite 213, Columbia, MD 21045. Author of "M.L.M.—A Shorcut To Financial Freedom"

STARR III, P.O. Box 962, Big Harbor, WA 98335. Publisher of "How to Build a Large Successful Multi-level Marketing Organization"

C. AUSTIN, RD 1, Blemont, NY 14813. Coupons and Refund Plans

KRIS VANTATEHOVE, 881 Windermere Rd., San Dimas, CA 91773. "Food Stuffs"

COMPUTER, P.O. Box 12132, Roanoke, VA 24022. Computer Software and Video Game Cartridges

SCOTT REPORTS, 2025 Northwest, Lansing, MI 48906. "MLM Mail-order Plans"

MULLINAX, 1274 E. Leafland, Decatur, IL 62521. "MLM Buying Club"

ROGER HANSON, P.O. Box 85, Fontana, WI 53125. "Modello Distributor of Radio Watches"

DMS & ASSOCIATES, Box 11511, Santa Ana, CA 92711. "Pure D'Lite Food Beverages"

AIM MARKETING, P.O. Box 882, San Diego, CA. Food, Diet and Vitamins

RICHLINE INC., Box 3479, Zanesville, OH 43701. "Aloe Vera Products."

A GUIDE TO MLM TERMINOLOGY

Each industry has its own terminology, and multi-level marketing is no exception. Here, then, is a glossary of buzz-words to help you communicate with MLMers on their own terms:

Bonus volume (or B.V.) An extra amount assigned to a distributor in order to help offset the effects of inflation.

Downline: The people directly enrolled by an MLM distributor plus the people they enroll. The rule of thumb is that any distributor you can track back to you is part of your downline.

First level: The people a distributor directly recruits when building an organization; the first level in an MLMer's downline. The second generation is made up of people recruited by the first generation, and so on.

Go direct: In some companies, the point at which an independent distrubutor is permitted to bypass his or her sponsor and buy directly from the company. Most MLM pros prefer to buy direct.

MLM: Multi-level marketing. People who do business this way are often called MLMers.

Multi-level marketing: A system in which the manufacturer sells directly to the consumer through an individual distributor rather than a retail outlet. MLMers increase their production (and therefore their income) by "multiplying themselves"—that is, sponsoring other distributors. Multi-level marketers are paid in direct proportion to the sales volume they and their organization produce. The more people an MLMer sponsors and the more those people sell, the higher the level of compensation and recognition that person achieves in the company; hence, the term "multi-level."

Networking: A technique by which MLM distributors share

information for their mutual benefit and profit.

Opportunity meetings: A gathering at which represenatives of an MLM company present the benefits to be derived by joining that company; these meetings may include filmed or live success stories and an explanation of the firm's marketing plan.

Party plan: A selling method used by some companies in which a party-plan manager recruits hosts and hostesses who invite friends to their homes for a showing of product(s). The host(ess) receives merchandise, money or both.

Pirating: Actively recruiting another MLM company's distributors.

Pyramid sales: A sales structure, illegal in most states, in which all profits flow to a single point.

Purchase volume (or P.V.): The monetary value of merchandise ordered by a distributor or his/her downline. MLM companies use this figure to calculate how much in discounts, commissions and overrides to assign its distributors.

Recruiting (or sponsoring): Inviting others to join an MLM organization; offering someone an opportunity to profit personally and in so doing to help build your organization.

Sponsor: A person who signs someone else into an MLM company.

Stacking: Placing a series of different MLM distributors downline from each other to control the rebates available from a company; the original sponsor then receives little reward for his/her efforts.

Rallies (or seminars or motivational meetings): Gatherings to "recharge the batteries" of MLM distributors, who attend for information, education and motivation; major speakers are often successful MLMers.

Royalties (or bonus checks): Incentives (over and above regular commissions and overrides) offered by an MLM company to encourage its distributors to strive for certain volume levels; these rewards are often luxury items and may include automobiles, trips, jewelry, cash, etc.

Upline: A distributor's upline consists of the person who directly sponsored him or her into an MLM business plus the person who sponsored the sponsor, and so on.

Warehousing: Stockpiling enough merchandise to supply an entire organization. (This technique is used mainly by successful distributors with large downlines who want to expedite and simplify product distribution.)

OPERATING AN
AT HOME CONSULTING BUSINESS

After several years of working in any given profession, you will have acquired specific skills that may be marketable as a vital service. Consulting is big business in the 1980s, and promises to continue to be in the years ahead. Specific knowledge is in big demand in this age of specialization.

CONSULTING IS A CONTRACT LABOR
BUSINESS—TIME IS MONEY

When you agree to offer your expertise to another at a pre-determined fee for a pre-determined amount of time, you are establishing a contract-labor arrangement. This type of business gives you a vast amount of freedom in determining your work schedule. Of course, to be successful you must wisely allocate your time. In this business, time is definitely money. It is wise not to allow friends and relatives to dominate your precious time. Many have fallen into this trap, offering free advice and services in the beginning, only to regret this later as increasing demand has been put upon them.

WHO TO SELL YOUR
CONSULTING SERVICES TO

Almost every type of business needs assistance from time to time and can benefit from the advice of a consultant. When the need for specialized assistance arises from time to time, it makes no sense for a company to hire permanent help. The overall cost of using a consultant to solve specific problems is usually less than creating a regular new job.

To find firms who will pay you handsomely for your expertise (and remember, almost any kind of specialized knowledge is marketable), you must learn to sell your most important product—yourself!

Advertise! You gotta tell 'em to sell 'em! A sparkling, upbeat sales brochure can do a big selling job. This sales brochure should include a resume of your background, services that you offer potential clients and resources that are available to you. Spend a few extra bucks for typesetting and quality printing. Going first class pays dividends in a consulting business. A photo of yourself and/or the service you perform can also work well.

Watch your local newspaper for "help wanted" ads. Sometimes a company will advertise a full-time position in the field of your expertise. Often you can convince such a firm that you can fulfill their needs on an on-going part-time basis. This saves them money in the long run and allows you to earn regular fees while still having free time to accept other assignments.

Don't limit your employment seeking activities to newspaper. Do some research. Make a list of any firms that could possibly use the service you wish to offer and mail them your brochure with a brief letter letting them know who you are, what you offer and how to reach you.

Don't be afraid to make some "COLD CALLS." An example of this is: locate a firm that does business in a field you have knowledge in. Give them a call. If you offer marketing services, ask for the MARKETING DEPARTMENT; if you supply engineering services, ask for the ENGINEERING DEPARTMENT; if you offer maintenance services, ask for the JANITORIAL or MAINTENANCE DEPARTMENT, etc. Find out the name of the man or woman who runs the department, but don't speak to them yet.

Next, you can visit the company and look over their company manual and/or sales brochure. Through homework, identify specific products, services or problems that you may be able to help them with. Now call the department head and tell him that you would like an appointment to discuss the beneficial services that you wish to provide. Talk benefits—their benefit in hiring you, not yours in landing the job!

HOW MUCH TO CHARGE

Although each person must determine his or her own worth, don't short-change yourself. Any kind of consultant work is usually more intensive and of shorter duration, and thus you deserve to be paid more per hour, per day, etc., than would a regular employee working in your field. While some consultants actually demand and receive fees that are up to one hundred times what a salaried employee would receive, you don't want to price yourself out of work either. In the beginning, you may be willing to work for just a little more than the going rate in order to launch your new consulting business. After you're rolling, it is realistic to charge double the pay scale of a regular salaried employee. If a regular employee is paid $12.00 per hour, you are not out of line to charge $20.00 or $25.00. If $25.00 is the going rate per hour, a fee of $40.00 to $50.00 per hour for your intensive services is reasonable.

In the beginning you may have problems estimating time duration of jobs, so rather than give a figure to complete the task at hand, it may be wiser to contract your services on an hourly or daily basis.

You can make big money selling your expertise. You can use your home as your headquarters, and other than a telephone and some printed brochures and stationery, no overhead is required. It is your desire and dedication that will determine your success!

An excellent 395 page book that will give you the basics of operating your own consulting business, plus many advanced techniques, is "How to Succeed As An Independent Consultant" by Herman Holtz. Available at several bookshops, your library or direct from the publisher, John Wiley & Sons Inc. To order by mail, send $19.95 plus $2.00 postage/handling to John Wiley & Sons Inc., 605 Third Ave., New York, NY 10158

Another great source of consulting information is J. Stephen Lanning's outstanding bi-monthly tabloid, "Consulting Opportunities Journal." For subscription information write: COJ, 1629 K Street, NW, Suite 520, Washington, DC 20006

MAKE MONEY WITH "JUNK" GOLD AND SILVER

Here's a timely business that is perfect for 1984 and beyond. Gold and silver are heading in one direction—UP! Sure, there are frequent market corrections, and it's three steps forward and then two back, but the general direction is up. I predict $2,000.00 per ounce (or higher) gold prices by 1990 and $80.00 (or higher) silver before 1990 dawns.

You can make money with gold and silver and you can operate right out of your home.

MAKING UP TO $500 WEEKLY WITH "JUNK" GOLD

Using just a couple of hours of effort per week, you could make up to $500 or more. Almost everyone has an assortment of items containing gold lying about—items such as gold rings, watches, medals, brooches, earrings, tie tacs, cuff links, fountain pen points, money clips, necklaces, etc. Most people have no idea where to sell such items, much less how much they are worth. Your inquiries, plus small ads in local newspapers will usually bring a big response and great opportunity.

It is important that you become familiar with the following precious-metal terminology in order to conduct your business profitably.

TROY WEIGHT: Troy weight is a different measurement than the English measure. 12 ounces equal a pound by Troy weight. 24 grains equal one pennyweight (dwt); 20 pennyweights equal one ounce.

GOLD PLATED: An electroplating process. Gold plated items are virtually worthless since the amount of gold content is so small. Don't buy gold plated items.

GOLD ALLOY: Almost all of the gold items you buy will be a gold alloy since few items are 100% pure gold. Usually silver or copper is added to give "hardness." If nickel has been added, then it is called white gold.

KARAT: Karat is also represented by the symbol "K," 24 karats is pure gold. 12 karats is 50% gold, etc. A National Stamping Act requires all items containing gold to be stamped with the karat number, but in certain cases you will find items not marked—these you will have to test to determine their gold content.

GOLD FILLED: A process whereby thin strips of gold are welded onto another metal and rolled under pressure to produce a hard gold surface. Usually it is represented by the mark "GF."

ROLLED GOLD: Rolled Gold Plate, or the symbol "RGP," indicates a similar manufacturing process to gold filled. The difference is that even thinner strips of gold are used. These alloys for RGP and GF items must be 10 karat or more, and "$\frac{1}{20}$th to 10K."

STER: Don't mistake the letters, STER, for white gold. This is sterling silver.

You will need a troy weight scale and a few pieces of equipment to test the items for gold content. Scientific supply and jewelry supply firms listed in the yellow pages usually sell this type of equipment. Mail order firms that offer equipment are: William Dixon, Inc., 752 Washington Ave., Carlstadt,

NJ 07072, and Keene Engineering, 11483 Van Owen Street, North Hollywood, CA 91605.

When you get your equipment, you can test an item for gold content by filing a groove about ⅛ inch deep in the item. Put a drop of nitric acid in this groove. There will be almost no reaction if the item is 18 karat or better. If the acid turns a light shade of brown, then gold is present. If it turns dark brown, there is very little gold content. If the acid turns pink, you have silver in your hands, not gold. Copper or brass is present if the acid turns green. Determining the exact karat content is accomplished with other items you'll receive in your equipment kit.

While each refiner puts out his own quote sheet for the prices they will pay for old gold, prices should not vary too much. Check with several of the firms mentioned below and you'll have the going rate. As for the price that you pay for the gold you purchase, it's usually wise to pay ½ (50%) of what you can sell it for. In other words, most junk dealers are out to double their money on every purchase.

Once you have located folks with gold they wish to sell, go to their homes with your equipment and test and weigh items for gold content BEFORE buying, or better yet, ask them to bring all of their items to your home. While scrap gold will bring you the most profits, don't overlook items with heavy silver content. Scrap silver is in abundant supply.

You can get into this lucrative part-time vocation with little funds and low, low overhead. And there is no ceiling on your potential earning. A couple hundred dollar investment in equipment, ads, and the first few purchases, launches this business.

Following is a list of companies which purchase junk gold and silver. Write to several and request their current quotes.

Agmet, Inc., PO Box 523, Hazelton, PA 18201

Denron Ltd., 1200 W. Northbranch Dr., Oak Creek, WI 53154

Albee Lab., Inc., 640 Pearson St., Ste. 102, Des Plaines, IL 60000

Eastman Kodak, 343 State St., Rochester, NY 14650

Englehard Industries, 429 Delaney St., Newark, NJ 07104

Federal Alloys, 2930 Dental St., Detroit, MI 48211

Grand X-Ray Co., 833 N. Ottawa, Grand Rapids, MI 49502

Handy & Harman, 845 Waterman Ave., E. Providence, RI 02914

Merry X-Ray, 1617 E. Jefferson, Phoenix, AZ 85034

New Orleans Silver, PO Box 52556, New Orleans, LA 70150

Southwest Smelting Co., 1712 Jackson St., Dallas, TX 75221

R.E. Van Valey, 1317 Republican, Seattle, WA 98109

Handy & Harman, 850 Third Ave., New York, NY 10022

Handy & Harman, 1900 Estes Ave., Elk Grove Village, IL 60007

Industrial Silver Co., 1717 Fourth St., Berkeley, CA 94710

Industrial Silver Co., 497 Scott Ave., Brooklyn, NY 11222

Industrial Silver Co., PO Box 18231, Hollywood, CA 90038

International Recovery, PO Box 33187, Houston, TX 77033

Jax Metal Shredding, PO Box 2187, Jacksonville, FL 32202

Donald McElroy, Inc., 9573 Williams St., Rosemont, IL 60018

Merry X-Ray, 3738 E. Grant Rd., Tucson, AZ 83716

Professional Equipment, 1386 NW 29th St., Miami, FL 33142

United Refining Co., 3700-20 N. Runge Ave., Franklin Park, IL 60131

West Coast Silver, 390 McGlincy, Space F., Campbell, CA 95008

RECLAIM SILVER AND PROFIT

Silver is found in photographic film and fixer solutions. Printers, photo labs, dentists, hospitals, and newspaper publishers are just some of the sources of reclaimable silver. In fact, every business that uses photographic copy film is a potential source of supply. Up until a few years ago, the sharp operator could haul away this "waste" free. Now, many supply sources recognize it has some value. Nevertheless, you can still buy their waste materials for pennies on the dollars you will eventually make.

To recover silver from used photographic film is a very simple process. You simply dump the film into a fire-proof container and burn it. Then collect the ashes and ship them to a refiner.

A gallon of waste fixer solution will yield approximately one ounce of recoverable silver. One easy method to recover silver from this kind of solution is to wrap a piece of copper wire or untreated copper mesh around a piece of wood. Then drop this into the solution and let it sit there for three days. The copper attracts the silver and you can extract most of it in this manner.

If you plan to go all out in this home business, you probably will need more sophisticated equipment. A commercial silver recovery machine will allow you to obtain more silver in less time. Such a machine will quickly pay for itself. Write the following companies for descriptions, quality-control and prices on their recovery machines.

Midwest Refining, 123 St. Paul Ave., Duluth, MN 55301

States Smelting Co., 1550 Elida Rd., Lima, OH 45805

Snook Corp., 751 Loma Verde Ave., Palo Alto, CA 94303

X-Rite Corp., 4101 Roger Chafee Dr., Grand Rapids, MI 49508

MAKE ORIENTAL RUGS AT HOME—
PROFIT THREE WAYS

Thanks to a progressive manufacturing company in Hong Kong, you can create your own oriental rugs; the kind that sell for $100.00 to $500.00 at auctions, exhibit shows, flea markets, etc.

You can profit from this machine in three profitable ways:

(1) Manufacture oriental rugs and sell them yourself.

(2) Manufacture oriental rugs and sell them to whole-salers, stores, flea market dealers, swap meet sellers, etc.

(3) Sell the machines and materials to people who would like to make money at home.

For information on the machine and materials write to:

Kin Yuen Metal Engineering Works
36 Sung Chi Street, G½F
Hung Hom Kowloon, Hong Kong

RENT FENCES

Pilferage is a big problem on "on the job" sites. Workers steal 10% to 20% of the goods that disappear. A bigger problem is the 80% to 90% carted away by outsiders. Construction sites are among the hardest hit.

In 1967 Anthony Ortega, who owned a small fencing company, came up with a bright idea. He approached a local housing project and offered to put up a cyclone fence for a nominal fee. "If my fence doesn't cut down pilferage, I'll leave it there free for a year." The construction boss took Mr. Ortega up on his offer. Soon after the fence went up, he admitted on-site thievery was drastically reduced. Thus, Ortega's "Rent-A-Fence" business was formed. Offices are now all over the nation.

For more information write to: RENT-A-FENCE, 1236 EAST LOS ANGELES AVE., SIMI VALLEY, CA, 93063.

GOLDEN PROFITS FROM THE GOLDEN GATE

When the Golden Gate Bridge authority decided to replace the heavy duty suspension cables on the Golden Gate Bridge after they were in use over forty years, a group of San Francisco entrepreneurs went into action. They bought the old cable, sliced it into 4-inch chunks and successfully sold them as momentos of San Francisco's past at $35.00 to $50.00 per chunk.

$35.00 got you a plain piece sitting in a leather covered presentation tray. For $40.00 you could get a chrome plated piece and for fifty dollars you received a gold plated chunk. Each chunk was numbered and represented a true collectors item. Close to two million chunks were sold. You figure up the amount; it is really overwhelming!

Now what does this have to do with you? Think about it! The day will probably come along in your area when a histor-

41

ical site will be demolished or taken down. Old parts of historical value, be they bricks, stones, wood, rail or chunks of cable from a bridge, are very saleable to collectors.

Original material brings the biggest bucks, but don't overlook "authentic replicas," either. The state of Illinois made a tidy profit recently when they first took down and sold their old Route 66 signs and later when they produced and sold thousands of Route 66 sign replicas.

WEALTH-BUILD WITH LOG HOMES

History has a way of repeating itself. Who would have ever thought that log homes would be back in demand in 1984? After all, this "primitive" form of building was big in 1784! Believe me, today the log house has returned.

As housing costs continue to soar (the average price of a new home today is fast approaching $100,000.00) many Americans and Canadians are returning to relatively inexpensive dwellings that once housed their ancestors.

You will find log cabins in the rural areas and you will also find them in suburban Cleveland, Chicago, Minneapolis-St. Paul, Dallas-Ft. Worth, or just about anywhere a home owner wants sturdy, low-price shelter. In the great state of Kentucky, log homes represent 2% of all new construction.

While some log homes are built from chopping down nearby trees, many more are purchased in pre-assembled kits. In addition to considering a log home for your dwelling, profits can be made in both selling them and contracting for their

42

construction.

Three of the leading suppliers of log home kits are: Alpine Log Homes of Victor, Montana; Authentic Homes of Laramie, Wyoming; and Lincoln Log Homes of Karnapolis, North Carolina.

MAKE BIG BUX IN THE
BLOOMING HEALTH FIELD

The college of Life Science says, "you can quickly master this 100% effective health system of Life Science, and help overcome ailments such as acne, asthma, tumors, diabetes, heart ailments, high blood pressure, overweight, backache, venereal disease, psoriasis and almost anything else."

The college offers a nutritional science course and doctorate degree and will show you how to be a PH.D. in just one year.

The college publishes a dynamic monthly magazine. Healthful Living" plus a newsletter, "The Health Science Newsletter." They offer many health-related programs. If interested, write for full details to: College of Life Science, Manchoca, Texas 78652.

Another institution offering ways to profit as you serve is the Holistic Massage training course available from: Kripalu Center for Holistic Health, P.O. Box 131, Summit Station, Pa. 17979.

200 hours of residential training in one of the nation's lead-

ing holistic care centers will equip you for a certificate in meditative massage, reflexology, acupressure point work and other related therapies. And that certificate can launch an exciting new vocation. And one that can be performed in your own home.

BELIEVE IT OR NOT: THEY PAY FOR DUST!

Hollister-Stier Laboratories, 3525 Regal St., Spokane, WA., 99220, has a problem—the company gladly pays cash money for common, everyday house dust to the tune of 50¢ a pound. That's a fact! The problem is, convincing folks that they will buy dust! Most people cannot believe anyone would pay money for something most homeowners would like to rid themselves of. The company presently buys dust from five collection points in Yeardon, Pa.; Downers Grove, IL.; Atlanta, GA.; Dallas, TX.; and Burbank, CA. Paper bags or vacuum cleaner sacks are the preferred means of collection. Plastic trash bags are not desirable because the dust in them tends to get too moldy.

If you can convince yourself that this firm means business, you can reap some easy profits.

The amount of dust in an ordinary vacuum cleaner bag is worth $1.50 or more.

Remember, they buy dust and not dirt (that would be too easy). The average household will net a tidy sum. However, you will have to collect dust from other sources to really cash in big. Perhaps you could run a little ad offering to pay, let's say, 25¢ a pound collecting dust from others or how about making a deal with a large janitorial service? The possibilities, like dust, are endless.

VINYL REPAIR PROFITS

Here is a nifty parttime or fulltime occupation that can be run from your home or your garage—repair vinyl. At home earnings can range from $20 to $30 per hour.

Wallace Brown of Mankato, Minnesota reports one job that required repair and recoloring of six booths. "It took two of us three days and was close to a $4,000. job." Those kind of earnings demand attention.

Vinyl PRO, 436 West Hopocan Ave., Barberton, Ohio, 44203, has a process approved by Ford, General Motors, and Chrysler. The company claims that you can get started with them for less than you can make on your very first job.

To find out on how you can cash in providing this in-demand service, write the company and request full details on how you can make good bux in vinly repair, recoloring and refinishing. The company says information is FREE and no sales person will ever call.

We know of a husband and wife team in El Cajon, California, who are doing extremely well in this business. It may be worth your while to look into this.

LET THE IRS
HELP YOU MAKE MONEY

Today the Internal Revenue Service takes a big chunk out of every dollar you make. Too big a chunk methinks, but that's another subject. My point here is that you can actually make a handsome income preparing tax forms for others. Some training is required, but once you have the knowledge you can earn steady income at home and with a little cost-effective advertising, folks will beat a path to your door.

Imagine going into business with a powerful money-hungry partner (IRS) who develops customers for your service year-after-year. It is estimated that 90 million people filed 1982 taxes and that at least 30 million of them paid an outside service for professional assistance.

Knowing how to prepare tax forms is important, but equally vital is promoting services to people in your community. A Chicago company (Federated Tax Service, 2021 West Montrose Ave., Chicago, IL., 60618) specializes in teaching ambitious homeworkers how to do both. Write them for free information on their fast-learning tax training and practical methods for obtaining business. You don't have to be an accountant or mathematical whiz to make money preparing tax forms.

BE A CONSUMER HERO
AND MAKE MONEY TOO

Here's a powerful money making concept from Robert J. Sturner, founder and director of "People's Discount Club Of

America." Economic conditions are ripe for this plan. Mr. Sturner claims a man or woman can earn $500 per day part time while saving consumers huge amounts of money on their everyday spending. At the same time merchants greatly increase their business.

We have looked over this plan and feel it does have real potential. P.D.C.A. now has "clubs" in all 50 states plus several foreign countries. They have been in business since 1976 and are the largest discount club in the world. Obviously, Mr. Sturner and company are doing many things right.

For more information on this organization and their money making plan, write:

Robert J. Sturner
People's Discount Club of America
7216 Manzanita Street
Carlsbad, CA 92008

VIDEO TAPE WEDDINGS AND OTHER SPECIAL OCCASIONS

Luna Video of Los Angeles, California, has found success in video taping weddings and other special events; so can you.

Brides and grooms enjoy a permanent record of their special ceremony and reception and are willing to pay handsomely to have their day of bliss recorded for posterity.

I believe this service will continue to boom in the years ahead. Video taping also lends itself to other services. Recently several people have pre-recorded their last will and testimony. Other events; graduations, confirmations, baby christening, etc., also offer good profit potential. Within a few years almost everyone will have a disc player hooked up to the TV set.

While I believe that with the necessary equipment and a flair for promotion, anyone could set-up their own business, it also may be wise to get help from a pioneer in the field who can help you avoid the pitfalls and give you a shortcut to success.

For free information, write: LUNA VIDEO, PO BOX 85324, LOS ANGELES, CALIFORNIA 90072.

BLOW UP YOUR PROFITS

Making fast cash is child's play when you sell popular helium balloons. Working out of your home you can earn up to $50. or more an hour selling at shopping malls, fairs, bazaars, parks, flea markets, swap meets, beaches, parks, churches, schools, carnivals, stadiums, arenas, even standing on a busy street corner or in the lot of an active corner gas station.

Marjorie Miller of Sacramento, California, earned a good living with a small flower stand. When she added a line of popular balloons to decorate her stand, as well as to earn additional profits, she was amazed that she soon was selling more balloons than roses!

Listed below are three leading firms you can contact if you are interested in balloon selling:

CREATIVE BALLOONS, INC., PO BOX 1165, CARMEL VALLEY, CA., 93924

SILVER SAILS CO, 671-13 MILE ROAD, SPARTA, MI., 49345

ACME PREMIUM SUPPLY CORP., 4100 FORREST PARK BLVD., ST. LOUIS, MO., 63108

COUPON CLIPPING

Now let's give you the lowdown on a dynamic new 1980s concept to make fast cash, easy!

Manufacturers "cents off" coupons began turning up everywhere during the late 1970s (in newspapers, magazines, as well as inside or on the backside of boxes of merchandise). America has gone "coupon crazy", and this trend is expected to continue for several years to come.

Here's how a Chicago woman has turned this boom into a windfall of profits! She finds her local paper carries $10 to $15 or more of "cents off" coupons in the food section, once per week. She buys several papers and clips every available coupon. She then sells these coupons to grocery stores, usually the independents, at about 15 cents on the dollar. Fifty newspapers with $15 worth of coupons in each one of them would yield $750 at face value, which in turn would net her $112.50 (15% of $750). Her only cost would be 25¢ times 50, which is $12.50, the cost of the papers. Even this can be reduced if friends and relatives will save papers for you.

While not all merchants will buy, this Chicago lady has found there are enough who will to make it more than worthwhile to clip and clip. She believes they use these "cents off" coupons to offer to their customers. $100 profit from about two hours "work" adds up to sweet profits.

Opinion: It is illegal for you to send in coupons for cash refund, unless you are selling the products named on the coupon. Using this plan, you simply sell to stores and the responsibility becomes theirs. We believe this is legal but suggest you consult your attorney to make certain you're not violating any laws, should you decide to use this plan.

SEMINARS IN THE HOME— MONEY IN THE BANK!

The thirst for knowledge on thousands of different subjects by millions of people has created a booming new home enterprise—seminars/workshops in the home for adults!

What type of home seminar could you offer that people, in small groups, would pay for? Chances are good that you, like most folks, have valuable knowledge on one or more different subjects that people would gladly pay to receive.

Here is just a brief sampling of the home based instructions now being given here in my "backyard" (the San Diego area):

Home based classes, seminars, workshops, etc., currently include: Language skills (Spanish is the most popular, attended by people from the Midwest and east who have recently moved to Southern California); Rapid Reading & Recall, Solar Heating Information, Interior Decorating, Car Care For Women, Protection from Violence, How to Properly Use Firearms, Public Speaking, Negotiation Skills, Hairstyling, Advanced Makeup Techniques, Skin & Eye Care, Modeling, Male-Female Relationships, How to Cope After Divorce, Initiating Relationships, Touching, Overcome Shyness, Creative Writing, Portrait Drawing Instructions, Watercolor Painting, Hand-formed beads, Sewing Skills, batik, Pine Needle Basketry, Photography, Acting, How to Operate Your Own Business, Bookkeeping for Beginners, Typing Skills, How to Incorporate a Business, How to Start a Business, Consulting, Country Western Dance Lessons, Gourmet Food & Wine Course, Meditation, Sailing, What You Should Know About Casino Gambling Before You Go To Las Vegas... and that's just for starters! Are you beginning to get the picture? The only people who probably do not have special information that many others want to obtain, are people who have lived their life in a cave somewhere!!

The fee charged for home-based instructions vary greatly. I know men and women who hold occasional classes in their homes or apartments for a "little extra spending money" monthly (often $100 to $300 per month), while others have turned their home seminars into a full-fledged enterprise, raking in thousands monthly by holding several classes or seminars each week. Fees range from $5 to $50 per attendee for each session (usually 2 to 4 hours in length.)

Advertising for attendees need not be expensive. Small ads, even classified ads in daily and community newspapers work well, and some dollar-conscious entrepreneurs obtain free advertising by tacking up circulars in laundromats, grocery

51

stores, and other places where people congregate. If you do a good job teaching people skills they want to learn, much repeat business will be forthcoming via word of mouth. Size of groups who attend home classes/seminars vary, but most instructors feel less than six is too few and more than 15 is too many, per session.

A NEW CONCEPT IN TRAVEL AGENCIES AND VACATION EXCHANGING

The high cost of travel and the slow economy of the past few years (1981-1983) has brought "hard times" to many traditional travel agencies. However, this also can mean opportunity for home-based entrepreneurs.

Alternative travel can become popular since high costs have driven potential globe trotters into looking for a better and cheaper method in which to get from here-to-there. The idea here is in the sharing of private vehicles and resources.

There is a real need for an agency to mastermind and coordinate this kind of travel. When you consider the millions of cars, planes, trucks, boats, motor homes, etc., owned by private citizens, you begin to comprehend the fabulous profit potential available.

The key here is to play travel matchmaker. Matching people looking for travel, facilities, lodging, etc., with those who can provide the services, equipment, and facilities required, for a fee.

Acting as a clearing house, the operator of the alternative

travel agency charges a fee for matching clients.

For example, let's say a driver is going from Los Angeles to New York—He lists his or her origin, destination and date of departure with your agency, agreeing to pay a fee if you can place one or more people who are interested in traveling with him/her to share expenses. Fellow travelers need not travel every mile of the trip—although this may be desirable—the driver also could pick-up riders who paid you a fee to list their travel needs in cities along the route. In this example from Los Angeles to New York, many cities in several states would provide pick-up and drop-off spots along the way.

Then you have a second listing (and fee) from this driver on his return trip from New York to Los Angeles a few weeks later, repeating the process lining up riders.

The fees you charge can be determined on distance, or you may opt for a flat rate. Naturally the people providing the transportation will have to base their charges on distance traveled. Using our New York to Los Angeles example, let's say both the driver and rider paid you $25. each for your service, then the rider paid the driver $75. in transportation fees, he or she would be able to make the nearly 3,000 mile trek from Los Angeles to New York, for only $100., less than ½ the price of traveling by bus and only about ⅓ the air fare cost.

CHECK REFERENCES—If you decide to book alternative travel, you must absolutely check references. Your clients have every right to anticipate a safe journey with a "normal" rider or driver. Although you will take reasonable precautions, you must get a disclaimer form printed so that it relieves you of any responsibility for accidents, thefts or other problems between the parties.

PRIVATE AIRPLANES

Anyone who pilots their own aircraft could offer the same service as auto drivers. Many business persons fly regularly, owning or leasing their own planes; many would welcome other business persons to share expenses. On the other side of the coin, many business and sales people, professionals and general travelers would be happy to share expenses with a pilot who can give them time saving and money saving air transportation. Here again you could provide a valuable service to both.

MOVING TOGETHER

More people than ever are renting their own trucks and moving themselves. As an "Alternate Travel Agency" you could match people who wanted to share a large truck or van to a common destination, or a location along the route. Since it is cheaper to return a van (round trip) than to pay for a one way trip, you could arrange for booking the return. If two parties moved from Seattle to St. Louis, you could arrange for one or more parties in the St. Louis area to return the van to Seattle—all parties paying you a nice fee for your match-up services.

TRANSPORTATION AND
LODGING EXCHANGES

Exchanging of vehicles and residences is another profit source for anyone starting an alternative travel agency. People in Minnesota who wanted to visit the mountains of Colorado would exchange their lake front home and auto for a Rocky Mountain condo and car.

Vacation home exchanging is already gaining popularity throughout the free world. Arranging such exchanges between Americans could net big profits, with the possibility of going international in the future. This type of service could match people all over the world. America is the nation most foreigners want to visit and Americans love to travel almost anywhere.

START-UP

Getting into this business will not cost a fortune. Advertising and promotion is the key to success. Ads in the travel section of large metropolitan newspapers, plus direct mail could build volume quickly. Word of mouth from satisfied clients can help keep business rolling. Although this type of business could start almost anywhere, I do believe a major city would offer a better chance of gaining quick recognition. A smaller town, but one near a desirable vacation area—lakes, the mountains, tourist attractions—should also work well.

HOW MUCH TO CHARGE?

Your fees must be reasonable enough to attract clients and at the same time substantial enough to afford you a decent profit. While there are many ways to handle fees, it may be wise to handle your services in a fashion similar to the activities of an ad agency. Fees are determined by individual listings. It is reasonable not to charge the same fee for someone exchanging vacation homes in, let's say, New England and New Mexico, as you would for someone who only wants a ride from Milwaukee to Chicago—less than a one hundred mile trip.

A low membership fee to help process paper work, listings, check of references, etc., may also be a great idea.

A basic fee for each particular type of service could be established, based on the value of the service. Advance payment of all fees is a must. Get paid before any travel or other services are performed. A small computer to keep track of various services offered and desired, plus application processing would be required once volume picked up. A card filing system probably would suffice for the few months of operation.

There is real potential here. The concept may need more fine tuning, but I really believe several entrepreneurs can develop a big money-maker from the alternative travel, rental and vacation sharing business.

This type of business can be operated from your home on a part-time basis. Later you may wish to expand into a downtown office space.

The possibility to set-up a network of agencies in major cities is real and this concept would also lend itself to franchising and national/international promotions.

This kind of opportunity is definitely not for everyone. Let your imagination run wild and give it some serious thought. It may be just right for you!

BUYING AND SELLING ALMOST ANYTHING! BUY CHEAP—SELL HIGH!

No one ever lost money buying cheap and selling high. It is another basic philosophy of mine that I have personally prospered with! Don't allow the simplicity of this statement to throw you, it is a proven wealth-building approach.

Wheeler-dealers are making big money today. Bargains are available in good used items and closeout new merchandise.

(1) Attend all available closeout sales (not the kind held by retail stores, but the kind offered by wholesalers and distributors—look for "closeout notices" in the classified section of large metropolitan newspapers.) Also shop all nearby auctions, garage sales, flea markets and swap meets, searching for good under-priced used merchandise.

(2) Use the "shotgun" approach to under-priced buying. Buy almost anything that is grossly under-priced, if you believe you know where to peddle it at a substantial profit. Space may be a consideration. Don't load up on items that will require expensive storage.

(3) Also, use the "rifle" approach. While being willing to buy almost anything at a super low price, it is usually wise to find a niche in the market. Start specializing in specific goods to a defined market. Your specialty could be used cars, typewriters, office equipment, tires, furniture, jewelry, antiques, rare coins, stamps, books, art, clocks, bikes, electronic gear, appliances, television sets, or whatever else turns you on and lends itself to a quick resale at at least double what you paid for it!

In spite of a somewhat depressed economy, bargains are still available if you dig for them. In fact, you're surrounded by them!

How much money can you make buying and selling? Easily a couple thousand dollars per year on a very limited basis. I have known some very active, very sharp "horsetraders" who make up to fifty thousand dollars a year in steady buy-sell transactions. The sky is really the steady limit. Your income will only be restricted by (A) the time you invest in your buying-selling activities, and (B) by how well you can spot super bargains and then turn them over at substantial profits.

IMPORTANT BUYING GUIDELINES

(A) PURCHASE ONLY MERCHANDISE, FAR BELOW MARKET VALUE. A "good buy" is not "good" enough. You want a fantastic bargain! A friend of mine buys and sells used, reconditioned typewriters. It has become a very lucrative sideline business. He runs little ads in various newspapers and shoppers guides:

WANTED used typewriters, must be in good condition. CASH. Phone #000-0000

He receives dozens of calls from eager sellers each week. Almost all of them offering to sell a good machine at a reasonable price. He recently told me, "I could make a substantial profit with about 90% of the machines, people wish to sell me. However, I don't want a good deal, I want a GREAT DEAL! By only purchasing about 10% of the typewriters I am offered, I generally triple my money and am still able to give my customers (he sells to both individuals and businesses) a bargain price—way below!!! There are enough "highly motivated" sellers around—people who want fast cash money—that you can buy goods at huge discounts.

(B) KNOW THE VALUE OF WHAT YOU BUY. Don't put yourself in the "trick bag" by buying items that you "think" are at bargain basement prices. It is vital that you know the approximate value of anything you purchase. You will often have to make a fast decision and may have to make an "educated guess", just make darn certain you can "ballpark" the potential value. I knew a fellow who once bought 5 gross (720) "mood rings" at .25¢ each. He had bought a similar mood stone ring for his wife a few years before at $5, and reasoned he was making a fantastic buy. What he didn't know was that the "mood ring" craze had burned out and his rings were in little demand. He was unable to find a jeweler or novelty store to buy the rings, even at his break-even price of .25¢ each. He finally sold them to various California swap meet sellers at his cost, but considering his time and effort to get rid of his rings, it was a losing proposition.

The lesson for all of us who buy and sell goods; Know today's approximate values and stay away from "fad" items that are at the tail-end of their selling cycle.

(C) KNOW THY MARKET! It's only a great buy, if you know where to sell it at a great profit. While it is not absolutely necessary to know who your exact buyer will be, it is wise to have a darn good idea where to locate your potential buyers. This factor alone, makes a strong argument for the selective approach to buying and selling. Don't buy ANYTHING that you don't have some idea as to where and how it can be sold!

PYRAMID YOUR PROFITS

While many moneymaking ventures require several thousands of dollars to get started, not so with my "grass roots" buying and selling strategy. You can get started for "peanuts" and pyramid your profits—fast. I have personally bought small items (watches, tools, etc.) for less than $50 total and sold them for $300 within one week. If you reinvest most or all of your profits during the first few months, you can turn a "chicken-feed investment" of only one hundred dollars or even less, into many thousands, in a very short time. And the beauty of this is, you can devote as little or as much to your buy-sell activities as you desire. While running your regular fulltime business or working at your regular job.

Buying and selling is the basic, profitable independent, home-based business. Its free enterprise with a capital F! It is easy to start, requires very limited funds and offers you truly unlimited potential!

My advice: Get involved! Its fun and profitable!

PROFITS FROM PLANTS

Janet Murphy's home is a vegetable jungle of palm and fig trees hanging ferns, ivy plants, spider plants and other assorted lush green plants, succulents and begonias. Janet has a sweet green thumb and she is cashing in on her talents with her own interior plantscaping business. The only thing that seems to be growing faster than her many plants is her bank account.

Miss Murphy's customers include both small and large offices, restaurants, and an indoor shopping mall.

People like to be surrounded by plants and other foliage because they personalize business establishments, soften appearances of otherwise sterile doctors and dentists offices and "dress-up" any location with their color and charm.

Working out of her lovely southern California home, "two thousand square feet, but the plants have taken over fifteen hundred," she informs you she has parlayed her magic thumb and an original capital investment of only two thousand dollars into a green business with a deep black bottom line. Could this be a home-based opportunity for you?

Although Janet does not service residential clients, I have heard of others in this blooming business who do—specializing in providing plantscaping for upper middle class and downright wealthy people. It has been reported to me that one couple who specialized in plantscaping for the nice, rich and refined folks of Beverly Hills, California, earns over a hundred grand per year working out of their home. That seems quite high, but there is no debating that plantscaping offers relatively low risks and high profit potential.

PLANTS TO STOCK

The key to success in this business is to handle the type of plants that hold up well and require only minimal care. All of the multi-varieties of the dracaena family (including dracaena marginata, a beautiful tree-like plant) do extremely well and are readily available. Fig trees (ficus) are always popular for their leafy, weeping effect. Palms are also always in big demand. Many clients choose the smaller, less expensive plants or trees. Boston fern and asparagus fern are very popular for hanging baskets, even though they are a bit finicky and require additional care.

PLANT DESIGN

Although designs can be standardized, every home, office or commercial area presents unique advantages and/or problems. The plantscape designer must consider lighting, temperature, humidity, traffic density and space limitations.

PLANT SOURCES

Most people who operate a plantscaping design business buy their stock from local growers. You will discover that most nurseries carry a large variety of plants and trees. Once you really get your fledging enterprise off the ground, you can consider buying plants and trees from leading wholesale nurseries in Florida. There are shipping companies who specialize in bringing plants from Florida to all parts of the USA. Once you establish credit, orders can be placed with Florida growers by phone.

Caution: Any nursery who ships plants is only responsible for plants until they are loaded on a truck. You must check with people who have already used the trucking services to be sure you are dealing with a reliable transporter.

People who enter this potentially lucrative enterprise soon discover that it is wise to use sterilized artificial soil for potting. Too often the soil in your backyard is contaminated with undesirable organisms (nematodes, grub worms, ants, fungus, centipedes, and bacteria), which can eat or decay your plants. Organic material such as vermiculite also should be added to your potting soil to make it looser and more aerated.

PLANT MAINTENANCE

Although substantial original profits are obtained from initial plant sales, your business will probably require plant maintenance services in order to thrive. These are the "bread and butter" of the business and include such services as pruning, fertilizing, watering and spraying.

It is usually wise to offer various "service contracts" to clients. One contract can be for basic maintenance; water, spray and fertilize if necessary. Plants are maintained under this agreement but usually without any guarantee. A monthly fee of $20 to $50 for weekly service is reasonable, and is dictated by how many plants a client has.

A more elaborate contract which guarantees the plants—offering replacements as needed, would out of necessity, demand much higher monthly charges. It is not uncommon for a large establishment with many plants and trees to pay up to $300 monthly for guaranteed care.

The prices you charge for interior plantscaping to earn a profit depend on the "on-site" considerations. If nearby windows offer plenty of sunlight, plant care will be quite easy. Many establishments do not afford this ideal atmosphere. You must figure the wholesale value of your plants and the probable loss over a year (which can be as high as 20% in some places) and your time, effort and supplies involved in your plant care. Don't overlook or underestimate unusual circumstances. Some plantscapers are required to climb ladders to hang and water plants in high ceiling restaurants, office buildings, and homes.

Your hourly wage should be penciled into all service costs. Only you can decide how much per hour your time is worth, but the range seems to be from $12. to $30.

Chances are that it would not be worth your time to charge less than $20 or $25. monthly to any client, including a single family home.

The best way to estimate any job is to figure all wholesale costs, including your overall cost of operating your business and then adding what you consider to be a fair profit. It is recommended that you add 50% to your overall costs to put your business in black ink and keep it there.

Plantscaping can be started as a one-person operation. Later you may wish to expand and hire others to help you. Since basic service and maintenance skills are learned quite easily, the going rate for hired help is quite low, in the $5.00

to $8.00 per hour range. If you don't provide transportation (a van is an excellent vehicle in this business and can be leased at a substantial tax write off, you will have to pay any assistants you hire an extra transportation allowance for providing their own transportation.

It can also be a smart idea to bond yourself and any employees you hire. It assures customers that you are trustworthy. Liability insurance is a must both on the site and in transit to jobs.

An excellent source of important information for prospective plantscapers is the Interior Plantscaping Association, 1601 Washington Plaza, Suite 14, Reston, Virginia 22090.

Many universities are offering courses in horticultural design. Also, your local library is a rich source of horticultural information.

GOURMET PROFITS FROM CATERING

Staying in the kitchen at a party while everyone else is drinking, eating and having fun, may not be your idea of a good time, but it certainly can be profitable.

The new breed of social caterers often earn a net income of $200. to over $5,000. for their orchestrated part and planning and culinary expertise. Americans love to eat and be entertained and those folks with enough money to indulge will pay handsomely to have their special dinners and parties planned, prepared and served within their own homes.

Many people who love to dine out and be entertained have been turned off by fine restaurants which are overcrowded and impersonal. Several have found it is better to "bring the restaurant" into their homes.

Here's a home based business that can bring home the big lettuce for people who like to work with food and who have a flair for promotion.

AN EXPANDING FIELD

Today social caterers offer everything from breakfast in bed for two, to lavish dinner parties for 200. Although still a relatively new concept, great expansion is underway and anyone wanting a big slice of the pie should get established as soon as possible. And yes, you can get started in your own home.

LUNCHEON OPPORTUNITIES

In the past, business people limited their lunchtime catering to placing a call to a local deli and asking that "a certain number of salami sandwiches and hot or cold drinks be sent over". While this practice still continues, more and more business executives are going first class. Enter the personal caterer.

The secret to success in catering is to get paid BEFORE the food and drink is purchased and prepared. The host or hostess must inform you in advance how many guests are expected and pay either half (50%) or all of your total charges several days before the luncheon, dinner or party. Thus, you can use the clients' money to cover all or most of your services.

HOW TO GET STARTED

The first thing a professional caterer must do is know how to plan. Advanced planning, right down to the smallest details is required for success. Printed forms that give you a check list on all planning, preparation and serving can be an invaluable helpmate. Last minute surprises only cause hassles.

Perhaps the best way to do the cooking is right in the clients home. However, some clients do not allow this, demanding that the food be prepared elsewhere. Naturally, you absolutely must prepare business conference luncheons in your own home or elsewhere. This is usually no problem, as cold salads, sandwiches and snacks often comprise luncheon servings.

Personalized service is a must! The caterers who are making the really big money have found out success comes as much from catering to the host or hostess as their guests. Clients love personalized service and being made to feel very important.

In addition to providing the food and service, some professionals arrange for the liquor, soft drinks and juices, hire bartenders—sometimes even musicians and other entertainers, etc. One successful Seattle catering service specializing in astrology parties, complete with special zodiac decorations, etc., and also bring a professional astrologer with them to entertain guests. Another service in San Jose has turned a handsome profit in specializing in the catering of bridal showers, with appropriate decorations and a hired photographer. A specialty can often help a beginning caterer get into business quickly with minimum advertising and promotion costs.

Should you decide to go into this business you will need promotional skills every bit as much as the ability to plan, prepare and serve delicious food.

Your local librarian can point you to several books on the subject of catering. This can be a super profitable business to enter, but in the final analysis it is the kind of business that requires you to offer personal service in which your own personality and organizational ability will determine your success or failure. It is a business that can be operated from your home without regular employees. Most caterers cultivate a list of people who work as independent contractors to prepare food and serve it on a party-to-party basis.

Catering is not for everyone, but is it possible that it is right for you?

$25,000 IN 30-DAYS—
STARTING FROM SCRATCH

Here is one of the most exciting and profitable HBO's we have ever uncovered.

This opportunity offers one of the fastest methods to make big money starting with little or no investment capital. Here is a system that can put up to $25,000 in your pocket in 30-days. This is a unique method of publishing and distributing coupon books.

I don't have to tell you discount coupons are red-hot now days. Supermarkets, restaurants, drug stores, gas stations, home repair firms, etc., almost every merchant is running coupon advertising on either a regular or semi-regular basis. Already several sharp entrepreneurs are hustling ads from local merchants for targeted local direct mail offers (a very nice mail-order enterprise). However, this setup is different, a new twist that has recently earned a bundle for a home-based promoter in San Francisco. Here is how it works: This profitable new twist is in having the coupons distributed through church, charity and civic organizations as a fund raising activity. There is absolutely no selling. The group members give the coupons away free and even are paid to do it! Groups reportedly jump at this deal. And why not! In place of selling candy, cards and gifts (some of which is not too easy to sell anyway), they sell nothing. They sell absolutely nothing and they are not bothered cooking and baking, or doing other chores associated with most fund raising activities.

69

You sell the program to local merchants. Your offer is almost irresistible. You will have leading churches and civic groups in the community distributing their advertising. In effect, they are receiving an endorsement from the groups. And to top off your super offer to them, they actually pay less for this ad service than traditional newspaper television or radio ads would cost.

Here's how Jack White in San Francisco worked it, starting from square one. He successfully worked a four-step program:

(1). He contacted his local church and found them receptive to the idea of being paid 25¢ each for every "local merchants coupon book" that they gave away free.

(2). He contacted other charitable and civic groups and asked them if they would distribute free coupon books to their members, friends and families if they were paid to do so. Many answered yes, some even offering to distribute such discount advertising to their members, family and friends without charge. However, Jack assured them they would be paid for their efforts at 25¢ for each coupon book they gave away. No wonder they were all ears.

(3). Jack contacted several printers for bids on a multi-paged coupon book. He asked for bids on various numbers of pages and total quantity, since he didn't have any way of knowing how many ads he could expect to print in his first book.

(4). He approached local merchants and sought their advertising support for his plan. At first he found his reception a little on the cool side, due to the fact he was asking them to "pay up front" for an advertising program they were unfamiliar with. Jack then changed tactics. He went back to the printer whom he had selected to print his coupon books and explained the problem. The printer agreed to print the job without advance pay and receive full payment when Jack collected upon publication. After all, the print shop owner knew the local merchants, and knew all or almost all—there are a few deadbeats—would honor their commitment once they saw their discount coupon ads in print. Now asking for no money in advance, signing up advertising was easy. "I once nailed fourteen out of twenty merchants in one afternoon." It is easy selling this setup when you ask to be paid AFTER the ads are published.

Jack's venture was a "qualified success!" "I made four thousand dollars in thirty days, but I worked my tail off, eighty hours a week, nearly 200 hours for the month." Still not too bad for a guy who was working virgin territory.

Soon Jack was ready to go after the big bux. The second time around he was 100% smarter. He contacted several leading civic groups to greatly expand his distribution network. Although he continued working with local business people, he included every type of business and professional. Eye doctors, dentists, psychologists, and chiropractors placed discount ads side-by-side with food markets, bookstores, flower shops and dance studios.

He also turned his attention to administrative duties, and hired a dozen "ad consultants" to sell advertising. Again, no up-front expenses. His advertising staff (some of which came from the ranks of the clubs and organizations who distributed his coupon books) worked strictly as "independent con-

71

tractors'', earning 20% commission on every ad they sold. If the merchant or professional paid up front—and many now did to obtain a slight additional discount, also knowing Jack had "previous experience in this field—the ad people were paid up front. If not, they were paid after publication.

The results were amazing. Jack White took in over $58,000 in less than 30-days. After paying his printer, the organizations for their distribution efforts, his advertising people and all other expenses, his net profit before taxes was slightly more than $25,000. Approximately 40¢ profit on every dollar received.

"If you work it right, you can make a grand a day", Jack says. Jack knows how to work it right, and now so do you. $25,000 within 30-days, starting from scratch. Some people work hard all year for that sum or less. It just goes to prove, you don't need lots of money to make money, but you do need profitable ideas!

GAMBLING INFORMATION EXPLOSION

Are you into any form of gambling? Do you play the horses, bet on football games, shoot dice, take your turn at the blackjack table, or any other gambling activity? If your answer is yes, and if you're above average in your skills and winning ability, maybe you can get very, very rich selling your expertise to others.

Mike Warren of Baltimore, Maryland, has earned millions of dollars—we have seen his federal tax returns—selling his expert gambling advice. Since Mike handicaps many sports (racing, football, basketball, etc.), he has an offer for almost any bettor. Other gambling information pros often zero in on a specific activity they excel in—pro football, craps, the dogs, horses, etc.

With over forty million active gamblers in America, ranging from the guy who dunks two bucks into the office world series pool to the guy who bets twenty thousand bucks because he doesn't believe the Dallas Cowboys are four points better than the Minnesota Vikings, gambling (both the legal and illegal variety) is BIG BUSINESS and getting BIGGER!

TWO FORMS OF
INFORMATION SELLING

Here are two popular ways that thousands of so-called "experts" are cashing in on the gambling boom:

(1). *Packaged Information:* This includes books, booklets, manuals, reports, newsletters, etc., that are sold—primarily by mail order—to the gambling public. If you have a "system" to beat blackjack, horse racing, stud poker, etc., it can be packaged in a printed format and marketed. The printed form can be a four page report or a 400-page manual, and the price need not have very much to do with the size of the printed literature. We have seen "dice systems" of 24-pages sell for $100 a pop, even though the actual printing costs didn't amount to 50¢ and that yields an incredible 19,900% markup!!

(2). *Game or Event Predicting:* This form of gaming information selling concerns itself with an actual event—a specific race, football game, boxing match, etc. Although you may advertise for clients by mail, the actual prediction is usually made by giving the client a number to call you a day or two before the game or event.

Both methods of selling gambling expertise are profitable. Obviously more research, effort and expense are involved in producing printed matter. Predicting the actual result of a specific event requires very little startup capitalization, with the exception of advance advertising to secure clients. Selling printed information will also require considerable advertising.

The real risk involved with making individual prognostications is that a string of bad (losing) releases will soon find you without clients. On the other side of the coin, if you released several consecutive winners to your customers, or at least maintain a respectable winning percentage (55% plus!), you will get both repeat business plus new word-of-mouth business!

In selling printed matter, you "grind out" your profits over a period of time. Also, you probably will have to prepare "backup-offers" to increase profits. Any person who buys one system or book from you is a leading candidate to buy another, and your customers list can be your most precious asset.

Selling gambling information is not for everyone, but for some it spells big, impressive returns. Up to $100,000 and more per year is rather common for a good hustler who has reasonably reliable information.

Startup capital: Advertising (either space ads in gambling publications or national general-interest tabloids and magazines or a direct mail campaign to a rented mailing list of known players) will not be cheap. Even a shoestring start will probably require expenditures in marketing of at least $2,000 and quite likely more.

This business can be operated inside the home. In the case of giving information by phone, it is advisable to install a separate number. A "hello" from your small child would label you a rinky-dink operator by a hardcore gambling customer.

If you're thinking about selling gambling information, visit your local newsstand and look over the many ads in publications such as MILLIONS, GAMBLING TIMES, PRO FOOTBALL WEEKLY, COLLEGE AND PRO FOOTBALL NEWS, AMERICAN TURF MONTHLY, AND TURF AND SPORTS DIGEST. These and other publications will give you a good idea how leading operators advertise their services.

Just remember this—effective advertising will bring you clients, but only accurate information will keep them spending money with you.

Caution: Never agree to place actual bets for clients. The laws against bookmaking are enforced and the penalties (including jail sentences) are severe.

Perhaps only one person in a thousand is suited for this type of moneymaking enterprise. It has been presented here only for the right person. It can be so very profitable.

If present trends continue, more and more states will be turning to one form of gambling or another, looking for additional revenues. Business is good now and soon will be getting better.

METAPHYSICAL MONEY

David Jones of Los Angeles is doing his best to turn "PYRAMID POWER" into the kind of smashing success enjoyed by "PET ROCKS" several years back. The concept that pyramids have the secret power to collect and focus unknown universal energy force and thus bestow special power or blessings on any person or object placed inside their influence, is attracting great interest to all shapes, sizes and kinds of replicas of those magnificent wonders that are found in Egypt along the Nile.

With more and more interest in pyramids being generated by TV and radio programs, movies, magazines, books and

newspaper articles, Dave Jones launched PYRAMID POW-
ER, INC in 1982 and already business is booming. The twen-
ty-eight year old entrepreneur, long a student of metaphysics
and unusual phenomenon, launched his small manufacturing
firm with less than $3,000 of his own capital, plus another
$3,000 from a friend who originally became his partner, but
who later allowed Dave to buy him out for only $500 above
his original investment.

"When we were only showing a very small profit after
three months of hard work, my friend came to me and asked
if I would buy him out for his investment plus an extra $500. I
borrowed the money and took 100% control", Dave explains
and then with a boyish smile, he adds, "I think my friend
made a mistake." That's putting it mildly! With total sales of
over three million dollars projected by 1986, Dave's buddy
will soon be crying in his beer, if he isn't already.

With tons of publicity built into the items he manufactures
and sells, Mr. Jones produces over two dozen varieties of
pyramids ranging in size from standard size plastic glass to a
huge model large enough to engulf a king size waterbed.
Dave's most expensive model includes the waterbed, complete with headboard and heater and his biggest pyramid for
a retail price of slightly over eleven hundred dollars retail.
Several waterbed stores across the nation have introduced
this item and initial sales have been encouraging. Dave is pro-
jecting four hundred thousand dollars profit, before taxes for
himself yearly by 1986. Already his income is approaching six
figures annually. Not bad for a young man who started with
less than three thousand dollars and one big idea.

Is pyramid manufacturing and/or sales for you? Probably not—even though the concept is growing fast enough to warrant some competition. The real point here relates to the boom in metaphysical merchandise and items and gadgets that are related to the occult sciences. From astrology to witchcraft, the western world has renewed its interest in the unusual and unknown. A husband and wife in Chicago hand letters, then print and distribute "Astrology Scrolls" to dining establishments and earn instant success; a St. Paul man long obsessed with the occult begins reprinting ancient occult manuscripts in booklet form in his basement and within five years builds a vast publishing empire; A Mesa, Arizona, Indian woman handcrafts and sells Indian "Good Luck Charms" and immediately prospers; while another husband and wife team in St. Petersburg, Florida, earns a fortune from importing "Sacred Charms" from India and selling by mail at ten times their original cost; another company in southern California reportedly is earning millions by mail selling tiny vials, each containing a few drops of the "Healing Water" taken from the springs in Lourdes, France. Beyond a reasonable doubt, there is a widening market place for all kinds of metaphysical items.

While some will snicker and label many of these entrepreneurs "charlatans" there can be no doubt they have discovered a market and are filling an expanding clientele. And who among us can really say just how valuable a service is being provided?

THE ESSENCE OF SUCCESS

Why will many people pay up to $100 per ounce for perfume? What special, magic, appealing ingredient makes a dab of oily substance worth mega bucks? Snob appeal for sure, plus the feeling of "treating yourself royally." Not to mention the seductive advertising campaign that attracted you to buy the stuff in the first place.

There is a big audience for high-price fragrances that women are anxious to buy and wear. But the economics are beyond the vast majority. JOY costs over $100; NOrell is $75; and Chanel #5 is $55 per ounce. Most people cannot afford these prices.

The fragrances, extracts, oils and essences that create these odors are now possible to reproduce at substantial savings. They are being duplicated by an enterprising company that sells these desirable products under their own PARFUM de NAUDET label. Prices range 80% or less than expensive famous brands.

There is important money to be made in creating a line of perfumes and colognes, using ingredients that mimic the expensive originals. Any kind of discount, especially one of 50% or more off the original price, should appeal to the affluent as well as to those people who would like to wear the high price brands, but who cannot do so because of a limited budget.

To succeed in this field, you must buy the essences at rock bottom wholesale, and cleverly package and promote like crazy. Party plan selling works well for colognes and perfumes, with perhaps a smart jewelry line to increase sales.

For more information about the fragrances and extracts, you can write to: Essential Products Co., Inc., 90 Water Street, New York, NY 10005.

TYPESETTING—A $100,000 A YEAR COTTAGE INDUSTRY FOR FAST FINGERS

You can set type for books, manuals, reports and magazines in your home with new photo-electronic typesetting equipment. All you need is a spare room, a relatively small investment and the ability to type. The moneymaking potential is awesome—from $30,000 to $100,000 per year!

A little space, fast fingers and good time management can turn a one-woman or man Cottage Industry into a gold mine. A modern computerized photo compositor is simply a super typewriter that produces professional type in various sizes and styles on light sensitive paper. The paper is then run through a relatively small developer. Thus, an entire book can be prepared for photo-offset printing. Most typesetting machines are no larger than a small desk. This process is much faster and far more cost-effective than the now outdated traditional metal typesetting methods.

Typesetting machines sell for anywhere from $2,000 to $200,000, depending on their speed, output and variety of type. The average price for a modern machine that can handle most composition jobs is in the $20,000 to $40,000 range. While equipment buyers face a substantial investment, most manufacturers will lease equipment and accept monthly payments. Also, in a computerized field that is experiencing constant technological advancements, leasing is usually the best decision. A good service contract is another must.

While a home-based typesetting can be far more lucrative than an ordinary typing service, covered previously in this manual, some forward thinking operators offer both services. Both typesetting and typing services also lend themselves to the employment of outside helpers. Although an operator would be wise to get an opinion from a tax attorney or competent accountant, several operators do use outside help on an "independent contractor" basis, thus avoiding a standard employer-employee relationship that would require various employee benefits, tax withholding, etc.

Some typesetters work closely with a free lance graphic artist, since some publishing clients and printers like to receive their type in "camera-ready" condition. The product of photo-typesetting is text strung out in long strips of paper—known in the trade as "galleys" which must be arranged with headlines and/or artwork that will eventually appear as pages.

Several typesetters find that their profit picture is brighter through specialization. Jack Lilly of Portland, Oregon, has carved out a nice niche for himself in setting technical reports; Betty Brown of Boise, Idaho, specializes in company newsletters and Ginger Julian of RUSH TYPE in Lakeside California, has discovered that by setting straight textual material, she can increase her volume many times over than if she were setting complicated material requiring frequent changes of type fonts. Marilyn Denson of Vista, California, is living proof that if you are willing to handle most all types of typesetting jobs, you soon will grow beyond a one person setup. Marilyn got started in this business in 1978, and within 5 years saw her equipment more than triple. She now also has six busy typesetters, plus a large shop, to help her keep up with the workload. Marilyn's brother, Dave is an offset printer. This has worked well for both, with each referring clients to the other. It is a good idea for anyone going into the typesetting business to strike up referral service with one or more printers in the immediate area. Some printers will send you customers, others will bill out the complete printing and typesetting package and then pay your invoice. Many print shops like to present their customers with one billing that includes typesetting. In this way, they can add 20% or more to your basic charges. Likewise, some printers will allow you commissions of 20% or more on customers you direct to them. It's one set of hands helping the other.

If typesetting sounds interesting to you as a part or full time profitable home enterprise, and there is no doubt big profits are possible, get in contact with local representatives of the leading systems in your area. These would include COMPUGRAPHIC CORP, IBM, ADDRESSOGRAPH-MULTIGRAPH and others.

Good used machinery is also available in most large cities from printing and office equipment brokers. Often used equipment can be bought at a fraction of the original price. However, keep in mind new technology is forever changing the state of the art, and also don't forget the importance of a service contract to avoid major expenses and "down time." In this business, "down time" means money down the drain!

Here's a company very active in buying and selling used typesetting equipment:

Locker Typesetting Equipment
122 Van Houten Ave.
Passaic, NJ 07055

OPERATE A "IN-HOUSE" FURNITURE STORE

Here is a real eyeopener. While many businesses are operated in or out of the home, many of them are service oriented or concern themselves with manufacturing, distributing and selling small items. Now Mr. & Mrs. David P. Perry of Fargo, North Dakota, have added a new twist. Dave recently started his own unique furniture business part time right in the couples six room condominium. After working several years at a large local furniture company, Dave suddenly found himself out of work as the big company's business faltered in a depressed economy.

Dave had two ideas. One was to give real bargains to people who wanted to buy furniture and secondly, display items in a home-like atmosphere.

Inquiries to furniture manufacturers in nearby Des Moines, Iowa, and Minneapolis-St. Paul, Minnesota, proved fruitful. He found that he could get 40% to 50% off manufacturers suggested retail prices on most of the articles (functional low-priced items) he wanted to stock. Dave's logic was sound. He felt most of the fancy showrooms in the Fargo-Moorehead area were specializing in luxury articles that only a small percentage of buyers could afford. He would offer inexpensive items geared to the taste and pocketbooks of mid-income apartment dwellers.

Because he had a good credit reputation he was able to obtain items he wished to sell with only a small advanced payment and 30 to 90 day credit on the balance. He immediately ordered three complete bedroom sets, living room, dining and kitchen sets. With his wife's help, he furnished every room in his condo, complete with beautiful carpet and drapes. Although, they lived in the "showrooms" their lifestyle enabled them to maintain all the rooms in excellent condition. Naturally, their condo was "over-furnished", but sales—not personal use—was Dave's objective.

Dave's marketing plan was direct and simple. He telephoned friends to come by and see his collection; next, he placed small ads in local publications:

BUY FURNITURE AT WHOLESALE. LARGE
SELECTIONS, LOW PRICES. CALL 000-0000

Dave decided to only markup items by 25%, so his wholesale claim was valid. Although his condo was loaded with furniture, his in-house selection could hardly be called large. However, Jack had catalogs and sales sheets from two of his manufacturing sources that allowed him to order from their extensive product line. In fact, no deliveries were made on site. All deliveries came from the manufacturer, or by Dave himself, who began making regular trips in a rented truck to Des Moines, Chicago, the Twin Cities and other source cities within a 400-mile radius.

Within ten months Dave had his home-based furniture business going so strong that his wife quit her secretarial job and joined him in his new business. Although Dave and his wife did eventually expand to a retail sales location, it was not required. Dave simply decided that a far greater selection of articles could be displayed in a large downtown outlet, and that his move would eventually triple the couples profits.

Mr. and Mrs. Perry have proved, beyond any doubt, almost anything can be merchandised from the home. All you need is a good idea and the git and grit to see it through. Furniture sales, are they for you? Perhaps, but again, the concept is what is important.

Almost anything sold in a store can be sold from your home!

SOUND PROFITS

How about a home-based business that is in demand year round, good times or bad times? That's the way it goes when you sell, install and service car stereo systems.

Since the mid-1970's drivers have been able to receive the same high quality sound as previously only available in home-stereo equipment.

Modern technology allows manufacturers of automobile stereo equipment to offer quality radio and cassette receivers, total-sound stereo speakers and first-class amplification equipment.

85

High-tech innovation has increased the mass-market appeal of auto stereos to the discretionary income market.

Start-up costs to set up a car stereo shop could easily run $15,000 or more, but a lucrative home-based business can be started for $2,000 or less, if the entrepreneur is willing to plow profits back into the business to achieve steady growth during the critical first year of business.

The automobile stereo business is growing by leaps and bounds. Frank Vizard, editor of "Autosound and Communications," recently stated "as home audio and video became non-profitable, many of these guys moved into car audio." The Wall Street Journal reported in March, 1983, that computer, video and home-stereo retailers are in a slump. This is not the case in the car stereo market. Business is booming, 1984-1985 are expected to be great years, and the upward curve is expected to last until at least 1990.

Write to manufacturers found in the Thomas directories and other reference books found at your library to obtain the very best prices. Your goal should be at least a 50 percent markup on sales plus extra money for installation. A garage with ample room is a necessity.

Small ads in local daily newspapers and weekly shoppers will bring in business, especially if you emphasize quality equipment at reasonable prices. Stress low-overhead that allows you to knock the sox off your retail shop competitors. But do pay a little extra for "name brand" equipment. Customers will in turn pay more for quality equipment and components.

Car stereo sales and service is a good times/bad times business because when the economy is blowing and going, people (most sales are to 18 to 45 age group) will spend money on new equipment or to upgrade present equipment. When times are tough, car stereos are stolen at a staggering rate. This too, is good news for the entrepreneur that lands the job of replacing them.

One secret to success is to work with local insurance agencies. When a victim loses his equipment to a thief, he or she fills out a damage claim and then takes it to a dealer for replacement. Why shouldn't that dealer be you? Talk with several insurance agencies. Convince them that you offer fast, dependable service, and at reasonable prices. If they like you personally and find your prices competitive, they can steer a lot of business your way.

The best way to make "*Sound Profits*" is to both sell and service equipment. Selling is one thing. Even installation is reasonably simple. Service and repair is another matter. If you're not mechanically suited for fast repairs, you would have to have someone who is, work for you. This could possibly be on a "per job" basis, where this person would not be considered a traditional employee (who wants the hassle of deductions, etc.). You certainly also could learn to do your own servicing. You don't have to be an electronics whiz to make it in this booming business. You will need product knowledge (easily obtained) and some mechanical aptitude (also obtainable to private or public adult schools).

If this business opportunity turns up your amps, I have given you the basics. Now it's up to you to do some fine tuning.

HOME RETAILING

Home based retailing or "Party Plan" selling, as it is often referred to, is alive and well throughout the United States and Canada.

Women are still buying tupperware, but they are also buying clothing, health products, jewelry, cosmetics, sexy lingerie and just about anything else you can buy in a retail store.

Not to be left out, many men have also gotten into the home retailing business. Many husbands and wives have joined forces to build profitable parttime or fulltime home businesses.

New buying trends have many retail store owners concerned. Increased direct selling and party plan selling, often fueled by some form of multi-level marketing, is changing the buying habits of millions of consumers. Add to this the current mail-order boom and it's easy to understand why retail store sales are slipping.

Tupperware now earns its parent company, Dart Industries, over 50% of its yearly profit, Mary Kay Cosmetics saw sales reach 200 million in 1982 (250 million is their 1983 goal), and a southern California cosmetic/personal care product company parlayed an eighty thousand dollar investment into sales of eight million dollars in less than two years. This form of selling is hot!

Profits are available for couples or individual representatives, who go with either a good established firm, or a bright new shooting star. Representatives are independant contractors responsible for scheduling sales parties. $300 in sales at a party is about average for this form of selling and will bring the representative 25 to 30 percent. ($75 to $90). Some representatives earn as much as 50 percent on sales, however 25 to 30 percent is the industry average.

If you are not overly excited by these numbers, keep in mind parttime representatives often hold three or four parties per week and fulltime entrepreneurs will often hold as many as ten or more parties (some by day, others by night). Also, sharp home-based party plan retailers work constantly to improve their promotional skills to bring more people to each party. One San Diego lady, well experienced in party plan selling, remarked "If I'm not earning $25 or more for every hour I put into this, I'm not realizing my potential."

People who agree to open their homes and invite their friends and relatives in, are given a nice discount on their own purchases. A small price to pay to folks who do a lot of the work for the party sales representative.

These parties not only provide "expected sales" but future parties and future sales. This is why high incentives and cash bonuses are often offered to representatives who recruit other sales people.

Good money is definitely available to sales representatives, but the really big bucks go to the capable recruiter. Top recruiters who reach supervision levels often earn $100,000 or more annually.

Home retailing is a money maker in both "good times" and "hard times". In times of economic recession, home party plans seem to continue to flourish. Perhaps because recruiting becomes easier. In difficult times more people are interested in new sources for additional income.

The boom in home retailing has attracted the attention of many power conglomerates. Colgate Palmolive now offers Princess House, Gillette has Jaffra Cosmetics and Ralston Purina has introduced Deco Plants. While it's too soon to tell if these big companies or others will have a major impact on home retailing, party plan experts have not rushed to sign up with the giants. Dan Schroeder of St. Louis Park, Minnesota, a leading recruiter in party plan selling, asks a question that no doubt is on many representatives' and recruiters' minds, "Are some big conglomerates jumping into home retailing just to grab some extra profits, or are they committed to both the people and products involved?" The answer to that question is still blowing in the wind.

Home retailing is a no overhead business with wide consumer appeal. Soft selling techniques are applied since the people at the house party are basically all friends or at least know each other. As a representative, little or no investment is required as a local distributor (sales manager) usually provides product as required. This is a people-oriented business that offers friendly, personal service. A woman (over 90% of sales representatives are female), man or couple can get started for next nothing and build a respectable income-producing business based on sales. Even larger profits, much larger, are available to the individual or couple who is successful in recruiting others to hold parties and sell products.

If you can sell products and convince others that they can do likewise, you will prosper!

90

PROTESTING PROFITS

Protesting is as common to America's heritage as apple pie. From a famous tea party in Boston many years ago, to hunger strikes and picketing in the 1980's, the freedom to protest seems to be inbred in our citizens.

Jerry Baumburger of Detroit, Michigan, noticed several auto workers picketing "unfair" hiring and layoff procedures at a local plant and the light bulb of creativity went on inside his brain. Why restrict the idea to picketing exclusively to union gripes. Many other people have plenty to protest about. Baumburger decided to start his own picketing service—a new service for people who want to complain publicly.

Two small ads; one in a local daily newspaper and another in an "alternative" weekly, got the ball rolling. Baumburger remembers his first job was picketing a used car dealer for a client who strongly felt that he had been saddled with a lemon. Baumburger had his girl friend, an art student, design an eye-catching sign. The words "don't buy here or you'll be sorry" were imposed on a large lemon, complete with wheels. Jerry was paid $50 for four hours of walking and standing in front of the dealership. "I could have made a hundred bucks, Jerry reports. "I was offered another fifty dollars by the car dealer to get my (*bleep*) away from his lot." Jerry declined, of course. "In this business your loyalty belongs to the man or woman who hired you."

Not all picketing business is negative. Jerry Baumburger claims almost 50 percent of his picketing is positive. A local pizza parlor hires Jerry on a regular basis to tell folks "*Fol-*

91

low Me For the Best Pizza in Town." A two block hike often has up to ten people in tow. Before the people enter the parlor, Jerry passes out discount coupons—50¢ off a medium size pizza, $1 off a large one. The coupons he hands out are "keyed" and although he works only on commission with the pizza shop owner, Jerry's cut—also 50¢ and $1 per customer, often brings him up to $40 in one hour.

Sherry Evans of Hollywood, California, also employs pickets (paying them $5 to $10 per hour, depending on the job.) She, of course, charges clients much more ($20 to $35) but for Sherry, positive or protest picketing is just a new twist to her main business—a singing telegram service.

A picket is a stiff cardboard sign, approximately 24 x 30 inches. Lettering must be neat and as few words used as possible to make the message easily readable. Attractive graphics, while not essential, certainly are desirable. This is a business that can be started on a shoestring. Anyone with a few dollars for advertising, a telephone and a willingness to be visible, can quickly be in business for himself or herself.

The laws governing picketing are not necessarily restrictive. A picket must keep moving and not block street or sidewalk traffic. The biggest negative in this business is the potential irate actions of a shop owner who is the object of someone's protest. A young man in Gary, Indiana was punched out by a restaurant owner who became livid when he noticed the picket sign read, *"If You Love Pets—Don't Even Let Your Dog Eat Here."* The young man was doing his own picketing after consuming "Food" at that establishment. However, the punches thrown could just as easily have decked a hired picket. Let the would-be entrepreneur beware!

Protest (or positive slogan) picketing can bring quick cash. It's a novelty-type business that could be operated parttime or fulltime from the home. The potential is there for expansion and much larger profits would be available to the creative promoter who hustled "new accounts" while hiring others to pound the pavement with a sign in hand.

MAKING AND REPAIRING DOLLS

One of the largest hobby groups in the United States are the "Dollers," people who collect, produce and/or repair dolls. There are hundreds of thousands of "dollers" in America today and their numbers are increasing each year.

The oldest varieties or antique dolls, usually from the old world (Germany, France or Holland) are the most expensive of the group, demanding prices up to $2,000 and more apiece. One of America's all time favorites, the original Shirley Temple doll, in excellent condition, will bring $600 or more from a serious collector. While this hobby is not for poor folks, making and repairing dolls can be started with limited capital. High quality reproductions will usually sell in the $100 to $300 range. Not cheap, yet affordable for many people.

The head is of primary importance in the reproduction of a doll. Material used to cast the head is usually china, ceramic or porcelain. Plastic molds are used for casting. The ceramic is poured into a mold as a liquid. It condenses on the sides, and is removed while still damp. It is then fired in a kiln at an extremely high temperature. Lashes and eyebrows and "skin coloring" are applied prior to the final firing. Limbs can be made by the same process, however, total composition bodies—even leather bodies that are exact copies of antique bodies—may be purchased and may be combined with homemade bisque heads.

Molds are available for almost every antique doll in demand. Making your own mold is the alternative. Kiln and molds are expensive, but you need not go to this expense. You can buy "greenware" (this is unfired ceramic), do the painting yourself and hire an expert to fire it.

Sources of supplies for everything from glass eyes to heads to complete dolls can be found by subscribing to *"Doll Reader"* (published 6 times per year by Hobby House Press, Ind., 900 Frederick St., Cumberland, MD, 21502 and *"Doll World"* P.O. Box 337, Seabrook, NH, 03874). The "bible" of the industry concerning pricing is the *"Blue Book of Doll Values"* by Jan Foulke (published by Hobby House Press Inc., who also publish "The Doll Reader.")

If you would rather repair than make dolls, operating a doll hospital can be a very profitable venture. Top repair prices deal with restoring antiques. Lesser rates are usually charged for less expensive dolls. Hair must be washed regularly and curled, clothes sewn or replaced, glass eyes restored to brilliance and cracks in composition heads and bodies filled and blended in.

You need not wait to become an expert before you get started repairing dolls on a parttime basis. Novices begin by making simple repairs on popular dolls, but not antiques. Probably the most common problem is worn out elastic in the ball-joint bodies, missing eyes and damaged hair. Sewing clothes for dolls also pays quite well. A woman in El Cajon, California, figures her time at $10 profit per hour. Business is readily available from doll owners and antique dealers who wish to display a doll dressed well in order to command the highest price.

In addition to antique shop owners, get to know the folks who own doll shops in your area. These dealers may offer a repair service of their own, but are often kept so busy that they will be pleased to "farm out" extra work to you.

Another great source for doll selling and doll repairing are the many doll shows held in almost every community. You will find dates and locations of these shows in the magazines previously mentioned.

Earnings of $10 to $20 per hour are realistic for doll making. Somewhat less, $5 to $15 per hour for doll repairing. This business is definately for a somewhat narrow audience, but if you already love dolls, you can cash in on this growing hobby.

Facilities and equipment required will vary according to your own specialization. A sewing machine is important. You probably will eventually want to own your own kiln since the making of a good bisque head is the key to creating a valuable doll. Artist brushes are needed to paint skin, lips, eyelashes and brows. An air brush usually works best for very delicate cheek tints. Everything needed, including hand tools, should not cost you more than a few hundred dollars. Shop around for good used items.

RECIPE REWARDS

Do you have a special recipe that friends rave about? Do you get your thrills by pleasing people with home-made goodies? Are you a gourmet cook or at least a person that can prepare a secret recipe or two?

If so, you can make substantial kitchen profits. Opportunity lurks everywhere for the home-based profits! You can enter the multi-billion dollar food preparation industry on either a full-time or part-time basis.

You will be able to set your own business hours and go just as fast or slow as you wish.

The best food in the world is cooked in the kitchens of America and Canada, and more and more folks are sharing their "goodies" with strangers—for a big profit! Here are just a few success stories:

Rufus S. sweet and sour barbeque sauce for years was the hit of family summer outings. Thanks to his enterprising cousin, he and cousin Tom are in business in Cleveland, Ohio selling Rufus's tasty concoction to food stores in Ohio, Indiana and Kentucky.

Edgar and Betty B. of Chicago, Illinois specialize in a dozen varieties of pickles. And their small kitchen canning operation grew so fast during the spring-summer of this year, that they now must either cut back sales effort or expand to a commercial location.

Bess Peterson of Duluth, Minnesota, also became a kitchen entrepreneur by accident. After giving friends and relatives delicious home-made "fudge baskets" for years, her niece opened her own restaurant and talked Bess into making extra fudge for sale. Soon afterwards other cafes and diners in the Duluth-Superior area were clamoring for her candy. Next a large candy and cookie company approached Bess for exclusive rights for the big St. Paul-Minneapolis market. But Bess refused. She said she already was earning more than she and hubby Bob needed, and did not want to leave her home kitchen for a commercial kitchen.

Get started right! If you are going after home-made kitchen money, decide that type of food you will handle. It's usually a good idea to stay with items you know best and have a reputation, even if only among friends and relatives, of preparing well.

Make certain you select something that can easily be prepared in large quantitites, without undue problems. If your oven space is limited, you don't want to offer baked hams, for example. Also pick dishes that can be easily packaged and safely delivered to stores and/or customers.

If your food items are found only in your own section of the country, or are made from vegetables, nuts or fruits unique to your region, you may be able to earn nice profits by selling to souvenir shops, gift shops, hotels, airport stores, etc. Some examples of regional products could include local honey, wild rice, wild berry products, maple syrup and exotic fruit and nut products.

Know your complete costs! A common pitfall of a kitchen entrepreneur is underpricing goods. At-home cooking or baking will greatly reduce overhead, still, many different costs are involved. You must know the exact cost of all ingredients that go into your dishes. Also every cost concerned with packaging and delivery. Add to this any help needed, increased electrical and water costs, right down to a little built-in amount for repairs, additional equipment and increased insurance.

Pricing your product can be tricky business. If you deal with one or more wholesale distributors, you can afford to accept a smaller percentage of profit per food item, based on volume, but don't cut your prices to a point that you are cooking for a hobby. No matter how much you love to cook, turning your pleasure into a business represents real work! Bess Peterson says she loves to cook, but would not work that hard for less than $20 per hour of her time, over and above actual production costs. Only you can decide how much you think is reasonable compensation for your effort, but certainly, anything less than $10 per hour is probably too little. When possible a good rule of pricing is to mark up your items double the actual cost of production.

If you are good at dealing with people, you should consider handling your own distribution, at least in the beginning. Once you find the specialty shops, stores, restaurants and/or delicatessens that will handle your hams, the public will tell you quickly if your product is as good and as fairly priced as you hope it is. (Most retailers will mark up food stuffs 30% to 50% and restaurants will often double your price when they serve to their customers.)

As your business develops, stay in close contact with your customers. If you offer several products and find that one of them greatly outsells all others, you may be wise to specialize, giving it a big push. Try to get free publicity from local newspapers, radio and television stations.

When you go after kitchen profits almost anything can happen. Your specialty food item could go from a local hit to a nationwide sensation. That kind of success would force you out of your home kitchen, but what the heck, for a million bucks or more per year, maybe you could get used to a huge commercial complex? Just maybe!

"RENT-A-HEAP"

If you own a lot zoned "commercial" with nothing on it or know someone else that does, you could cash in with a junk car rental business.

The big national new car rental agencies are getting between $18 and $35 per day and up for their rental automobiles. It's not hard to understand why used cars renting at low rates ($7 to $12 is the current national average) have become so popular.

Here is a business with real potential. Investment is quite modest (remember; you would be offering cars that are several years old and without frills.) And you just might get started without any investment on your part, like Dave Kingley of Denver, Colorado did.

Dave had an ideal vacant lot, perfect for used car rentals. Trouble was, young Dave, age 25, did not have the money to purchase a half dozen or more used cars. Not one to let a lack of cash stop him from grabbing a good opportunity, Dave began hunting for a partner. He soon found one.

Dave's eager partner turned out to be a used car lot owner. He liked Dave's idea and decided to go into business with him, using Dave's vacant lot, while at the same time offering rentals at his used car sales lot. Although he did not cut Dave into a partnership at his own dealership, he did split 50/50 with Dave at his place. Not too bad since not one penny of investment was required from Dave Kingley.

If you have capital to invest and have a vacant lot or know where one is that can be rented at a cheap price, you can be in the used car rental business for less than ten thousand dollars. Maybe even less than five grand it you're willing to plow back the profits to keep the venture rolling.

The primary requirements are:

(1) A good location—one with plenty of visibility.

(2) Used cars that are in good working order—they don't have to look good but they must run well.

(3) Competitive rates—keep your rates at or below other used car rentals (remember; anyone who rents junkers is price conscious) and substantially below new car rental agencies.

(4) Cleanliness—junker or not, folks want a clean car inside and out.

(5) Insurance—protect yourself from legal hassles by carrying a good policy. You can also earn a small premium by making an arrangement with an insurer to offer individual daily and weekly policies to people who rent the cars.

(6) Advertising—the way to get the most for your ad dollar is distributing flyers to bars, laundromats and other places where people congregate. Small classified ads in daily newspapers and weekly "shoppers" also help drum up business. Dealers in this business claim 80% of their business comes from locals and only about

20% from tourists. Major new car rental companies find that visitors account for over 50% of their rentals.

Another big consideration in operating a used car rental business, will be car repairs. Older cars do break down often. You or someone you know is going to have to keep the cars operative. Some mechanical ability would be a big asset. If you're not into monkeying with autos, you certainly better know someone who will repair your cars at a reasonable price.

Additional profits are available to used car rental owners who offer to help sell privately-owned cars for a commission. If you have a choice location, you can allow a seller to park his car on your lot and put a "for sale" sign on it. Ten to fifteen percent of the selling price is a good commission to request.

"RENT A HEAP" and make a heap of money with this new booming business.

"PRINTING" MONEY

Yes, it's illegal to print your own money, but here's a money-making venture that is almost as good, and it's 100% legal!

It's a well-guarded secret that many printing brokers are earning bigger profits than printers. We know a huge printing company with plants in Los Angeles, San Francisco, Denver, and St. Paul, which employs almost two thousand people. They also lost almost two million dollars during 1982-1983.

We also know a fellow who works out of his home in a suburb of Los Angeles, who made over one hundred thousand dollars during that same time period as a printing broker with no employees and very little overhead.

A printing broker owns no expensive presses, needs no employees, and yet can handle almost any type of job a client may want. A print broker can easily work out of his/her home or apartment, and can be in business for peanuts. In fact, this extremely profitable venture can be started with no investment whatsoever. It sounds incredible, but it's the truth.

THE ADVANTAGES: Nearly all print shops are specialists today. Those with the small sheet-fed presses (the "instant printers") charge higher prices—per page—and handle the small jobs. The firms with the big sheet-fed presses (such as the rotary press), work on volume and deal with longer runs. The web-press plants specialize in newsprint catalogs, newspapers, tabloids, etc...); the four-color press shops reproduce color photography; the big card stock printers handle specialized card stock tickets, etc...); the label presses roll out the gummed and pressure-sensitive paper or foil labels. There are other classifications to be sure, but this gives you a pretty good overview. There is some overlap of work, but primarily specialization is the order of the day.

It would take millions of dollars in equipment inventory to cover all the types of printing that clients want. Even then it's impractical for even a multi-million dollar printing company to cover all bases. Each specific type of printing requires singular skills and technical expertise. The big companies and the small shops agree on this; they can't be all things to all

103

men. The printing broker can be, and therein lies his big advantage by making contact with several printers in your area. (Your area can be as small as a 25 to 50 mile radius if you live in a large city, or up to several hundreds of miles if you live in a small town.) You want at least one and preferably two sources for almost any kind of printing job a client can hand you.

Be up front with each printer you call on. Tell the owner or manager that you have started a printing brokerage and you want to add them as a potential source of supply. In today's tough market, most shops will welcome you with open arms. They have little to lose and much to gain by giving you the red carpet treatment.

WHAT TO ASK FOR: First, of course, ask for the biggest sales commission they will allow off their regular price sheet. Twenty or twenty-five percent to a printer's broker is somewhat standard in this industry, but thirty percent or more is not uncommon. Secondly pin them down on delivery time. Printers are notorious for not meeting their deadlines. As a printing broker you'll give yourself a little time, (if the shop says 5 days, you'll tell your client 7 or 8!) Nevertheless, you can't afford to lose business because the shop is very loose about honoring it's commitments. You must only deal with printers of high integrity and good work habits. Another major consideration is quality. As important as price and fast delivery is, quality is too important to overlook. Also insist any shop you work with guarantees to protect your accounts.

By checking samples of the shop's work, you'll have a good idea about what quality standards they maintain. If possible, also talk to some of their recent customers. This is a darn good way to check quality control and deliverability.

THE MONEY-MAKING PLAN: Once you have secured a relationship with several different shops that handle a wide range of work, you're ready to go after business. Armed with lots of determination and plenty of business cards (your card can identify you as a printing broker, i.e.—TIM HUNTER PRINTING BROKER, or as a printing company—TIM HUNTER PRINTING COMPANY. Zero in on your most likely customers. You can obtain orders from almost every type of business (almost all businesses use printing—some use a little, many use a lot), but the big bucks comes from landing the big jobs.

Give special attention to mid-size companies. The mom and pop outfits only use small quantities, and the huge live-chip companies probably are already tied in to a contract with one or more large printing companies. In the medium size manufacturing companies, financial institutions, etc..you will find excellent customers that use many different forms of printing (including special brochures, catalogs, catalog sheets, price lists, booklets, etc..). These firms can spell p-r-o-f-i-t, and lots of it, for you!

Your strong pitch is this; "I can handle almost any printing job you'll ever need. Let me quote your next project."

GETTING PAID: If you're starting on a shoestring, and don't want to (can't) handle the financial arrangements, (some clients will gladly pay 50% in advance and 50% on completion of the work—others will expect to pay only upon completion), you would be wise to turn the order over directly to the printer who will do the work. (Make certain he agrees to protect your accounts.) Later, when you build up a strong cash flow, you can handle all the paperwork and payments.

As a printing broker your moneymaking potential will be unlimited. Each printing company is restricted by their equipment limitations. Each printer offers specific work but as a broker you can cover a wide spectrum. Very seldom will you find yourself saying "I'm sorry, we can't handle that type of job." With several good sources of supply, you can smile and say "No problem, we can do it!"

Here is a moneymaker that can be started without any investment (except a fistfull of business cards). Business is available everywhere, in big cities or small towns, and there is no ceiling on how much money you can make.

If your goal is to earn $50,000 or $100,000 during the next twelve months starting from scratch, not too many home based business opportunities offer that kind of potential. This one does!

BECOME A MILLION-DOLLAR
REAL ESTATE BROKER

Nearly a million American men and women own a real estate license. However, less than half of them are active. And only about 10% of this potential sales force (about 50,000 to 60,000 people) are making big money selling properties. Nevertheless, big bux are available to a real hustler who goes out of her or his way to establish good contacts.

106

One method to make the long green is to deal exclusively in properties (commercial or residential) valued at one million dollars or more. A home office and some expensive calling cards puts you in business.

THE PLAN: Obtain the necessary licenses from your local state control board. In many states you will have to "work" as an agent before you can become your own broker. If this be the case, you will find several brokers happy to have you on a parttime basis. After all, they don't pay salaries and your only income is upon a sale. You can easily work part-time as a real estate agent while involved in another occupation. Once you serve this apprenticeship, go after and get your broker's license.

Create the illusion of wealth. Have an artist and printer prepare beautiful stationery and business cards. Next put on your finest clothes and visit the most exclusive properties for sale in your area. You'll find these properties in sales listings, multiple listing books, etc., available to you as a broker. Call on the owners of million-dollar real estate and ask them to list their properties with you once their current listings expire (most listing periods are about 90 days, but expensive property can take much longer to sell). Tell these prospective clients that you cater to the wealthy and that you have excellent contacts.

Six percent is the going rate for most real estate commissions. The selling broker and the listing broker split this amount 50/50. By just listing million dollar plus properties, you will make $30,000 or more upon their sale. And you don't have to sell them.

Obviously, you stand to make it bigger, if in fact, you cultivate rich contacts and do some of the selling yourself.

I met a dapper gentleman from Beverly Hills who spent his summers at the Del Mar race track who explained this concept. With a twinkle in his eye and a martini in hand, he told me "I like money, but I don't like hard work. I have found listing expensive properties compatible with these likes and dislikes".

Sounds like this dude has a good thing going for him. Seems to me this same basic concept could also be applied to selling insurance and financial planning for the wealthy.

A big opportunity to make big bux and make some rich contacts.

SWEEPING DOWN THE PROFITS

Here's an opportunity to go into business for yourself, select your working hours, and even wear a regal top hat on the job. The profit potential? Very high! The investment? Moderate. About $2,500 or less! The demand? Rapidly increasing!

Tommy Lee Pelcher in Baton Rouge, LA. pockets a tidy $250 for 8 hours work, and Edward Stillman of Austin, TX. demands—and gets—$400 for the same amount of time. What does Tommy Lee, Edward, and hundreds of other innovative businessmen (it seems that this field is dominated by men but there are couples too who work together) do for the nice bucks they receive. They are chimney sweeps!

Sweeping chimneys may not be your idea of having a good time, but...

The work really isn't that bad and the pay is excellent. Parttimers generally clean two or three an evening plus four or five more on weekends. Most "sweeps" now charge $50 for cleaning the first chimney and $35 or $40 for each additional one on each job.

Why will people "being of sound mind" pay some strange character in a black suit and top hat, fifty bucks or more to clean up a chimney? Safety is your answer!

When solid fuels (wood, coal, etc.,) are burned in a stove, furnace or fireplace, soot and creosote build up. Unless a chimney is cleaned regularly, flammable soot and creosote will accumulate in the flue. This can drastically weaken a chimney. If left uncleaned for a long time, the results can be destructive. A home owner can eventually lose the entire chimney. Worse yet, unwanted fire in the chimney could ignite a blaze that turns the whole house into an inferno.

Soon after *World War II*, America and Canada switched almost completely from solid fuel to more convenient oil, gas and electricity. It appeared the day of wood and coal burning heat was over forever. But alas, history has a way of repeating itself. The "energy crisis" of the seventies abruptly sent millions of people into at least supplemental heating of their homes with wood and coal.

Electricity, oil and gas may be "cleaner" and more "convenient" than wood or coal but they are also a lot more expensive. The entire nation may not be ready to return to the heating method used by their parents or grandparents, but several million are starting a trend in that direction. This means thousands of more chimney sweeps will be in big demand. The real risk of a devastating fire in solid heated homes makes this service a necessity.

TOP HAT AND TAILS
FOR A POSITIVE IMAGE

Any chimney sweep worth his salt will wear the proud and ancient european garb of "black hat and tails." Modern-day opportunists tell me this also pays off with a highly visible image that is easily recognizable. Free publicity in local newspapers and magazines or on radio or television, seems to come easy for the "fully dressed" sweeps. This can really give the new home-based biz a big send off.

THE JOB ITSELF

Chimney sweeps knock loose and scrub out ever particle of soot and creosote that can be removed from the flue. How best is this done? Ask ten sweeps this question and you'll get ten different answers. Some sweeps recommend round brushes, others insist the square ones are better. Some like hard brushes, others prefer the soft ones. Some say you sweep from the bottom up, others snicker and say a good sweep starts atop the roof. All good chimney sweeps get the job done right, but they certainly have many different means to reach the same end.

110

Sweeping chimneys may not be your idea of having a good time but it sure can be profitable. $500 to $1,000 a week is a realistic goal for fulltime work and parttimers are reporting earnings in the $200 to $700 range. We've even heard an unsubstantiated report out of Columbus, Ohio, of a young man who, along with his wife and brother, started sweeping chimneys in 1983 and earned a ten thousand dollar profit—split between them—their first month. This seems a mite high, but the possibilities in this new (old) business are truly remarkable.

Once you own the "tools of the trade", and you do need specialized tools, you are ready to advertise. Use newspapers and local shoppers. Also go after free publicity in any and all local media. Another source of jobs can be a little ad in real estate publications in your area. Realtors also can be a good source of referrals.

THE TOOLS OF THE TRADE

The nice people at August West Systems, Inc., P.O. Box 603, Westport, CT. 06880, will be happy to sell you a big pac kage of all the special tools, operating information, and promotional ideas you need to make good money as a flue cleaner. For a free copy of their report *"The August West Story"*, write to them.

I would like to offer several sources of supply, instead of just the August West Company. However, they are the only company I know of offering a complete setup. I am told they have everything needed to get started, and that they are nice to do business with.

FOSSIL FINDING
HAVING FUN—AND MAKING MONEY

Rocks contain a great deal of history. They also offer unusual profit potential in the form of fossils.

Fossils can be the petrified remains or impressions of entire humans or animals or of their bony parts, skin, features, or tracks, or any telltale evidence of the presence or passing of creatures from the past.

Among the most valuable to collectors and museums are the trilobites. They roamed the world's oceans some 500 million years ago, and ranged in size from about one inch to 18 inches or more. Though the trilobites haven't been with us for millions of years, their fossilized remains are commonly found all over the country.

Also quite popular and not too hard to find, are the ceohalopod—a shelled forefather of the octopus and squid—that lived in Missouri some 350 to 400 million years ago.

WHERE TO LOOK Fossils can be found everywhere,—every hillside, quarry, and water bed is a potential "finding grounds." Even the rocks in your field or home garden can contain rare specimens. However, the more you know about fossils and the geological formations where they are likely to be found, the more treasures you'll be able to locate.

The best place to find fossils is where you find sedimentary rock that was laid down under a prehistoric body of water and is characteristically layered. Many of the creatures that once lived in and near the pond, lake, or sea, will be preserved within the solidified sediment. This is especially true if they had hard parts on their bodies such as carapaces, shells, or bones. The creatures' remains will have survived the millions of years since their demise as impressions (casts or molds). Sometimes they will be partially or completely "replaced" by dissolved minerals. Since organic matter disintegrates very slowly, these replacements can sometimes create an exact replica in stone. Even down to the cellular level.

The fossil finder will sometimes find specimens "weathered out" on the exterior of rocks. Usually, however, it is necessary to split the strata in your search. Tightly embedded specimens must, of course, be extracted with extreme care.

Always keep in mind the discovery of one preserved organism will suggest that others could be nearby. Remember, too, that fossils are almost always close to what once was the creature's natural habitat.

TOP FINDS Following are the more popular fossils among the commonly found varieties.

Trilobites look like chubby insects and are usually 1½ to 4 inches long. Their heads (cephalons), segmented bodies (thoraxes) and tails (pygidia) are often discovered separately, since these creatures would shed their shells to accommodate growth much as crustaceans (lobsters, crabs, etc.) do today. Complete specimens are highly prized.

Cephalopods have big cylindrical shells. This group includes nautiloids, ammonites, and straight cephalopods. They often have intricate and ornate ridges and markings.

The shells can range from a couple of inches to several feet in diameter or length.

Crinoids are delicate flowerlike sea creatures that have heads, arms, and stems. Finding stem sections are quite common and of very little value to the serious collector. Intact they bring a decent price.

Other fossils include fish skeletons, insects, animal and bird tracts, sharks teeth and petrified wood, among others.

REWARDS Payments for trilobites can be as little as $5 or less or as much as $400 for a "perfect" specimen. The same is true of cephalopods. Some shells are so common as to be virtually valueless but an unusual specimen will always find a buyer. Crinoids, when whole and intact, command a price of $40 to $100.

If my description of various fossils mentioned here, including how to find them and profit from them, have you stimulated, but still somewhat uncertain, you'll need to start digging for more information.

An excellent book for beginners is "*The Weekend Fossil Hunter*" by Jerry D. La Plante. Mr. La Plante's book is filled with helpful information on rock identification, tools needed, map study and fossil extraction. It also lists the very best fossil areas in all states. Published by Drake Publishers, Inc., it is available in most rock shops.

The "bible" of the industry is "*Index Fossils of North America*" by Harvey W. Shimer and Robert R. Shrock (M.I.T. Press). This monumental reference guide is available at many libraries.

HOW TO START AN
ENTREPRENEURS' CLUB
IN YOUR CITY

There are Elks Clubs, Press Clubs, Toastmaster Clubs, and 1001 other clubs found in cities across the nation. Why not start a new club for business people and entrepreneurs in our city. The trend has already started in many California cities. Some have started as non-profit organizations, others are strictly for the profit of all concerned, including the promoter.

While it is too soon to tell if existing clubs are operating profitably, I see great potential and you can get started on a shoestring.

Here's the plan. In a mid-size or major city (I don't think prospects would be good in a small town,), make inquiries with local hotels concerning a free meeting room (hall) in exchange for their serving lunch to everyone who attends. Select the establishment which offers the nicest facilities and the best price for a simple, but good, lunch. A promoter in Columbus (a mid-size town), told us he averages 100 people at the hotel, provides the room and caters the meal for $6 per person. Since the promoter charges each "member" $12 he doubles his money, less expenses.

Your only expenses are related to building attendance. Go for all the free publicity you can get (television, radio, newspapers). Also you can get your cause a real boost by seeking speaking engagements before business-oriented groups (Chamber of Commerce, neighborhood business organizations, etc.) Tell everyone your story: You are launching a business/entrepreneur club for everyone in business for himself or herself, or anyone hoping to start a business—any kind of business. You will meet regularly (once a month on a weekday) and provide an interesting speaker, lunch, and an attractive setting for people to mingle and exchange ideas. All for a reasonable amount. (Keep your charge in the $10 to $15 range).

If you make a dedicated effort to obtain publicity, you should get plenty with this novel promotion. The more publicity, the more people who will attend. Lots of people in business will realize the importance of attending, even more who want to start a business will recognize the opportunity.

On a parttime basis, working only a few hours a month, you can drum up some good money with this promotion. And the service you provide is terrific. All sorts of good and highly interesting things happen when a bunch of entrepreneurs get together to hear a good speech, break bread, and talk business with one another.

A keynote speaker at your meetings is a must. By massaging an ego or giving a man or woman with a hot new product, a chance to address an eager audience, you can often land a great speaker for peanuts, or even scott free! It will be important to pay very little, if anything, to your speakers during your first few formative months. Later you may decide it is wise to pay a good fee to land a great speaker who can help build your audience.

You can go on a month-to-month basis, allowing folks to reserve by phone a day or two before the meetings, or even walk in without reservations. Just make sure you know your hotel's policy. Some hotels are pretty flexible, others want to know how many they will be serving in advance. The more flexible your hotel and its catering arrangement is, the better!

Have all guests sign a book that will give you a valuable mailing list. A postcard reminder a week or so before each meeting will help these folks become repeaters.

Later, after you firmly establish your club, you may want to sell yearly "memberships". For example, by subscription a person could be allowed to attend 12 meetings, complete with lunch, for the normal price of ten. Since business folks do travel quite a bit, you could issue "tickets" and allow your "member" to give them to others to use, if she or he chooses.

One more vital point. In operating any kind of club it is very important to maintain the same date, time and place. Example: "the last Friday of each month, 12 o'clock noon at the Ramada Inn." (Friday is your best choice of days since many people will have lunch, listen to your speaker, rap with fellow members for a while and then go home early. Saturdays are great for seminars (workshops) for many people, but not for the self-employed. They prefer weekday meetings.

Starting a business meeting club in your city could mean good business for you. Perhaps, just as important, it would help establish you as a business leader in your community. Think about all the great contacts you'll meet! You'll be on a one-to-one, first name basis with many of these movers, shakers and money makers (say, that's not too bad a name for a business entrepreneur club) in your area.

MAKE MONEY WITH A MICROCOMPUTER

The computer revolution of the 1970's has delivered the computer explosion of the 1980's! It also has paved the way for a new, very lucrative cottage industry.

In his book "The Third Wave", author Alvin Toffler predicts that the electronic cottage may be the mom and pop business of the future. Increasing numbers of home-based entrepreneurs are making his prediction their reality. Here are just a few examples on how people are profiting.

Computer Services—to do accounting, taxes, financial planning, word processing, mailing lists, inventory, etc.

Selling Computer Hardware and Related Items—in 1982, over 1,600,000 microcomputers were sold, and the demand is rapidly rising! Printers and other add-on computer devices also experienced huge sale increases. Computers are the fastest growing segment of the American economy, and should continue to be throughout the 1980's.

Marketing Programs—The huge number of microcomputers generates a large need for programs (software) that provides the computer with the instruction necessary to perform a given task. This is probably the fastest growing segment of the computer industry.

Information, Please—Many people want knowledge about computers. This promotes a market for providing information in the form of computer camps, schools, courses, books, publications and workshops.

Providing Supplies—supplies such as labels, forms, paper, disk cleaners, etc. are also an expanding market area.

Computer Repairs—The increasing number of computers has resulted in a skyrocketing demand for repair centers. Anyone who can repair these little electronic monsters will seldom, if ever, be unemployed.

The above represent just a few of the obvious ways the electronic cottage industry tycoon can prosper in this field. There are many, many others, all associated with a computer and man's desire to become quickly informed on almost anything.

SELECTING YOUR MICROCOMPUTER

First things first! Before you can profit with a small computer, you must own or lease one. Competition is heavy, and the ads can be confusing. What's a person to do? Get your hands on a good computer selection book. This subject is too detailed to be presented here, so I am listing a trio of excellent books on this important subject. Look (study) before you leap. No two microcomputers are alike. Buy or lease only when you know exactly what you will be getting. These books will help you make an informed decision.

COMPUTER SELECTION GUIDE—choosing the right hardware and software by Dan Poynter. The versatile and talented Mr. Poynter (he's also a publishing and aviation sports expert) has written another excellent book, this time on selecting your own computer. This book is basic and yet very complete, very easy-to-read, and understand. You'll be a very informed buyer after you read this excellent short course in selecting both hardware and software. The price: $11.95 plus $1.00 postage/handling from: PARA PUBLISHING, P.O. Box 4232, Santa Barbara, CA 93103.

COMPUTERS FOR SMALL BUSINESS—A step-by-step guide on how to buy by Gary Bencar is another great reference book and selection guide. Mr. Bencar owns his own computer consulting business and gives the reader, literally, several hundred dollars in expert advice for only $9.95 in this highly informative paperback manual. This book will teach you how to analyze your computer requirements, locate and evaluate the correct software, get the most value for your money plus much more. Only $9.95 plus $1.00 postage/handling from LA CUMBRE PUBLISHING COMPANY, P.O. Box 30959, Santa Barbara, CA 93105.

CHOOSING A COMPUTER by Tom Alfred is another very useful guidebook. It is filled with problem-solving advice and valuable buyer-beware information. Unlike Poynter's or Bencar's books (both trade paperbacks), this offering comes in hardcover only. The price is $16.95 plus $2.00 postage/handling from NORTH STAR PRESS, P.O. Box 1324, North St. Paul, MN 55109.

Once you have wisely selected your new microcomputer, you are ready to provide the service of your choice. Here are some insights into what you may offer your customers:

PAYROLL SERVICE: A computerized payroll can save a company both time and money. Small firms (probably your most likely clients) of 5 to 50 employees can be expected to pay from 80¢ to $1.50 per employee per week for a payroll service. And many small business people will jump at the chance to get out from under the burden of preparing their own payroll.

ACCOUNTING: Accounting services are not as easy to set up and operate as a basic payroll service. Again, small to mid-size firms are your most likely customers. An individual program must be put in operation to fit the client's singular needs. Knowing computer hardware and software may not be enough to set up and maintain a sophisticated program. Going into business with an accountant could solve this problem.

One of the best sources of programs for computerized accounting is COMPUTRONICS, South Pascack Road, Spring Valley, NY 10977.

For assistance in charging for your computer services, write for current information on the valuable pricing manual, "Charging for Computer Services", available from PBI BOOKS, 384 Fifth Avenue, New York, NY 10018.

Another excellent method to determine your fees is to query several competitors to discover the going rate in your area for professional services.

INCOME TAX PREPARATION: In addition to a good microcomputer, you'll need to complete a basic income tax preparation course, easily obtained through a local school or a correspondence school. There are a number of good software programs now on the market. You may write to these program headquarters for more details on software:

EZ TAX, 2444 Moorpark Rd., San Jose, CA 95128
MICRO TAX, P.O. Box 4262, Mountain View, CA 94040
OMEGA TAX SERVICE, 222 S. Riverside Plaza, Chicago,
    IL 60606
FEDERATED TAX, P.O. Box 1004, Port Huron, MI 48060

MAILING LISTS: Many small publishers and active mail order firms must make regular mailings to their customers or
subscribers. These firms need their mailing lists constantly
updated—no easy task if done manually, but a snap for the
correctly programmed microcomputer.

In this type of business you will face established competition,
but business is always available to the operator who is an ag-
gressive sales person. Business can be obtained locally or
through the use of mail order advertising or direct mail. Keep
in mind, many companies are using direct mailings for at least
part of their sales, including wholesalers, manufacturers and
retailers.

Fees do vary. The range seems to be 5¢ to 10¢ per 3 or 4 line
name and address for data entry and $10.00 to $20.00 per
thousand name print out, depending on the label format.

You can write the following companies concerning mailing
list programs:

PRECISION PROTOTYPES MAILING LISTS,
    12221 Beaver Pike, Jackson, OH 45640
SOFTWARE CONCEPTS, 105 Preston Valley Shopping
    Center, Dallas, TX 75230
POWER SOFT, 11500 Stemmons Freeway, Dallas, TX 75229
COMPUTECH, 975 Forest Avenue, Lakewood, NY 08701

122

In addition to servicing and maintaining lists for others, profits are readily available to anyone who compiles their own lists for rental. Regardless which type of list you would compile—lawyers, doctors, accountants, teachers, students, etc., and the possibilities are endless—only offer to rent your names. This keeps customers placing repeat orders. Prices you can charge for list rentals can vary from $25.00 to $100.00 or more per 1,000 names, depending on the list and how easy or difficult it is to obtain.

A reliable and competively-priced source for all sorts of paper and mailing labels is MAIL ADVERTISING SUPPLY COMPANY, 1450 S. West Ave., Box 363, Waukesha, WI 53187.

PUBLISHING YOUR OWN SOFTWARE

A computer is only as good as the program that is given to it. The writing, production and marketing of software could make you very, very rich. Competition is fierce, but this is one arena where the individual can compete with the giant corporations. If you are creative and persevere, success can be yours.

You may have heard stories of people making a bundle through writing a computer program. A Minnetonka, Minnesota man was recently paid sixty thousand dollars for a new game program he wrote over just four weekends. A Mason City, Iowa college student wrote four game programs in one year and was rewarded $150,000 for his brilliant efforts. A Tucson, Arizona young married couple have reached millionaire status in less than four years writing game programs, and they "went into business" only as an extension of a hobby they so dearly love.

Not everyone can expect big money, but the profit potential is truly endless. Games offer the fastest rewards but are also the hardest to sell in a very competitive market.

The demand for new and well-written business and educational programs is increasing. Customers are demanding a wider level of program support along with well-written instruction manuals. The successful software companies must excel in all phases of production, marketing and support in order to survive. In the past, companies could get away with producing a sub-par product. Today's strong competition makes this impossible.

If you become a competent programmer, you can write and submit software programs to the various vendors. If you have no programming knowledge, you can teach yourself to program. Many good programmers were self-taught. I recommend that you stay abreast of the latest programming techniques by subscribing to programming journals and examining the software of others. These journals keep abreast of new trends and what's currently hot. Joining a local "Microcomputer Club" in your area, and thousands of clubs have come into existence in the past few years, can provide you with great source of new knowledge.

Before you spend many hours writing a new software program, you may wish to survey the market first. Find out what programs are in demand by talking to software vendors, computer clubs and individual personal computer owners. This will help you determine what to concentrate your time on for the greatest potential profits.

SELLING MICROCOMPUTERS

In 1982, over one million, six hundred thousand micro-computers were sold. Conservative estimates are that over three million were sold in 1983 and that well over five million will be sold in 1984. Sales are soaring!

An obvious way to sell computers is to open your own computer store. This requires a substantial investment. A Radio Shack franchise (available from Tandy Corporation) will cost you in the neighborhood of $50,000 (dealership cost, initial inventory, etc.) plus building rent, fixtures and insurance.

A low-cost way to sell computers, ideal for the home-based entrepreneur, is to make sales without carrying inventory. There are several companies, both new and established, who will dropship hardware and/or software directly to your customer. No stock, no franchising fee, and hopefully, no hassles. These manufacturers can usually provide beautiful catalogs and professionally prepared brochures.

You can expect to earn 10% to 30% profit on your sales. Also, you may qualify for additional bonuses based on volume. Many of these companies also allow you to sign up other sales distributors and earn commissions on their sales via the multi-level marketing approach.

Here are three companies that market computers through independent distributors:

NOVATRONICS—full range of software—P.O. Box 7352, Minneapolis, MN 55407

TECHNICOM—computers and software—P.O. Box 15068, Salt Lake City, UT 84115

TRONICS—markets Texas Instruments, computers and software—2536 E. Loop 820 Worth, Ft. Worth, TX 76118

Word processing and the microcomputer revolution offers the home entrepreneur almost unlimited opportunities to profit in new technology.

Probably the best book available on the subject of word processing is WORD PROCESSORS AND INFORMATION PROCESSING by Dan Poynter. This marvelous guidebook is designed to be used as a selection tool in purchasing word processing eqquipment, products and services. It also will give the reader a planning guide that will help determine your requirements plus an understanding of word processing technology. Add to this a comprehensive resource directory of available products and you have an important manual on this subject. You may order this great book by mail for only $11.95 plus $1.00 postage/handling from PARA PUBLISHING, P.O. Box 4232, Santa Barbara, CA 93103.

SOURCE DIRECTORY
COMPUTER MANUFACTURERS
(A PARTIAL LIST)

Alpha Micro
17881 Sky Park North
Irvine, CA 92714

Altos Computer Systems
2360 Bering Drive
San Jose, CA 95131

Apple Computer Inc.
20525 Mariani Avenue
Cupertino, CA 95014

Applied Digital Data Systems
100 Marcus Blvd.
Hauppauge, NY 11788

Atari Computers
P.O. Box 61657
Sunnyvale, CA 94086

Basic Four Corp.
P.O. Box 11921
Santa Ana, CA 92711

Brother Industries
333 South Hope Street
Los Angeles, CA 90071

Burroughs Corporation
95 Horse Block Road
Yaphank, NY 11980

Canon USA
One Canon Plaza
Lake Success, NY 11042

Casio
15 Gardner Road
Fairfield, NJ 07006

Colonial Data Services
105 Sanford St.
Hamden, CT 06514

Commodore Business Machines
487 Devon Park Road
Wayne, PA 19087

Compal Computer Systems
8500 Wilshire Blvd.
Beverly Hills, CA 90211

Compaq Computer
12330 Perry Rd.
Houston, TX 77070

Compucolor Corp.
P.O. Box 569
Norcross, GA 30071

Compucorp
1901 South Bundy Drive
Los Angeles, CA 90025

CompuPro, Godbout Electronics
P.O. Box 2355
Oakland, CA 94614

Data General Corp.
4400 Computer Drive
Westboro, MA 01581

Digilog Business Systems
Welch Valley Industrial Road
Montgomeryville, PA 18936

Osborne Computer Corp.
26500 Corporate Avenue
Howard, CA 94545

Hewlett-Packard Corp.
1010 NE Circle Blvd.
Corvallis, OR 97330

Otrona Corp.
2500 Central Ave.
Boulder, CO 80301

Information Systems
P.O. Box 1328
Boca Raton, FL 33432

Panasonic
One Panasonic Way
Secaucus, NJ 07094

Northern Telecom, Inc.
P.O. Box 1222
Minneapolis, MN 55440

Quasar Electronics
9401 West Grand Avenue
Franklin Park, IL 60131

Ohio Scientific
1330 South Chillicothe Rd.
Aurora, OH 44202

Quay Corp.
P.O. Box 783
Eatontown, NJ 07724

Novation Corp.
18664 Oxnard Street
Tarzana, CA 91356

Radio Shack/Tandy Corporation
One Tandy Center
Fort Worth, TX 76102

Olivetti
155 White Plains Rd.
Tarrytown, NY 10591

Sharp Electronics
10 Keystone Pl.
Paramus, NJ 07652

Olympia
Rt. 22, Box 22
Sommerville, NJ 08876

Sinclair Research Corp.
Two Sinclair Plaza
Nashua, NH 03061

Sony Corporation
9 East 57th St.
New York, NY 10019

Tektronix
P.O. Box 500
Beaverton, OR 97077

Televideo Systems
1170 Morse Ave.
Sunnyvale, CA 94086

Wang Laboratories
One Industrial Avenue
Lowell, MA 01851

Timex Computer Division
P.O. Box 2655
Waterbury, CT 06725

Xerox Corporation
1341 West Mockingbird Lane
Dallas, TX 75247

Toshiba Systems
2441 Michelle Dr.
Tustin, CA 92680

Zenith Data Systems
1000 Milwaukee Avenue
Glenview, IL 60025

Vector Graphic
500 North Ventu Park Rd.
Thousand Oaks, CA 91320

SOFTWARE HOUSES

(Write for their latest catalog.)

Aspen Software
P.O. Box 339
Tijeras, NM 87059

Broderbund Software
2 Vista Wood Way
San Rafael, CA 94901

Ashton-Tate
3600 Wilshire Blvd.
Los Angeles, CA 90010

Century Micro Products
P.O. Box 2520
Mission Viejo, CA 91690

Computer Exchange
P.O. Box 23068
Portland, OR 97223

Cornerstone Software
P.O. Box 5151
San Jose, CA 95150

Designer Software
3400 Montrose Blvd.
Houston, TX 77006

800 Software
3120 Telegraph Avenue
Berkeley, CA 94705

Lexisoft, Inc.
P.O. Box 267
Davis, CA 95616

Liberty Inc.
740 Main St.
Waltham, MA 02154

MicroDisk, Inc.
P.O. Box 1377
Gardnerville, NV 89410

Peachtree Software
3 Corporate Square #700
Atlanta, GA 30329

Programming International
505 Hamilton Avenue #107
Palo Alto, CA 94301

Standard Software
CO-RI Bldg.
Avon, MA 02322

Structured Systems Group
5204 Claremont Avenue
Oakland, kCA 94618

Systems Plus
1120 San Antonio Road
Palo Alto, CA 94303

Taranto & Associates
121 Paul Drive
San Rafael, CA 94903

Vandata Business Software
17544 Midvale Avenue No. #205
Seattle, WA 98133

Wholesale Suppliers
P.O. Box 22428
Carmel, CA 93922

SOFTWARE BUYERS

Aardvark
2352 S. Commerce
Walled Lake, WI 58088

Manhattan Software
BX 1063
Woodland Hills, CA 91365

CDC
13715 Vanowen St.
Van Nuys, CA 91405

Powersoft
11500 Stemmons Expressway Ste. 125
Dallas, TX 75229

Instant Software
Peterborough, NH 03458

BOOKS

Basic Books
10 East 53rd Street
New York, NY 10022

Computer Book Club
Tab Books
Blue Ridge Summit, PA 17214

Boardroom Books
500 Fifth Avenue
New York, NY 10110

Computer Books
50 Essex St.
Rochelle Park, NJ 07662

Byte Books
70-P Main Street
Peterborough, NH 03458

Computer Reference Guides
2706 South Hill STreet
Los Angeles, CA 90007

Carnegie Press
100 Kings Road
Madison, NJ 07940

Essex Publ. Co.
285 Bloomfield
Caldwell NJ 07006

Gale Research Co.
Book Tower
Detroit, MI 48226

La Cumbre Publishing
P.O. Box 30959
Santa Barbara, CA 93105

Data Dynamics Technology
P.O. Box 1217
Cerritos, CA 90701

Datapro Research Corp.
1805 Underwood Blvd.
Delran, NJ 08075

Datasearch
730 Waukegan Road
Deerfield, IL 60015

Dekotek, Inc.
2248 Broadway
New York, NY 10024

Design Enterprises
P.O. Box 27677
San Francisco, CA 94127

Knowledge Industry
701 Westchester Avenue
White Plains, NY 10604

Lifeboat Associates
1651 Third Avenue
New York, NY 10018

Micro Books
P.O. Box 6502
Chelmsford, MA 01824

Missouri Indexing, Inc.
P.O. Box 301
St. Ann, MO 63074

North Star Press
P.O. Box 1324
No. St. Paul, MN 55109

Prentice-Hall, Inc.
General Publishing Division
Englewood Cliffs, NJ 07632

Howard W. Sams & Co. Inc.
P.O. Box 7092-P
Indianapolis, IN 46206

Sybex
2344 6th St.
Berkeley, CA 94710

Synergetics
P.O. Box 1077
Thatcher, AZ 85552

John Wiley & Sons Inc.
605 Third Avenue
New York, NY10158

PUBLICATIONS

(A partial list of magazines and newsletters dealing with hardware, software and/or word procession.)

Byte
P.O. Box 590
Martinsville, NJ 08836

Business Computer Systems
Cahners Publishing
221 Columbus Avenue
Boston, MA 02116

Classroom Computer News
341 Mt. Auburn Street
Watertown, MA 02172

CLOAD Magazine
P.O. Box 1267
Goleta, CA 93116

Computronics
50 N. Pascack Rd.
Spg. Valley, NY 10977

Creative Computing
P.O. Box 789
Morristown, NJ 07960

Cottage Computing
Home Business News
12221 Beaver Pike
Jackson, OH 45640

Data Communications
1221 Avenue of the Americas
New York, NY 10020

PLC Magazine
One Park Avenue
New York, NY 10016

Softside
6 South St.
Milford, NH 03055

ON-Line
24695 Santa Cruz Hwy
Los Gatos, CA 95030

Software Authors Quarterly
Fowler Services, POB 240
Wytheville, VA 24382

Superletter
POB 3121
Beverly Hills, CA 90212

Video Print
30 High Street
Norwalk, CT 06851

Word Processing News
1765 North Highland #306
Hollywood, CA 90028

The Word
Word Processing Society
P.O. Box 92553
Milwaukee, WI 53202

Words
Intl Info/Word Processing Assn.
1015 North York Road
Willow Grove, PA 19090

SELLING VENDORS

Recent issues of computer magazines, rapidly taking over huge sections of space on the book shelves and newsstands of America, will give you the names and addresses of several computer program vendors who just might consider handling your programs. Obviously, you would query only those firms who sell software similar to what you have written. BATTERY LANE PUBLICATIONS, Box 30214, Bethesda, MD 20814, can supply you with an updated list of software vendors and the type of programs they require.

Once you have several potential buyers for your programs, contact them by mail or phone. Tell them what you have and see if they desire to evaluate your program. Try to get several different companies to evaluate your work. Don't accept the first offer that comes your way. Be certain to fill out a non-disclosure form before sending your program to any company. This prevents the software vendor from revealing your program to anyone else.

Another way to protect your program is to get it copyrighted. This is an easy procedure. Write to the COPYRIGHT OFFICE, LIBRARY OF CONGRESS, WASHINGTON, DC 20559, and ask them to send Application For TX along with instruction form Circular R1. These forms are very easy to fill out and will cost you only $10. Send the completed forms, 2 printed listings of your program and the $10 fee back to the Copyright Office. Your program will then be "protected" by law.

You must also include the copyright notice in the program listing. It should be in the following form: Copyright John

Smith, 1984.

Once you submit a program to the software vendor, a waiting period of 5 to 10 weeks can be expected. If your program is accepted for publication, another royalty agreement will then be signed.

Royalty payments vary from vendor to vendor. The average is in the 15% to 22% range of the selling price of the program. Needless to say, if your program turns up hot, you can make lots of money—and quickly!

A good software publisher will help you polish up your program for marketing. They will suggest improvements and aid in perfecting the manual. If your program is very complex, the vendor should also be willing to provide telephone assistance to the customers. We recommend that you investigate the software vendors very thoroughly before singing any final agreement. You may want to hire a lawyer to look over the offered contract.

Do not expect to earn a fortune with just one program. However, even though there is a lot of software being published, there is still a wide open market. For the person who is not experienced in marketing or has little time, marketing your program through a vendor is the best method.

DOING YOUR OWN SOFTWARE MARKETING

If you prefer to market our own software, you must be prepared to do all the packaging, marketing and program support. Marketing puts you against the leading vendors, and program support can be a big hassle unless your programs are extremely well-written.

If you are going to do it yourself, scan the leading computer publications to discover your competition. You probably should buy and evaluate competitive programs to determine if yours is as good or better.

Keep your prices in line with similar software that is on the market.

Decide how you are going to market your product—by mail or through software stores (off the shelf). Programs that are sold through software or computer stores will require better, more expensive, packaging. Software sold exclusively by mail will not need fancy packaging.

Almost 50% of all software is sold through mailorder. However, as the number of software stores increase, so will the percentage of software sold off the shelf. This means more expenses in software packaging to you. There are a number of companies which will help you prepare good software packages. You'll find them advertising in various computer publications.

If you intend to market software through computer stores, you must allow them a 40% discount off the intended retail price. You may also give an extra 5-10% discount for large volume purchases. The best way to contact computer stores is in person. Direct mail may overall be more cost effective but will not produce the high percentage of initial results that person-to-person contact will.

Consider person-to-person sales calls on all stores within a 100 mile radius and use direct mail (an attractive brochure and a strong sales letter is a must) for all other stores you want to reach. Being available to answer store owner or manager questions regarding a new program is the major reason personal sales calls work so well.

(If you intend to market software by mail, study well my mail order section in this book. It will give you the basics of selling by mail plus some of the advanced techniques.)

One of the best ways to market your software (and many other products also) is to produce a catalog. A small catalog can be easily and inexpensively produced. You should include a number of related programs, i.e. several educational programs, business programs, etc. If you only have one program, locate other similar programs and write the owners. Tell them what you are doing and ask for wholesale prices on their software. Using the catalog approach can cut your advertising costs while gaining extra sales. Just be certain your catalog is both attractive and informative.

You must decide what type of software you will handle: all types, games, educational, scientific, business or utility. It is usually wise to stick to what you know. In the beginning of your fledging business, it may be a good idea to restrict your software to just one or two brands of computers. Make it for only the more popular computers. Later, you can broaden your market if sales warrant expansion.

CONTROL

Full control over the programs you write and/or market is not easy. Software can be copywritten, but a copyright only offers protection against exact duplication, and even that "protection" is somewhat minimal.

The biggest problem today is software piracy. Large numbers of people are making illegal software copies for their own personal use. Even worse, some companies actively duplicate and resell programs without paying a royalty for the privilege.

There are ways to protect your software so that it cannot be easily copied. However, this is not fair to your customers who need back-up copies. Many people will not buy protected software. Also, sharp programmers can always discover your protection codes. This method will only deter a portion of computer owners, and it will result in lost sales.

One method some companies use is to make the customers sign an agreement stating they will not allow illegal copies to be made. Others price their software so low that it isn't worth the effort to make illegal copies. Including complex manuals, necessary for use of the program, makes copying more difficult. Other companies include or make available low-cost back-up copies to their customers.

You cannot prevent the persistent pirate from copying your software. However, you can and must take steps to prevent the average customer from giving away extra copies. However, today's consumers often think they have a "right" to make a copy or two.

I believe the greatest potential for software sales are in the following market areas: Business, Education and Financial. Although game programs still sell, microcomputers are now being put to more practical uses.

The following manuals and books could help you sell your programs;

HOW TO PACKAGE AND MARKET YOUR OWN SOFTWARE, Datasearch, Suite 108, 730 Waukegan Rd., Deerfield, IL 60015

MACHINE AND ASSEMBLY LANGUAGE PRO-GRAMMING, The Computer Book Club, Blue Ridge Summit, PA 17214

GAME DESIGN SYSTEM (ARARI), Frobco, P.O. Box 2780, Santa Cruz, CA 95063

HOW TO WRITE AN APPLE PROGRAM and HOW HOW TO WRITE AN IBM-PC PROGRAM, Datamost, 9748 Cozycroft Ave., Chatsworth, CA 91311

CREATING GAMES FOR THE APPLE COMPUTER, published by John Wiley & Sons, Inc., 605 Third Ave., New York, NY 10158

HOW TO SELL YOUR MICRO SOFTWARE, Essex Co., 285 Bloomfield Ave., Caldwell, NJ 07006

WORD PROCESSING

A word processing program can produce letters, reports, documents, even complete books, using your microcomputer and printer. It can do everything a common typewriter can do, faster and more accurately.

It allows instantaneous correcting and editing and has electronic recall capable of storing large quantities of information. Words need only be typed once. Words are arranged and rearranged on the screen. You then push a button and activate your printer. A final printout is made automatically without the need of error-ladden retyping and proofreading.

Here are just a few examples of how you can profit:

BOOKS, BROCHURES, NEWSLETTERS, ETC.

There are literally thousands of businesses that regularly need brochures, circulars, price sheets, etc. Add to these civic organizations, clubs and churches and you have a vast market for reliable word processing services.

In addition, several individuals and companies regularly or occasionally produce newsletters, bulletins, booklets, manuals and full-size books. While it is not easy to match everyone's typesetting needs with any given microcomputer, you can obtain hardware and software to fill many of these needs. Computerized typesetting is the wave of the future, and the technology is readily available today.

ADVANCED HOME TYPING SYSTEMS

Home typing has long been a popular cottage industry, although somewhat limited in profit potential. Now, through the use of modern electronic technology, you can offer new, streamlined home typing services that can greatly increase your net worth.

New services can include "repetitive letters". Many firms, clubs, etc. have need to send a form letter to dozens, hundreds or even thousands of members or clients. In the past, a standard form letter was used. Today, that form letter can be made to appear personal. To accomplish this, the letter must have built within it individual salutations (with individual names) for each member or customer. The customer's name can also be included in several places in the body of the letter. It is impossible to do this with offset printing, and typing each letter individually is out of the question. A word processor can easily perform this function.

There are a number of word processor programs which can be easily used to produce the form letter. These same programs can combine the form letter with a mailing list containing the names and addresses of the intended recipients. Each letter can then be printed out containing the proper salutations and names in the body of the letter. The mailing list can be used to address each letter. To the recipient, the letter appears to be individually typed (as long as you are using a letter quality printer). This letter personalization is a very valuable service for both large and small mailings. It is also a great time-saver and very cost effective. Most importantly, it has proven itself to be far more effective than a flat form offset

142

letter. Clients and members are far more likely to respond to this "personalized" appeal. Charges vary, with $2.50 to $7.50 for the first letter and 15¢ to 35¢ for each additional letter being the general range.

RESUMES

A word processor system is ideal for producing 10 to 50 copies of a resume. The resume is prepared and stored on disks. This can be recalled at any time, and the desired number of copies produced. If it becomes necessary to make changes in the resume, editing can be quickly performed. The necessary changes can be made and the resume stored or printed all within a few minutes! The big advantage of resume preparation with word processors is speed and the ease of making changes.

If you will write or assist your client in writing his or her resume, you can charge $10 to $25 for this service, depending on length, plus $3.00 to $10.00 for the first complete resume and 25¢ or more (depending on length) for additional copies.

Section Two—

Home Writing/Self-Publishing Opportunities

Introduction

This is the life.

Maybe there is a better way to get paid for self-expression. If there is, it remains a mystery to me. Don't misunderstand, it sure isn't all *fun and games* or *strawberries, cherries and a heavenly angel's kiss in Spring.*

No! There is an element of work to creating words on paper. Sometimes your thinking process gets real cute. The resulting "writer's mental block" is like running full speed into a stone wall. Sure, it's only psychological stuff, but no less frustrating. *THE PITS!* What do you do when you're playing hide and seek with your creative nature? Hang in there! It will come to you. Slowly at first, but then like a gusher. It is all stored up there in the marvelous computer that is your brain. And your brain is linked to the Creative Intelligence of the universe. You should worry? It is all here for your unlimited benefit.

This manual is written for anyone who would like to earn money, a little extra dough or whole bunches of long green, through the process I call *SELLING WORDS.*

John Steinbeck, James Jones, Taylor Caldwell and William Shakespeare are *writers.* I'm just a pencil-pushing word seller, but I'm making nice money and enjoying myself. And you can, too.

Don't let the "experts" trick you into thinking that you need an impressive training period and many years of formal education to write for pay. That's pure *horse manure!*

A positive mental attitude and an unyielding desire to succeed and "see it in print"—plus a willingness to share useful information can make you a winner in word-selling biz!

I offer no miracle get-rich-quick scheme, but in this manual you will find the techniques, tactics, concepts, guidelines and methods that can point you to success in writing and/or self-publishing.

Each person must decide what they want from their literary labors. A full-time writing/publishing lifestyle centered around the world's best stay-at-home enterprise? Or, simply, a nice spare time income to supplement one's regular income or how about productive retirement? You set your goals. My desire is to help you achieve them.

The big sky is the limit. No matter how much you accomplish, there is always something new to begin. Example: I'm earning good bread as a self-help and information writer and publisher. Additionally, I am well regarded nationally as a mail order and direct marketing advertising copywriter. This is challenging work and I love working with many stimulating fellow entrepreneurs. The kind of men and women who forsake mundane security to go for it in business and in life. My kind of people! I should be happy and content, right? Well, not exactly true. Sure, I'm basically pleased with my lifestyle and writing, but I'm not 100% satisfied and content. You see, I want to author a best-selling novel. *Isn't the grass always greener...?*

In several areas of life, it can be counterproductive to always want more. For a writer, I think it is healthy. It is important to keep new desires and goals in front of us, and maybe just a slight dab of creative unrest to keep us forever working on new and more challenging projects.

ALWAYS GIVE THANKS FOR ALL THAT YOU ARE, ALL THAT YOU ARE NOT AND ALL THAT YOU CAN BE!

FINDING SUBJECTS TO WRITE ABOUT

A work of fiction must be brought forth from deep within the author's being. To be successful, it must reek with originality. Good, solid non-fiction works must also be spiced with creativity; however, here the author relies heavily upon research and/or past experiences to produce a strong manuscript.

Information subject matter for articles, fillers, reports, booklets or full size books can be found anywhere and everywhere. For the very best results start with your own field of expertise or one you wish to read about and research. Don't kid me or yourself. If you're an adult who has not led a very secluded life, you have useful information on a subject or subjects that folks will pay you to learn.

Here is a partial list of what interests readers (people):

People Want To Be:	People Want To Obtain:	People Want To Do:
Loved	More money	Their own thing
Appreciated	Advancement in business	Start their own business
Admired	Security for the future	Express their
Beautiful	More leisure time	individuality
Creative	Improved health	Accomplish something
Powerful	Self-esteem	important
Respected	Peace of mind	Obtain affection & love
Productive	Self-control	Important tasks
Informed	Pleasure	Improve themselves
Free	Improved physical	Travel to exciting places
Successful	appearance	Have more fun
Recognized	More personal prestige	Do less work
Forgiven		Make a greater
		contribution

Focus on providing people with simple, understandable, and helpful information that will satisfy any of the above, or combination of the above "WANTS" plus a few other good ones that could have been added, and your work can become a BEST SELLER. More importantly, you will make money and also feel good about it. A super double pay off!

As both a writer/publisher and advertising consultant, I never cease to be amazed at the huge number of folks who have valuable information between their ears who don't consider packaging and selling it. Some just keep giving it away free, or much worse, they keep it to themselves.

This is the age of specialized information. People are ready, willing and able to pay good money for zillions of different forms of useful knowledge. Simply find a need and fill it. And needs are found everywhere. From spiritual bliss to how to have a successful garage sale, and from a super new diet to how to bake a better apple pie to improving your sexual performance, the list of topics is eternal. Never fear, you will never run out of available and saleable words to sell.

Here's a meaningful exercise. Grab yourself paper and pen and write down every subject you have some degree of knowledge about. Don't bother putting these subject headings in any order of importance. Just jot them down as they drop down from your mind. After several minutes, when you begin groping for more headings, stop. Now examine your list and pick the topics that most interest you and get busy writing!

FINDING THE TIME TO WRITE

I just don't find time to write." The No. 1 copout of all would-be authors. Your success depends on effective use of time!

You have heard the time-tested saying, "If you want something done, ask a busy person to do it." Busy, productive people who effectively manage their time will somehow get things done and meet their goals. At the same time the person who doesn't manage time will sit at the desk and stare at the work that should be done. Or perhaps shuffle papers without accomplishing anything or quite likely, make excuses not to start at all.

Misuse of time seldom involves an isolated incident; it almost always is part and parcel of a well-established pattern of poor work habits. God knows, changing or reprogramming our behavior is not an easy task. Learning to cope with the clock and make it work for us rather than against us is no simple behavior change. The potential pay off is so beneficial however, that we must turn destructive, time-wasting habits into rewarding habits that best utilize the precious gift that is time.

DOWN WITH CLUTTER

Many business people in general, and writers in particular, have huge piles of papers, envelopes and current work on their desks, somehow assuming the more important matters, like cream, will rise to the top.

For rare inviduals some clutter actually seems to work. Since clutter has often been a part of my own experience, I have often rationalized it. "I'd go nuts if I had to maintain a tidy desk," is my plea to anyone who will listen. However, after getting serious about effective time management, I no longer can justify all my clutter and "piles." My desk is still never really neat and some clutter prevails; however, I have come a long way. I intend to continue to improve in this vital area and I strongly suggest you do likewise. I don't want to preach perfection, mind you, I just want all of us to avoid that chaotic, sinking feeling. Clutter can create tension and frustration; it can make us feel "hopelessly snowed under." That feeling can lead to unproductive work or escape. When a writer gets frustrated his work will be sub-par, if that person works at all. A work bottleneck is often followed by the mind shutting down. This is the "mental block" ploy that writers too often accept as an uncontrollable occurrence thus giving it power in their experience. It is both avoidable and controllable. One excellent method to prevent the mental block syndrome is to keep both your desk and your mind free from clutter.

An effective means of dealing with your papers, projects, mail, etc., is to go through them and divide them into five categories:

(1) High Priority—Immediate Action
(2) Low Priority
(3) Pending
(4) Reading Matter
(5) Wastebasket

Put all high priority items on top of your desk. Put all other items out of sight. Put them in your desk, under your desk or on a side table, in any case out of sight! (Naturally, all items in category five are already off your desk and in the circular file. Excellent time managers make liberal use of the wastebasket.)

Now sort through your high priority items and choose the one that ranks No. 1 in importance and have at it. Don't go on to anything else until this is accomplished, and so on and so on. When all top priority matters have been handled pull up the stack of low priority items and work on them.

YOUR WRITING TIMETABLE

One more crucial thought on your "high priority" list. Set aside a time to work exclusively on your current topic. It doesn't matter what particular writing task you are working on. What is important is that you set aside a certain period of time daily to accomplish it. If you can only spend two hours daily on our new "word selling business," at least spend those 2 hours wisely. Perhaps one hour will have to be spent on the business aspects of writing. Set up a work schedule employing the five categories given. This would leave you with one hour daily (perhaps much more on weekends) to work on your chosen subject. For best results hold fast to this time-table and make it a daily routine. It is generally best to use the same work time each time (some writers do their best work very early in the mornings, others keep a pot of coffee brewing as they work in the wee hours of night). Find your best time and then stick with it. Most pros who write for a living (your ultimate goal?) keep a rigid schedule. My own "time to write" is both early and late. I have discovered 8 a.m. till 11

151

a.m. are three good morning hours for me, as are the late evening hours of 10 p.m. till around midnight. My concentration ebbs during "day time hours" and I use my time with routine business activities.

PRIVACY IS A MUST

You need a time to write and you also need a place to write. If you already have an office in your home or a spare bedroom to turn into one, you have it made. If no such luxury exists, see if room exists in your garage—if it has adequate lighting, heat, etc. If all else fails, use your own bedroom evenings and put it off limits to other family members for that hour or two in which you put words on paper. Some Word Sellers may set up shop on the kitchen table nights, but I have always felt the interruption factor there makes this household center a poor work area.

The kitchen table, for a start, is okay as a mail processing area if your writing is being marketed by mail order—in which case, family members are not "off limits." Their help is strongly solicited and will be much appreciated. You may even consider letting "sonny" use the family car Saturday night if he licks enough stamps and stuffs enough envelopes, etc. How you bribe your spouse is your own concern. By now, you should know how to *push the right buttons.*

Single people make fine writers. They also can conduct successful mail order businesses. The only thing they lack that a married person has (or should I say *may have*) is built-in cheap labor. The single person must either (1) do it himself or herself or (2) hire outside help.

In all fairness there are advantages and disadvantages in both cases. Sure your spouse and children love you, still a favor rendered means favors sought in return. Just think about all the trouble that boy might get into with your car Saturday night. On second thought, don't think about it!

STOP PROCRASTINATION—
TAKE ACTION *NOW!*

The "I'll do that later" mentality prevents a multitude of great accomplishments. It robs you of time, money and true success. If procrastination is your problem, don't put off doing something about it!

The fundamental reason most people procrastinate is because they have formed a habit of avoiding responsibility. Again we must be willing to change old unproductive habits. For the writer here are three solid suggestions:

(1) Decide to change—starting NOW! Starting today (not tomorrow) set aside your time to write and handle related business matters.

(2) To find the necessary hours in a week for putting words on paper, willingly make the sacrifice. In many cases, simply cutting out or cutting down on TV viewing (a major enemy of your Creative Force) will produce all the time you require to allow yourself to write for money.

(3) Don't give up. Too many people quit when they are drawing near a smashing success. Don't give up on yourself. You can do it! Also, if you find yourself slipping backward into old procrastinating habits, recognize your backsliding

and take charge of your life. At first it may be two steps forward and one backward. If you continue to reinforce positive new success habits, you'll soon take ten strides forward for every tiny step back.

DON'T LET OTHERS WASTE YOUR TIME

Since most of us are masters at wasting our own time, we damn sure don't want outside help. You owe a certain amount of time to your family and friends. Strong marriages and true friendships require time and effort. Just remember it was actually your own fault. You let them take your time.

YOUR TIME IS NOW

Effective time management is of paramount importance to all success-minded people. For writers it is absolutely essential. I trust the time I have spent on this subject has not been in vain. By taking charge of the time in your life, you'll soon be enjoying the time of your life! Guaranteed!

METHODS OF BOOK PUBLISHING

There are three primary methods in which an author's book may be published. They are:

1. Accepted by a standard publishing house for publication.
2. Published by a "co-op" or "Vanity" type publisher.
3. Self-published by the author or by an independent publisher with the author's permission.

CONVENTIONAL LEGITIMATE PUBLISHERS

If a regular, reputable publishing company accepts your manuscript, they will pay all printing, production and promotional costs of turning your manuscript into a book.

Your success will solely depend on your book's merits and their promotion and distribution efforts. With the possible exception of a prearranged "advance" payment (difficult for unknown writers to obtain) any money you earn will come by way of a percentage of sales—known in the book trade as "royalties." Royalties range from 4% to 10% or even more. Today's average is around 6% to 8%. If your book sells well you can earn a nice profit; if it doesn't sell well, your profits will be very small. In either case, be it a smash hit or a real flop, you will not lose money on the printing, distribution, etc., since your publisher will pay all these expenses. You can only lose the time and effort it took you to write your book. Depending on how you value your time and efforts, this, too, can be a substantial loss if your book does not sell well. However, you will not be required to come up with "up-front publishing money."

VANITY PUBLISHERS, SUBSIDY PUBLISHERS, CO-OP PUBLISHERS AND DISTRIBUTORS, ETC.

Most Vanity-style publishers could care less about your book or booklet. They are, however, another means to "break into print."

The game here, and it is a big money game, is to bring in the sheep and quickly flock them. By using all sorts of hard-sell tactics and super-psychology concepts, vanity-type publishers (they also often hang out under subsidy and co-op publishing labels) do a huge multimillion dollar business each year.

With few exceptions, I find "vanity" and "subsidy" publishers to be nothing more than literary con artists.

Regardless of the names they call themselves, the results are usually the same. The "publisher" implies that he will share the expenses with the author. He almost always is "thrilled" after reading the author's manuscript and strongly suggests the author sign his contract and "get published" at once. Usually, he states that many copies can be sold so that the author can not only get back his original investment but also earn a "huge profit." Come on, baby, we is going to make your book a best-seller. *Sure they will.*

In recent years competition has become so fierce between these operators that their sophisticated sales literature began making more and more irrational statements, all promising authors great rewards for signing on the dotted line. So many complaints were filed with various government agencies that

156

the Federal Trade Commission (FTC) finally was forced into action. They issued "cease and desist" orders against many Vanity and Co-operative publishing companies. Many of those still in business have suits filed against them, but still continue to operate while fighting legal battles.

Before signing with any "publisher" (regardless of what name they use) who wants you to pay all publishing expenses in exchange for "future royalties," please write one or all of the below listed agencies:

Federal Trade Commission
Washington, D.C. 20540
(Ask them for a copy of all "complaints and decisions" against Vanity-type publishers—then prepare for many hours of reading!)

Better Business Bureau of New York City
220 Church Street
New York, NY 10013
(Ask them for a report on "Vanity" publishers and also a reprint copy of "How to Get Published—More or Less" which originally appeared in Harper's magazine.)

Many books, booklets and articles have exposed the sordid dealings of "Vanity" type publishers, telling how gullible authors have been ripped off. One of the best appeared in Lyle Stuart's *The Independent*. Send 50¢ and a self-addressed stamped envelope for a reprint of the eye-opening report on one man's experiences with a "subsidy" house to: The Independent, 239 Park Avenue South, New York, NY 10013.

In the past 10 years that I have been active as a writer,

copywriter, self-publishing teacher and mail order consultant, I have talked with many, many authors who went through the Vanity publishing experience. Every person, with one exception, has told me they had a bad experience with a subsidy publisher. All had lost money and felt as if they had been taken. The lone defender of a Vanity publishing experience is a nice little lady in San Diego who had her collection of poems published at a cost of almost five grand with a vanity house. She freely admits less than 100 copies were sold and that she lost almost all of her investment. Still, she is happy. "I wanted my poems in book format without doing any of the production work myself. This they did for me, and I'm pleased." If she is happy, I'm happy for her. And if you are interested in "seeing" your work in print and are willing to cough up five thousand smackers or more for the privilege, you gotta right to do it. However, I'm sure most of my readers will agree with me when I say: I can't afford to mess around with these city slickers. Me thinks an author's money interests them a zillion times more than the words he applies to paper.

SELF-PUBLISHING

The third and often best method that can be used to get your book or booklet into print is the do-it-yourself publish and promote it method!

Using this concept you pay the full printing costs, but you also get all copies printed. You deal with a book printer whose only job is to print and ship you your books as soon as possible. You become the publisher, promoter and prime source. You alone take responsiblity for your book, booklet, report, etc., and the ultimate success or failure.

158

Self-publishing is not new. Among the great authors of all time are many who at one time or other turned to do-it-yourself publishing including Shelley, Mark Twain, Walt Whitman, Upton Sinclair, William Blake and Zane Grey.

In more recent years, Carl Sandburg, D. H. Lawrence, James Joyce and Robert Ringer have joined the ranks of the self-published. Conventional publishers told Lawrence his book **Lady Chatterly's Lover** was pornographic, James Joyce's *Ulysses* was just too long, Sandburg has a history of adverse relations with standard publishers and Bob Ringer's *Winning Through Intimidation* was rejected so many times he decided to go it alone. Single-handedly he made it a big financial success and then sold reprint rights for a fortune to the same type of conventional publisher who previously had only passed out a pink slip.

One of the greatest benefits of self-publishing is the total control you retain over the words you write. Successful books earn nice royalties for their authors, but conventional publishers always get the lion's share of a big, bold best-seller. As author and publisher, you can pick up all the marbles.

IS SELF-PUBLISHING FOR YOU?

Too many writers remain obscure and broke because they live in the secluded, unrealistic world of the "artist." If you look down your nose at the business end of writing and find something crass about making a profit, self-publishing is not for you! Chances are, you'll never make much money from your literary labors, regardless of how you market them. To make money you need a positive attitude about money. If you see yourself as a struggling author who disdains commercial success, rest easy. Success will not invade your private world.

If, however, you get excited about the do-it-yourself approach to writing and publishing, and even more pumped-up about earning a small or large fortune, self-publishing can be your road to riches.

Professionals (doctors, ministers, lawyers, college professors, etc.) often turn to self-publishing as a means to an end. Since greater recognition and prestige follow authorship, they often self-publish to build or maintain a professional image. While their book may not be a smashing commercial success, as an author they are elevated to the extreme in the eyes of friends, relatives and their peer group. A recent national poll showed how highly authors were respected in America. Among the "Most Admired Professions" writers ranked fourth highest. Only rock singers, movie stars and sports heroes ranked higher.

An author will be elevated to extremes in the eyes of friends, relatives and his peer group, regardless of whether his book is successful or not. Doctors, psychologists, lawyers,

160

teachers, ministers and other professionals often gain greater status by writing and publishing a book in a specialized field. A book written on a specialized topic often tends to make others believe the author is an "expert" in that certain area. Often this promotes increased opportunities, a better position, a large salary increase, public speaking or consulting fees, etc.

It's a fact! A large number of people secretly would like to write a book. An even larger segment of the population is impressed by those who do.

PUBLISHING FOR PROFITS

I certainly have nothing against folks who become authors because of the fame and prestige associated with publishing their own books. I accept this as a legitimate reason to go into print. After all, even if their books do not earn them a nice profit, better positions and increased earning potentials are often a byproduct of self-publishing. Thus, in the long run, their books or reports may pave the way for future substantial earnings.

Prestige and recognition is a worthwhile reason to self-publish. However, I do have a special fondness for the self-publishing author who "publishes for profits."

Making money is the name of the game! It's fun, too! This author has written more than two dozen books, booklets and manuals on various subjects: writing, publishing, mail order, direct mail, advertising, real estate, professional football, horse racing, etc. Add to this hundreds of published articles and fillers, and also newsletter and magazine publishing. Not to mention my main area of expertise—copywriting!—countless ads, circulars, catalogs, sales letters, et al.

The big money is here for the positive thinking, positive action self-publisher. Next to a burning desire to succeed and a good measure of knowledge and self-confidence, success is usually the result of one's willingness to get involved and master the business of promotion, sales, advertising and distribution. Writing your book or booklet is only step one on the long ladder that can lead to a smashing success in self-publishing. An author could write one of the greatest books ever, but if he stops there, his self-publishing venture will fail. Effective promotion and marketing are the major self-publishing success factors.

SUCCESSFUL BOOK DISTRIBUTION

Writing a book is only a job 10% to 20% complete. There is joy in seeing your literary labors "born" through the printing process. If you have decided to let a legitimate publishing company (not a flim-flam subsidy outfit, I hope, for your sake) publish your masterpiece and they have accepted, 80% of the work (marketing and sales) lies ahead, but your effort is completed. If you're going to self-publish, you had better get to work! A lack of sales, promotion and distribution effort can turn even a good book into a financial dud.

You gotta *tell 'em to sell 'em,* and that means hustle and bustle in the arena of sales and publicity.

While it's not that difficult now for writers to self-publish their own works, the novice publisher will soon discover publication is only the first step on the ladder of success in self-publishing. It is the vital areas of distribution and marketing that will decide ultimate victory or defeat of any publishing venture.

Too often writers/publishers order 1,000 or more books, manuals or booklets printed, and then ask themselves: "How Am I Going To Get Them Distributed And Sold?" Friends and relatives are only going to put a very small dent in a 1,000 book run, unless the author is immensely popular and has a huge circle of friends or fans. Successful distribution strategy begins prior to publication, not as an afterthought while staring at many boxes of your books stacked high in your garage or spare bedroom.

163

Here are just some of the proven ways to sell books, (many of them very innovative):

- Sell through a book distributor
- Sell direct to bookstores
- Sell to libraries and schools
- Sell via telephone solicitation
- Sell via mail order space ads
- Sell via direct mail
- Sell through radio and TV commercials
- Sell at swap meets and flea markets
- Sell door to door
- Sell at local parks and recreation areas
- Sell by handling out ad flyers at concerts, churches, conventions, universities, etc.

Every one of the abovementioned techniques of selling self-published books has been used successfully to market the written word. At first glance, a few of these methods may seem very unusual, but they have worked for others—why not for you? If you abhor lots of personal contact with potential book buyers, some of the above distribution techniques will not be your cup of tea. You'll have to try more conventional sales tactics (working with distributors, retailers, etc.); however, if you don't mind "getting involved" with people to sell your books, your means of distribution can cover the gamut of distribution methods. Many, if not all, of the above, plus many more you can experiment with.

The real secret of successful book distribution is to EXPAND YOUR THINKING. "Think Sales!!"

Get busy telling people about the merits of your book. "THE MORE YOU TELL, THE MORE YOU SELL." Remember William H. Johnsen's ten important two-letter words: "IF IT IS TO BE, IT IS UP TO ME!"

HOW TO SELL BOOKSTORES

Please take notice of the above heading. *It is not* about how to sell books through bookstore distribution. *It is* related to some of the proven methods of *how to sell bookstores* (the women and men who operate them, of course) your book. There is a big difference! I am discussing a full size book or manual. Small folios, reports, etc., may be excellent sellers via mail order, with folks eager to pay good money for the information provided. However, when it comes to selling your wares on bookshop shelves, your offering better look a lot like the competition—a book that looks like a book!

Once a bookstore owner or manager has agreed to handle your book, you have given it a competitive chance. It will either sell or not sell based on its own merits, or at least, based on bookshop customers' willingness to part with cash money for what you have written. True, further promotion and advertising, plus selective display can greatly enhance its salability. Still, just being allowed "space" on the shelves gives it at least a fighting chance in the open literary marketplace.

Self-published books, booklets and manuals are receiving more attention today than any time previously. They have now become *almost acceptable* in the book selling community. Some booksellers are still resisting the new wave of self-published books. While their reasoning is many-fold, a few "reasons" store owners offer are:

- Dealing with a book distributor makes bookkeeping easier
- Previous bad experiences with a self-publisher or "slow selling" self-published work

- Limited shelf space
- Book and/or author lacks recognition

SOME SOLUTIONS

The book dealer who objects to "billing" from many different sources should be told something similar to this: "Let's forget about billing. I'll give you an extra 5% discount for cash" (of course, you'll take a check!), *or* "Let's put 5 or 10 copies of my book here on consignment—you only pay after they sell, and if they don't sell, it hasn't cost you anything."

Both of the above techniques may break down initial resistance. You may win the dealer over in your flexibility and desire to do business on his terms. But be reasonable. Don't move into their bookstore. Maybe this guy (or gal) has had to contend with a "pushy" self-published author previously. Do get your book placed on the best display shelves available for maximum exposure. Don't drop in two or three times a day to "check on how sales are going." Once a week is about right, unless you have a good rapport with the dealer and he enjoys talking "shop" with you. If it's strictly a business arrangement and you perceive you are dealing with a cooly efficient type—play the game to the hilt. Let him know in advance, he won't see you again for at least "a week or more." This should put his mind to rest that he is not dealing with "a flaky, eager-beaver, bothersome writer!"

Lack of space is a hard objection to overcome, but where there's a will, there's just got to be a way! A friend of mine who operates a small book distributing company in the San Diego area showed me one great way to overcome the "lim-

167

ited space" syndrome for books he wanted placed at a certain downtown bookshop. The solution? Take off your sports jacket (if you're wearing one), roll up your sleeves—and get busy! Busy showing the bookshop owner or manager alternative display methods. Be careful not to give him the impression that he is not a good displayer. Simply, make a few calculated suggestions that can benefit him—and you! Using this approach, my distributor friend "found" shelf space for 50 titles he was distributing—surely you can find room for a few copies of your book!

Regarding the quality (the printing) of your book: If it is not a decent, attractive quality job, you're in trouble. The major publishers crank out high quality workmanship. To compete, you better make sure your book printer can produce a competitive product. Many self-publishers who deal exclusively in mail order sales may specialize in low quality books. After all, they often reason, "It's the ad that sells the book." This is not the case when your book is sitting on the bookstore shelf surrounded by thousands of other titles. Yes, the subject matter is very important but "looks" count big too. Very few poor-quality books sell at retail outlets. A well printed book with an attractive cover is a must! Also, don't neglect the back cover. Once a prospective customer has picked up some of the book's major benefits (reasons to purchase) can close the sale. More often than not, the front cover and the title get the attention, but it's the back cover copy that makes the sale! If you leave the back cover blank or indulge in only a little self-appeasing glory-seeking with much to do "about the author," you can miss closing the sale.

The above problems and some possible solutions all concern themselves with "face to face" direct selling. Now let's turn our attention to profitable ways to solicit book dealers by mail.

You forfeit an important selling tool—"Eye-ball to eye-ball salesmanship" when you solicit booksellers by mail. Now it is vital that you employ a nice printed circular and/or sales letter to make your presentation pay off.

Since retail bookstores are constantly being bombarded by book publishers and wholesalers, you will want to use every sales technique possible to get your message across and an order placed.

A nice topical book, well printed with an attractive cover, is a must! If the cover of your book is a real knockout, I recommend having your printer make a photo copy—approximately 2" x 3" and print it on your sales letter and/or circular.

Now what other sales inducement can you offer each prospective bookseller? What about your discount?

A 40% discount off cover price is the normal discount in the book trade. The big chain stores often get another 5%, but 40% off cover is pretty standard.

A 50% DISCOUNT COULD SWING THE SALE!

If you can afford to offer a 50% discount (or more!) on your book (and most self-publishers can!), by all means do it! This type of premium discount gets welcomed attention from many book dealers.

The extra 10% off will not get an order from the dealer who sees no other value in handling your book, but if he is seriously considering ordering, the extra discount could well "sell him" on placing the order. It can be the deciding factor!

I have had success with many of my self-published works in offering a full 50% discount, combined with a request for payment with order. I consider this a very productive trade-off. I give the dealer an extra 10% discount that he appreciates, and I get paid with receipt of the order, something I really consider a coup!

Since many booksellers are notoriously slow in paying their bills (some *never* pay them!), a check with order can eliminate a future hassle. Keep in mind, terms of payment with order will only be honored by the one-location dealers. Large chains of bookstores, drugstores, discount outlets, etc., insist on 30 day billing. Don't let this stop you. Large chains overall have a good record of paying their bills promptly. Individual bookshops comprise about 80% of all stores in the U.S.A. and Canada, but don't overlook the other 20% controlled by large chains.

This circular brought home the bacon! I had a good book tailor-made for California retailers. I offered an attractive full 50% off discount and mailed to the right list. I purchased a mailing list of 350 newsstands that sold the California edition of the Racing Form. In addition, my girl Friday spent one day at the local library and compiled a list of bookshops from various phone directories: Los Angeles, San Diego, San Francisco, Sacramento, San Jose, and other leading state-wide cities and towns. A mailing to 1,250 retailers resulted in more than 100 orders. Two weeks after the mailing, the best was yet to come as many dealers repeated with larger reorders!

SELL YOURSELF—
THEN SELL THE BOOK DEALERS

A positive, assertive approach is essential if you intend to convince bookshop owners that they are well-advised to carry your books. This is true in both face-to-face selling or mail order solicitation. If you develop self-confidence in yourself and really objective "good feelings" about your book, your oral or written sales pitch is going to be that much more powerful. If your book has any merit whatsoever, the only obstruction in your path is any reluctance of book retailers to stock and display it. The correct oral or written presentation will win them over. This can spell S-U-C-C-E-S-S for your book!!

SELLING WORDS TO
THE BIG CATALOG HOUSES

America's leading mail order catalog houses (Spencer Gifts, Sunset House, Hanover House, etc.) reach tens of millions of active mail order buyers yearly. These mass media catalog mailers specialize in mailing attractive gift and novelty catalogs 4 to 8 times per year. Each catalog is crammed with hundreds of items geared for impulse mail order buying. Additionally, most of the major catalog mailers also run "leader" space ads in popular magazines: *House Beautiful, Apartment Living*, etc., to generate new customers. While the majority of the items they carry fall into the gift, toy and novelty merchandise classification, they also sell millions of dollars worth of books, booklets and folios yearly. Recently I have noted these subjects were being offered: *Handwriting Analysis, Astrology, Winning Contests, Tracing Your Family Roots, Numerology, Writing and Self-Publishing, Playing Poker* and *Playing Bingo*. You can see, this represents a wide spectrum of subjects. No doubt, many other subjects are also being peddled or would be found acceptable for mass marketing by this often overlooked, but big-dollar market.

BIG DISCOUNTS FOR BIG SHIPMENTS

A few years ago, *Mr. Bingo* Gus Levy sold 30,000 36-page booklets to a dozen different leading catalog houses. He earned very attractive profits, even though his profit-per-book was very modest. You can't earn a whole lot per book when you're selling your wares at 40¢ per copy as Gus did. However, even 10¢ net profit per book (and Gus probably earned much more) ain't all that bad when you do it 30,000

172

times. Gus says he made out okay. In case you were wondering, the catalog firms sold his bingo book in the low retail price range of 99¢ to $2.00, with the "average" retail price being $1.50. Far less than the $3 per copy Gus received from his own advertising.

If you have the right book or folio for this wide-open market, you're going to have to bait your sales hook with a bigger than normal discount. The big catalog merchandise buyers turn their noses up at standard 40% and 50% book discounts. Nothing less than 60% is likely to be considered, and it may take discounts of 70% or more to really grab their attention.

If you enjoy low cost per unit publishing and if you have a stimulating, informational self-help or how-to-do-it title, this broad market could be tailormade for you.

Standard soliciting procedure is to send a sample copy of your book, any available advertising material and a personalized letter spelling out your offer and your best wholesale prices. Three prices should be sufficient: per 100, 500 and 1,000 units ordered.

Four of the biggest catalog houses are listed below (check out a recent issue of *House Beautiful* or other "homes type" magazine for other current advertisers.

SUNSET GIFTS
12800 Culver Blvd., Los Angeles, CA 90066

SPENCER GIFTS
1050 Black Horse Pike, Atlantic City, NJ 08410

HANOVER HOUSE
Hanover, PA 17331

FOSTER-TRENT
2345 Boston Post Rd., Larchmont, NY 10538

NEWSLETTER PUBLISHING

Kiplinger is given credit for launching the newsletter concept 20 years ago, and by the mid 1970s the tremendous newsletter explosion was in full swing. The 1980s promise to be the biggest and best decade ever for informative letters.

There seems to be a need for newsletter publishing under every possible subject heading. Folks today desire specialized information on a thousand and one different topics. From *religion* to *astrology* and from the *stock market advice* to *blackjack systems,* successful newsletters set the pace in providing fast-breaking news, inside info, tips and predictions.

SELL YOUR KNOWLEDGE— DON'T KEEP IT TO YOURSELF OR GIVE IT AWAY

Leading newsletter publishers like Howard Ruff of the *Ruff Times* (now called *The Financial War Room*),are cashing in big on selective knowledge. The *Ruff Times* currently has over 100,000 subscribers at $75.00 per one-year subscription. That puts yearly N/L revenue in the neighborhood of ten million dollars. A darn nice neighborhood to reside in. Sure, Howard Ruff is the exception, not the rule, nevertheless, hundreds of other newsletter publishers are making nice profits.

175

YOUR SUBJECT SHOULD
RELATE TO YOUR INTERESTS

If you're serious about entering the newsletter field, do so with a subject that you excel in. Be it business opportunities, stocks, entertainment, product information, self-improvement, consumer advice, or what have you? Just make sure you have the specialized knowledge to start your letter and a keen interest that will push you deeper into your subject and related areas. It will help if you are an avid reader. Usually one must read many books, magazines, newspapers, trade journals, etc., in order to cull new information of value to your subscribers. An elaborate filing system may be required to file interesting facts from your research.

FORMAT

The standard format of a newsletter is either one or two 11 x 17 sheets printed on both sides and folded to 8½ x 11 size.

A four-page letter is one 11 x 17 sheet and an eight-page letter is two such sheets. While most letters are either 4 or 8 pages, some publishers do produce a 6-pager. This is easily done. One 11 x 17 sheet printed both sides and folded, plus an inserted 8½ x 11 sheet printed both sides and left unfolded, makes a six-page newsletter. While there is no rigid rule saying all newsletters must be 4 or 6 or 8 pages in the 8½ x 11 format, 95% do fall into this format.

OVERALL NEWSLETTER COST

While newsletter production costs are quite low (1,000 copies of an 8-page newsletter can be typeset and printed for around $250.00, and if typesetting is not required you can cut that cost in half), subscription solicitation costs are very high. As 1984 begins, the average yearly subscription rate is approximately $76.00 according to a nationwide newsletter reporting poll. (The range greatly varies: from just a couple of dollars to a couple thousand dollars per yearly subscription.)

Newsletter publishers, even the top producers, often spend 70% of the subscription price for every new subscriber they bag! Thus a $48.00 per year letter may well spend *$33.60 for every new subscriber obtained.* How on earth can you make a profit if it takes 70% of all new subscription revenue just to procure new members, you ask? Your answer follows:

REPEAT PROFITS

While it is common in the industry to spend 60% to 80% or more of all new subscription money just to land those subscriptions, exciting financial gains are still available to the diligent publisher. The key to success here is in generating a *high renewal percentage.* It may have cost you an outlandish sum for every new member obtained, but you may only spend one dollar or less in receiving each renewal. Three of Four months prior to a subscription expiring, the dedicated writer/publisher begins sending out renewal notices. The first "notice" is a very soft sell. You simply inform your subscriber that his/her subscription expires soon and ask them to renew now.

177

If two such general notices haven't brought your subscriber back into the flock, you or an expert advertising copywriter must produce the right appeal that will convince the subscriber that he absolutely must continue receiving your valuable letter, that it is *vital to him* that he receive it without interruption.

Since it is 98% less costly to have a current subscriber renew than to obtain a brand new one, you must keep sending renewal literature. No less than four attempts should be made to reinstate a subscriber.

A high renewal rate spells S-U-C-C-E-S-S in newsletter publishing. A good topical letter should bring a high renewal rate. Most experts agree that you must have at least 55% or 60% of your clients repeat if you are to win the war of attrition and establish a self-sustaining, money-making letter. The super pros shoot for a 70% or better renewal rate!

MORE LETTERS FOR CASH

CREDIT AND COLLECTION WRITING SERVICE

While several major corporations maintain their own in-house collection agency or do business with a large outside bill collection service, most business people do not.

Thousands of firms need a freelancer who can help develop new business and establish credit for them. Also much needed, is a sharp writing style to induce slow accounts to *pay up!*

Drumming up business: If you live in a city or good-sized town, personal contact (go up one side of the street and down the other) will land you clients. If you live away from a metropolitan area, or just prefer not to play salesman, direct mail can be used to build your business.

WHAT MAKES 'EM PAY? Simple! *Pride, Guilt or Fear!* Good collection letters incorporate a strong appeal to one of those three motives. You'll have to play psychologist when analyzing slow-pays. Individualized letters bring the best results. Your first letter should always be short and to the point, but also quite friendly. A simple "you no doubt have overlooked this bill..." request usually will suffice. From letter #2 to the **Final Notice** (usually not till 3 or 4 previous attempts have failed), your persuasive skills can make you lots of money.

Standard fee for collection: 40% of debt owed your client. If the debt is quite current (120 days or less) you might take a smaller percentage. Likewise, you ought to receive no less than 60% if the debt is "cold", over one year old. You should also inform your customers that they must consider discounting old debts. Example: another firm owes your client $500 but the debt is 14 months cold. After all else has proved unfruitful, you may wish to offer a "final notice and proposed settlement." If the wayward company or person will pay within 10 days, you will discount the debt 40%, thus accepting $300 as payment in full. This action often brings fast payment on an otherwise uncollectable account. Just make sure all of the discount money isn't subtracted from your fee. Your client must share the discount with you, the collection writer.

There is no standard fee for establishing new business or arranging credit. You will have to negotiate your own best deal. One good method is to determine approximate time involved, making darn sure you receive no less than $15 per hour for this important service.

OPERATE A HOBBY LETTER

If you are enthusiastic to the point of being full tilt bozo on a certain hobby, game or sport, consider a letter on the subject. Successful word profits are to be made in almost every aspect of human recreational activity.

FAMILY NAME LETTER PROFITS

Here's a dashing new concept with unlimited fun and money potential! Why not take advantage of the *trace your own roots* craze that has hit America and Canada ever since Alex

Haley wrote his ten-million copy bestseller *Roots* a few years ago.

If you're interested in your own family tree and if you don't hate research, this is a natural! You begin by tracing your family name as far back as you can. You then solicit subscribers from folks with your name (city telephone books usually are the worst source of names for a direct mail campaign, but not so using this exciting plan—they give you a source of free names and addresses to mail to!) Since a person's name is like beautiful music to his or her ears, a family name newsletter is a potential source of huge revenue. Once you get beyond the historical aspects of your name, get full participation from your subscribers. Request that they send in a profile on themselves. Also you can print as many addresses in each issue as space permits, encouraging members to get to know each other better.

Regarding subscription rates: methinks a social newsletter like this is, demands a rather reasonable subscription fee. Perhaps $15 to $20 per year for a monthly letter (12 times yearly) or $8 to $10 for a bimonthly (6 times per annum would be about right!

RESUME PROFITS

In today's competitive job market, well-prepared resumes are increasingly vital in landing the better jobs. Resumes are designed to give employers a brief, but penetrating look at the background and qualifications of prospective employees. The busy employer saves time, effort and money by qualifying job applicants through the resume process.

The need for well-prepared resumes has created a multimillion dollar market for word sellers. The money is good and the work relatively easy when you *follow the wheel* (the established format).

Some writers found resume writing so very profitable that they have turned to it exclusively, often setting up storefront shops in busy downtown areas. Other word sellers use resume writing as just part and parcel of their total sales approach to writing for pay.

RESUME WRITING FACTORS

The main object of the resume is to get your job seekers hired. Great for word of mouth advertising! To accomplish this task you must embellish their positive past employment history and any and all other pleasing work and personal traits. Among key points an employer wants to see in a resume are:

182

1. APPLICANTS OBJECTIVE

   The exact position the applicant is applying for and his/her major qualifications for same.

2. EMPLOYMENT HISTORY

   List positions previously held with description of all services rendered. A full description of a person's last held job is required. Prior to this, the skillful resume writer may be somewhat selective in listing past employment. For example, it may be prudent not to mention a position in the past where the applicant was discharged or forced to quit, under undesirable circumstances.

3. EDUCATION

   Here we list data on our job seeker's highest education achievements. List name of the college or high school and subjects majored in and any degrees that were earned. Also, list any on-the-job education the applicant pursued, outside of his formal education.

4. PERSONALIZED INFORMATION

   Although optional, it is often well advised to list the civic, social and charitable organizations a person is affiliated with. Caution: if your client is a political or social activist, with membership in some highly volatile organization, it may be best to omit this information, unless of course, you know the person who is in charge of hiring shares a similar viewpoint.

The standard resume is only one or two pages in length. However, size and content vary greatly. Ten pages may be appropriate for the person seeking a "big job." The fee a word seller can charge for resumes also varies. On the average,

$7.00 to $12.00 for a simple "short form" resume of one or two pages would seem about right. Add at least $4.00 or $5.00 for every additional page over two. Often your clients will request several copies of the same resume you prepare. They should be run off on a good copier. If you don't own a quality desk model plain bond copier, make arrangements with a local printer who has one. Your client should not only pay the actual cost of making copies, but also a couple extra dollars for your effort. Example: You charge your client $10.00 for a two-page resume and $1.00 for each additional copy.

SOLICITING RESUME CLIENTS

As mentioned, some resume writers have opened resume stores in busy areas of cities, enjoying walk-in trade. Short of this, small ads in leading local newspapers, tabloids and magazines will usually attract eager customers. College papers and bulletins also produce clients.

Sample ad copy:

> **RESUMES.** Get that special job.
> Have your resume professionally
> prepared. Low cost! Call 000-0000.

Supplies needed are minimal: A ream of white bond paper, carbon paper, correcting fluid and your trusty typewriter will get you started. Also, if you don't own a copying machine, you must at least have the use of one nearby.

Following is a hypothetical resume to give you further insight into format:

184

James Hill
1202 Mission Street
San Diego, CA 90000
Phone: (619) 000-0000

OBJECTIVE

TO OBTAIN A POSITION WHICH OFFERS ME A CHALLENGE AND OPPORTUNITY FOR ADVANCEMENT.

EMPLOYMENT

FOOD TOWN MARKET   5/81 to 6/83
610 Main Street, San Diego, CA   Position: produce manager

As produce manager for the large (over 17,000 square feet) Food Town Market in San Diego, my responsibilities included supervision of the 2,000 square foot "produce department", including selections and purchase of all fruits and vegetables. During the two years I worked for Food Town, produce business increased 20%.

JACK'S FOOD MART   4/80 to 5/81
100 Pacifica Avenue, San Diego, CA

I worked in many different capacities while at Jack's Food Mart. I served as check-out clerk, stock man, meat counter assistant and produce worker. Also, I drove the company truck and accompanied owner, Jack Swanson, on meat and produce market buying trips.

DISCOUNT DRUGS   2/78 to 4/80
777 Seacliff Street, San Diego, CA

Worked part-time for Discount Drugs while attending business college. Approximately 25 hours weekly. While most of my duties were confined to the stock room, I also worked as a clerk in both the cosmetic and candy departments.

EDUCATION
6/78 to 6/80   SEASIDE BUSINESS COLLEGE
                                               San Diego, CA
                                    MAJOR: Business Economics
                                         Complete 2 year course

PERSONAL DATA
Height: 6'1"
Weight: 185 lbs.
Health: Excellent
Marital status: Married on March 16, 1983
Organizations: PTA, Helping Hands Association
Interests: Swimming, waterskiing, guitar, spectator sports

SHOPPER PROFITS

Maggie McCoy Turnbull owns and operates the *New England Express Shopper* that serves three small Massachusetts coastal towns. Her weekly tabloid began as only a four-pager, and with only six paid advertisers. By issue #3 she doubled size (8 pages) and could boast thirty-nine display advertisers plus over 100 classified ads. By issue #5, again she enjoyed double the pages (now 16) plus 60 display advertisers and more than 200 classified ads. More importantly, within five short weeks, she was making a profit. Not bad for a small three-person tabloid (two teenage daughters help her play publisher, editor, writer, advertising sales person, business manager, distributor (all copies are free), janitor and bookkeeper. Not bad at all when you consider she started her shopper with just slightly over two thousand dollars. Maggie's big secret? *"I worked 60 hours a week, mostly calling on local merchants for advertising. Most were afraid to go with an unproven new paper, even though my ad rates were very cheap. However, enough said O.K. that my shopper began to grow rapidly."* I hope many!

Most shoppers, like Maggie's, are tabloids, printed offset on the big web-fed presses. Standard format: 5 columns in width by 16 inches in depth. Approximately 80 column inches per page. The tabloid page size is much larger than a magazine, but smaller than most daily papers. An eight page shopper with five 16-inch columns per page will yield about 500 inches of ad space. Now let's say you kick off your weekly with a 5,000 circulation (it is risky to start any paper with less than 5,000 run). Here is an example of weekly costs and potential profits.

5,000 8 page tabloids (newsprint) typeset, printed and folded: $500.00

Distribution (the paper itself is FREE!) costs to deliver to homes and businesses: $125.00.

Overhead—office machinery and supplies, office rent, utilities, phone, etc. (per week): $125.00.

TOTAL: $775.00 each week.

POTENTIAL PROFITS

60 display advertisers, averaging 5 inches of space each—300 inches @ $6.00 per col. inch: $1,800.00

200 classified (business and personal) advertisers @ $1.00 per ad (Shopper publishers have found it is good biz to practically give away classifieds—some actually do give them away FREE—to get several people in the habit of using the paper): $200.00.

Okay, it is only hypothetical! Yet lots of people are making it work. If you spend $775.00 a week to do business and you take in $2,000.00 your weekly profit is very attractive. Most shopper publishers settle for a lot less, especially during the critical first few months. Our example did not include extra advertising sales people that many shoppers employ on a strictly commission basis. In our figures, we assumed the publisher was bringing in all the ad business. If you sign up another sales person or two, you'll have to allow them at least 20% of revenue from each ad they sell. And in order to keep a good *ad hustler*, many publishers offer up to 40% of money from ads they sell. This can cut into profits. Also, shopper publishers often have to "open accounts" for local business people. Some of these independent merchants go under without paying off their advertising account, others stay in biz and still refuse to pay, often claiming "no results."

RESULTS BUILD REPEAT BUSINESS

You have seen the profit potential on just 8 pages. Increase to 12, 16, 20 or more and the numbers soar! Even with more payouts and a few no-pays, the publisher can make the big bucks. Here are some major factors that bring success.

(1) You find a need (little or no nearby competition from another strong shopper or powerful daily). Anyone considering starting a shopper should spend as much time as possible "talking shop" with local merchants. Especially seek their reaction regarding their local advertising or lack of same.

(2) If you go for it, do it right—*publish an attractive paper.* Pay heed to overall design and select a "catchy" name or one that fits your locale.

(3) Pound the pavement. *Seek out your advertisers.* Once you're well established (in business over one year) and if your reputation as a customer producer is good, they will begin to seek you. Until then you must keep after them. The big chain supermarkets, drug, discount, and variety stores probably will ignore you until they have noticed you have a well-established paper. So, your main ad meat will be the small independent stores and shops of all varieties. Don't be too selective, go up and down the street.

(4) *Make sure the paper gets distributed.* Foolish indeed is the novice shopper owner who does a good job in getting a steady flow of ad dollars only to get sloppy in regard to distribution. No! You don't hire a couple of high school kids, pay them a measly amount and forget about it! Two reliable high schoolers may be great as your distribution crew, but if you're wise, you'll monitor their services. Even if your own son or daughter is one of your helpers, keep tabs on distribution. Repeat advertising is essential to a shopper's success. Repeat ad dollars only come from happy merchants who have received results! Good distribution brings buyers and sellers together.

(5) 120 Days To Success! *Stick with it if it shows any sign of possible success.* Most shoppers that do fold (well over half do) go under within the first four months. Some go down in less than four weeks! Hang in there. After 3 or 4 months, the odds switch over to your side. It is the old *winners never quit and quitters never win* syndrome that nevertheless is so true in many areas of business, writing, publishing—and life!

MORE POINTERS THAT LEAD TO PROFITS

- Seek out a reliable web printer for your tabloid. (Ditto for typesetting and composition.)

- Time the initial issue late in the month so that you can quickly bill your advertisers on the first of the following (this is a good trick to play if cash flow is vital from the start).

- Although advertising pays the bills and makes the profit, "save" at least 20% of each issue for human interest news reporting.

- A big tip! People love their names in print. Make an effort to list as many people in each issue as possible. Keep tabs on all local events—women's clubs, girl scouts, boy scouts, high school sports and activities, etc. At first you'll have to seek out newsy items. As soon as local folks realize you seek such items, they will bring them to you.

- Regular columns on local gossip, recipes, even astrology, can build reader interest. Yes, you may have to pay for this. You just can't be the cook, the chief gossip, the den mother and the star gazer too! Give local writers a chance. $20.00 to $40.00 is the going rate for a column (300 to 800 words) in a small local paper. Perhaps you can trade some left over ad space for the words you need.

You can prosper with a Shopper. Many factors add up to success or failure. Next to a burning determination to own and operate your own successful paper, location is the key. Following location is area to cover (it must be well defined) and then comes competition. If you discover an area with little or no competition or unimaginative competition, you have found a need. Fill it!

HOW TO OPERATE A
CORRESPONDENCE CLUB

A handful of sharp operators are making big bucks in this social field. Using either a newsletter (cheaper!) or magazine (probably better, once established!) format. The key to success here is threefold:

1. Advertising. Two sections in your publication offer ad space (usually sold by the word) A. Ladies wishing to meet guys and B. guys looking for social contacts with the fair sex.

When you're just getting started it is wise to offer very cheap ad rates. Since your first print run will probably be for only 500 or 1000 copies or less, 10¢ per word or perhaps 50 words or less for only $2 would be a reasonable ad rate. You can also charge to print an advertiser's photo. Most clubs charge anywhere from $2 to $8, depending on their circulation. Often, since single women apparently are less likely to advertise than men, some correspondence club directors offer discount prices to the gals. Some even OFFER FREE ADS for single women, with or without photos.

2. Subscriptions. Another source of revenue is subscriptions. The majority of clubs have subscription rates of $10 to $18 per year for a bimonthly or monthly subscription, to entice more advertisers, and club directors often offer a free 30 to 60 word ad when a person subscribes.

3. Forwarding Fees
With profits coming in from ads and subscriptions, this third area of extra profits is *pure gravy*. Most correspondence

clubs charge forwarding fees to readers who are writing their advertisers. The trick here is to assign all advertisers an ad code. Example: *L-202-Colorado.* This code could mean L (lady) Advertiser 202 from Denver.

Here is her hypothetical "lonely hearts" ad.

> L-202-Colo. Single lady, 30 years old. 5'7". 135 lbs, attractive. Never married, but may change that status for "Mr. Right." Desire companionship with athletic man, 30-35, who loves both indoor and outdoor sports, especially skiing. Photo with first letter, please.

The "fee" for writing this gal in Denver may range from 50¢ to $2. $1 per letter is somewhat standard. Clubs who handle all correspondence for a nice fee would require the person writing to enclose his letter to an advertiser (usually sealed) in a larger envelope with fee charged. The outside letter addressed to club headquarters. The inside letter or letters (some folks send a dozen or more off at once, seeking love and/or friendship) would simply carry the code number in pencil. The club would remail them to the advertisers in question.

Any writer who likes the social scene as well as making money, may want to look into the correspondence club scene.

You could order a few club magazines from ads in various supermarket tabloids (*National Enquirer, The Star, Midnight-Globe, Modern People,* etc.,) to give you a further feel for this type of specialty publishing. Likewise, if you launch

your own social correspondence publications, small classifieds in these popular tabloids can give you your start. Issue
#1 is your biggest obstacle. You may have to offer free ads to
one and all and cut-rate subscription rates in order to fill up a
pilot issue. Once a correspondence club gets rolling, the ads,
subscriptions and forwarding fees will have a snowball effect,
as will the dollars!

This form of social publishing isn't for everyone, but for
some it spells big fun and even bigger profits.

PROFIT FROM MAGAZINE ARTICLES

The late 1970's saw a publishing explosion of magazines in America. Readers soon saw many new titles compete for public interest. Today there is a magazine published on every conceivable subject—usually several magazines on *every* topic. In some areas it has become a little ridiculous *(The man's (or sex) magazine field, for example.)* By early 1980, no less than 269 different sexy mags were being published monthly, bimonthly or quarterly. Now that's a lot of words and bare flesh competing for reader and viewer interest. For the sophisticated adult article writer, it is also a vast paying market for free-lance talent. Not every *word seller* can crack the biggies like *Playboy, Penthouse, Oui,* etc., but some of the second-stringers like *Fling, Dude* and *Cavalier,* also pay cash money for articles, short stories, etc.

Maybe all these crazy *skin mags* aren't your cup of tea (I'm with you!), but how about earning nice checks from several of the thousands of other national, regional and trade magazines that are open to free-lance submissions? You have a wide open market available to you and unlimited topics.

START IN THE MIDDLE OF THE HEAP
AND WORK UP

When it comes to submitting articles to magazines, most new writers aim too high or too low. As an unknown typewriter tickler or pencil pusher, who hired a typist to neatly arrange words on paper, you have a chance to have your articles published in leading national magazines such as *Reader's*

Digest, Cosmopolitan, or *Playboy.* Your chances, however, are just slightly better than your chance to win the Irish Sweepstakes. Sure, it's possible, but the odds are mighty long. Wait till you build a solid reputation before hunting the big game.

While one group of novice writers address their manila envelopes to the biggest and most widely read national magazines, the other group sends off their manuscripts to only those little local magazines who offer small pay or no pay to their hapless contributors. Some say, get your feet wet. Get your work in print, at any cost (even no pay!). Yours truly disregards this thinking. I titled this book *SELLING WORDS*, and I wish to emphasize, you trade your words for financial consideration, and nothing else. Unless, of course, you wish to donate writing talent to your favorite club, charity or other non-profit organization. I have much more respect for those who keep getting rejected by aiming their articles at the heavyweight national magazines, than the person who writes articles just to see his or her name in print. The best route to steady flow of cash for your articles is to get started with middle-pack publications who can't pay the big loot but who do offer reasonable pay for accepted submissions. This great *secondary market* is an excellent media for breaking into print for a profit!

WHAT THE EDITORS WANT

After reading many market reports and writers guidelines supplied by hundreds of magazines, I'm convinced *human interest* is the numero uno magazine article success factor. Followed closely by *self-help, personality profiles* and *personal experiences.*

Even pragmatic business and trade journals want human interest interwoven in the success stories they print. Today's article writer must learn to write about real people while passing on information.

HUMAN INTEREST ARTICLES

Since fact can really be more exciting than fiction, readers want to feel the human drama in your informative writing. People never tire of success stories of men and women who started at the bottom (or battled much adversity) and rose to the top of the heap! You will never miss if you work on still another rags-to-riches true experience—yours or someone else's.

SELF-HELP AND "HOW-TO" ARTICLES

There is no end to the public appetite for good "how-to" and "self-help" articles on a thousand different topics. To crack this lucrative market you need only share your own true experiences or visit your library to research topics that interest you. You can also tie these articles into a self-publishing book effort. Many a shrewd article writer has expanded his article(s) into a report, booklet or full-size self-published book and enjoy resounding success. On the flip side of the money wheel, many a sharp self-publisher has raked in nice "extra profits" by spin off articles from a previously published book.

PERSONAL EXPERIENCES

All but the most withdrawn and secluded among us are constantly encountering experiences that can bring us recognition and reimbursement when shared in print. The outstanding feature of sharing life's personal experiences, is that we have lived them and are best suited to present them to our readers. Don't think that personal experiences must be momentous to be saleable to magazine editors. They need only be original, stimulating, creative and chuck-full of human interest. True, a stranger-than-fiction story of how you once lived in a haunted house filled with ghosts will spark high interest in many people, but some other folks will be just as interested in your childhood reflections on the coldest winter in St. Paul, Minnesota or the hottest summer in Tucson, Arizona. Or any one of a zillion other engrossing personal encounters.

Since experiences are on-going and because life tosses us many curves, change-ups and sliders along with the hard fastballs, the alert and reflective *word seller* never need lack personal experience subject matter. The world outside is filled with new happenings, personal contacts, and constant human drama. Then too, the inner world is forever creative. Let your ideas, thoughts, reflections, mind patterns and dreams be your guide. For it is in the *windmills of your mind* that the seeds of great new articles are ready to grow, bloom and be richly harvested.

MARKETING ARTICLES

Just as the self-publisher must *keep on keeping on* after writing his or her book, booklet or report, the article writer must keep revising and soliciting magazine editors until his piece has been accepted. A series of rejections must not intimidate the writer, though they may make the author consider a new rewrite, with perhaps a slightly different twist.

There are magazines and trade journals for *every* type of conceivable article or filler that you may wish to write. Two of the most comprehensive marketing books every *word seller* should own are:

Writer's Market, $14.95 plus $1.00 postage/handling from *Writer's Digest Books,* P.O. Box 42261, Cincinnati, OH 45242 and

The Writer's Handbook, also $14.95 plus $1.00 postage/handling from *The Writer, INc.,* 8 Arlington St., Boston, Mass. 02116.

Both of the above will be found in your local library, but as reference works, they cannot be checked out. I recommend ownership. Check for them in your favorite local bookstore, or order by mail. Another book very helpful to the article writer than I highly recommend is:

MAGAZINE WRITING—The Inside Angle, $10.95 plus $1.00 postage/handling from *Writer's Digest Books,* P.O. Box 42261, Cincinnati, OH 45242.

There is money to be made—lots of it!—writing magazine articles. I use article writing to help promote my self-published books and for "extra income." Many writers earn steady income selling words to magazines exclusively. In either case, magazine article writing deserves your consideration. It is a wide-open marketplace and very responsive. Go for it!

FREE ADVERTISING
AND PUBLICITY TECHNIQUES

The best kind of advertising is *FREE!* Editorial mention and reviews of your works on the printed page and "guest shots" on radio and TV programs can bring a swift and powerful cash response. Add to this ego-satisfying recognition and you have a dynamite combination!

KEY MEDIA CONTACTS

These are the publishers and editors of magazines, newsletters, trade publications, etc., in fields related to your own publishing and/or writing venture.

For example: If you're writing books, booklets or reports on *How to Collect Rare Books for Fun and Profit*, you would want to zero in on all publications that reported on this subject. Certainly, you would subscribe to the *AB Bookman's Weekly* and continually seek to have them review and mention your offerings. You also would be wise to cultivate a relationship with many book editors of large daily newspapers. While these book editors may spend 98% of their time reviewing new books, almost all of them have at least some professional interest, or at least curiosity, in antiquarian offerings. If they liked your work, many of them would give you free space.

P.I. ADVERTISING

P.I. (per inquiry) or P.O. (per order) advertising isn't really free. In this method, various magazines, TV and radio stations offer to plug your wares in return for a percentage of each incoming order. While "percentage deals" run the gamut from 20% to 60% of gross revenues, 40% is pretty standard. The publication or station working a P.I. or P.O. arrangement may demand 60% of a $5.00 "report" that they know you can publish at 25¢ or less, each. However, they may be happy to accept 40% on a full-sized book selling for $10.00 or more.

While there are hundreds of outlets for P.O. advertising in both the printed and electronic media, the market is constantly changing. The best way to locate a potential medium in your area is simply to contact all available media.

While it is true many book and booklet publishers have cracked the P.I. marketplace and made huge profits without "up-front" ad costs, it must be said the market is somewhat selective. Often before offering you a solid ad promotion, the media in question may ask you to show them a successful selling track record. It is always easier to hook up with P.O. deals after you have first proven that you have a fast-selling number. This makes good business sense. While the media in question is accepting P.I./P.O. advertising to fill "empty space" in their publication, or "open air" on their stations, they don't want to fill it with slow-selling items. Give them a winner and you will be given carte blanche with future proposals. Drop a bomb on them and they will hang up the next time you ring them.

ARTICLES FOR ADS

Many magazines, including several national publications, have a somewhat limited article cash budget. While they need a steady stream of informative and entertaining articles, cash resources are limited. Many times a writer/publisher will be able to trade a well-written article for either a commercial ad or editorial mention of the author's current work. Of the two possible choices, the editorial mention often will bring in far more orders than a regular ad.

Don't expect any of the major periodicals to jump at ad article/advertising trade offs. Best results are obtained in soliciting the smaller magazines and journals, especially those who are very specialized in their subject matter. Several opportunities exist in the business opportunity field, and in the areas of new technology.

An excellent means of obtaining free publicity is to offer to write a magazine article about your subject. In order to engineer such a deal, you should write to the editor of an appropriate magazine mentioning that you will be willing to write an article for his magazine at absolutely no cost to his publication. Say that you will slant it toward his magazine's audience. Tell him that all you would like in return is mention at the end saying you are the author and where readers can buy your latest publication.

You have two things going for you in such an arrangement. First, you as an author are considered an authority in your field, and magazines want authorities writing articles for them.

Second, most publications are on tight budgets, and mention of a "freebie" makes them sit up and pay attention.

RADIO AND TV APPEARANCES

The electronic medium (especially TV) is often seen as an enemy of the printed page. Statistics prove Americans are reading less as we head into the 1980s, while spending more time in front of the *idiot box*. Still, good works of fiction sell very well (witness the nearly 30 million copies of John Jake's *Kent Family Chronicles* that have sold over the past few years). A new nationwide drive by PTA groups also is signalling a return to the art of reading for pleasure. Educators now realize they can sell the joy of reading to grammar school kids. All they ever needed was attractive packaging.

Nonfiction material of the "how-to" and "self-help" varieties is commanding larger sales today than at any time in history. People are seeking specialized knowledge and overall self-improvement. And the demand keeps growing and growing.

SELL IT "ON THE AIR"

The big movie and TV studios and major publishing houses have recently joined forces to create many smash multi-media best sellers. Why shouldn't you get a little piece of the action?

While many authors regard television as an insidious creation that is slowly producing a generation of "non-readers" and "non-thinkers", other writers are using this vast video media to pad their bank accounts! Why not you?!

Everyone knows what's coming down when a leading laundry soap company is staging a 60 second spiel, where an "ordinary" housewife claims, "Tide got my wash cleaner and brighter than any other detergent!" It's called a commercial!

In the world of talk shows the big selling has only begun when the commercial ends. From *Today* to *Tonight* to *Tomorrow,* from *Dinah* to *Donahue,* a unique and highly effective form of advertising is taking place. While we viewers believe we are being entertained by an actor (who happens to have a new movie out) or informed by a psychiatrist (who's just written a book), it runs out that the talk-show guests are actually seeking publicity for themselves or their wares. And we are being sold by the softest of sells. The arrangement can be compared to a barter. In return for free (or nominally paid) guests, talk shows provide visitors with a platform for subtle, almost subliminal, plugs.

Maybe Merv Griffin or Johnny Carson won't beg you to be a guest on their network shows, still, you can make several TV and radio appearances if you aggressively pursue them.

There are about 300 "interview" oriented television programs in the USA, and well over 1000 radio talk shows. It takes an enormous amount of guests to keep these shows on the air. While personalities come from many walks of life (actors, singers, sports figures, politicians, etc.,) writers make the largest single profession regularly interviewed.

It is not difficult getting on local TV and radio programs. Like I said, this media needs a constant supply of fresh topics. Place a phone call (person-to-person calls often produce better results than letters) and speak to the station's program director. In some cases, the show's host must line up his or her own guests. If this be the case, you will be so informed.

A wide variety of topics are acceptable for discussion on the air. And the more controversial your subject matter, the better. At all times, helpful "How-to-do-it-Yourself" and good information always has a ready and receptive listening or viewing market, and the media knows this.

Do a good job of putting yourself and your topics over on the tube, and it's quite possible, an impressive local station manager just might help you arrange some national coverage. Many of the authors on the network show got their starts on the small, local talk circuit. Come to think of it, you just may get your shot with Johnny or Merv!

COPYRIGHT IT!

No matter what you create on paper, be it a one page "report" or a 1,000 page literary masterpiece, it is wise to protect your creative labor via the copyright method. This procedure is also simple and easy to obtain.

In 1976, after decades of confusion, the United States Congress updated copyright laws in this nation. Many new provisions were added, giving expanded protection to copyright holders.

Following is a brief, but hopefully, concise review of the new copyright law, plus information on how you can secure a copyright for everything you write.

WHAT IS A COPYRIGHT?

A copyright simply gives you the right to copy, distribute and sell an original work of authorship. It is a law protecting ownership. Generally, a person owns what he or she creates until he sells it, or assigns it to someone else, or until he or she accepts a salary for creating it (publishers often, but not always, hold the copyright). What we call copyright protection is the legal registration of that ownership. The copyright office, for a fee of $10, keeps a record of the date a property existed, to whom it belongs, and has on file in the Library of Congress two copies of the work. In cases of infringement litigation, these data are legal evidences that entitle the owner to obtain redress and collect damages. Copyright protection extends only to *works;* it does *not* extend to any idea, procedure, process, system, etc., regardless of the form in which it is described. That is, you can copyright sequences of words or sounds, of which a copy exists. You copyright the copy, not the content.

A person owns this right to copy only for a specific time. For works created after January 1, 1978, the new law provides a term lasting for the author's life, plus an additional 50 years after the author's death. For works made for hire, and for anonymous and pseudonymous works (unless the author's identity is revealed in Copyright Office records), the new terms will be 75 years from publication or 100 years from creation, whichever is shorter.

Under the old law, the term of copyright was 28 years, plus a second renewal term of 28 years, or 56 years in all. Under the new law, works in their first term must still be renewed, but they can be renewed for a term of 47 years, making a total of 75 years. Copyrights already in their second term at the time the new law went into effect are automatically extended up to the maximum of 75 years without the need for further renewal.

Among other features, the new law also

• incorporates into a single system proprietary copyright and what was formerly known as common-law copyright (ownership of unpublished works) and provides for the copyrighting of unpublished works;

• establishes guidelines for "fair use" for "purposes such as criticism, comment, news reporting, teaching, (including multiple choices for classroom use), scholarship, or research";

- creates a Copyright Royalty Tribunal which oversees royalty collections and payments to copyright owners for such uses as in jukeboxes, on public broadcasting, cable TV, etc.

WHAT CAN YOU COPYRIGHT?

Under the new Copyright Act, a claim of copyright is registered under a revised classification system. Instead of the fifteen classes provided under the old law, the new system provides for only five classes. Instead of the numerous application blanks and forms under the old law, the new law provides for only eight. They are:

1. CLASS TX· NON-DRAMATIC LITERARY WORKS. This category is very broad. Except for dramatic works and certain kinds of audiovisual works, Class TX includes all types of published and unpublished works written in words (or other verbal or numerical symbols), such as fiction, non-fiction, poetry, periodicals, textbooks, reference works, directories, catalogs, advertising copy, and the compilations of information.

To secure registration of copyright in this class, one uses application form TX, which replaces six old forms (Form A, Form A-B Foreign, Form A-B Ad Interim, Form B, Form BB, and Form C). You can obtain Form TX, or any copyright form you need, free of charge, by sending a specific request identifying the number of each form you need, to

Copyright Office
Libarary of Congress
Washington, D.C. 20559

208

2. CLASS PA: WORKS OF THE PERFORMING ARTS.
This category includes published and unpublished works prepared for the purpose of being performed directly before an
audience or indirectly "by means of any device or process,"
such as radio or television. The category includes musical
works, including any accompanying words; dramatic works,
including any accompanying music; pantomimes and choreo-
graphic works; and motion pictures and other audiovisual
works.

To register your copyright in this category use Form PA,
which replaces four old forms (Form D, Form E, Form
E-Foreign, and Form L-M).

3. CLASS VA: WORKS OF THE VISUAL ARTS. This
category consists of published and unpublished works that
are pictorial, graphic, and sculptural, including two-dimen-
sional and three-dimensional works of fine, graphic, and applied art, photography, prints and art reproductions, maps,
globes, charts, technical drawings, diagrams, and models.

If you wish to copyright a work of visual art, use Form
VA, which replaces seven old forms (Form F, Form G, Form
H, Form I, Form J, Form K, and Form KK).

4. CLASS SR: SOUND RECORDINGS. This category is
appropriate for registration for both published and unpublished works in two situations: (1) where the copyright claim
is limited to the recording itself; and (2) where the same copyright claimant is seeking to register not only the sound recording but also the musical, dramatic, or literary work embodied
in the sound recording. With one exception, "sound recordings" are works that result from the fixation of a series of

musical, spoken, or other sounds. This exception is for the audio portions of audiovisual works, such as motion picture soundtracks or audio cassettes accompanying a film strip; these are considered an integral part of the audiovisual work as a whole and must be registered in Class PA. Sound recordings made before February 15, 1972, are not eligible for registration, but may be protected by state law.

Use Form SR to register claim to a Sound Recording.

5. CLASS RE: RENEWAL REGISTRATION. This category is used for all renewals of copyrights that were in their first term when the new law went into effect. It covers renewals in all categories. Renewals can only be made in the 28th year of the first copyright registration and have the effect of extending copyright protection for an additional 47 years. Use Form RE for renewal registrations in all categories.

Under the new law, a genuine effort has been made to simplify the categories and red tape surrounding them, as can be seen by the one category/one form norm so far. However, the Copyright Office has found it necessary to create and use three other forms:

Use Form CA to apply for supplementary registration, to correct an error in a copyright registration, or to amplify the information given in a registration.

Use Form IS if you want to import copies of foreign edition of a non-dramatic literary work that is subject to the manufacturing requirements of section 601 of the new law, which requires with some exceptions and exemptions that works copyrighted in the United States must be manufactured in the U.S. or Canada.

Use Form GR/CP (for group registration for contributions to periodicals) as an adjunct to a basic application on Form TX, Form PA, or Form VA, if you are making a single registration for a group of works by the same individual author, all first published as contributions to periodicals within a twelve-month period, for example, a group of essays in a travel column, or a series of cartoons (cartoons would be registered in Class VA, visual arts), as provided in section 408 (c)(2] of the new law.

In order to qualify for this registration, each contribution must have been published with a separate copyright notice in the name of the copyright owner. This is only a convenience for columnists who wish to register a collection of their work; it does not affect the ownership of the contributions, which belong to the author all along.

A writer does not lose his copyright in a work of authorship by virtue of its being published in a periodical. Article 201 (c), "Contributions to Collective Works," reads: "Copyright in each separate contribution to a collective work is distinct from copyright in the collective work as a whole, and vests initially in the author of the contribution. In the absence of an express transfer of the copyright or of any right under it, the owner of the copyright of the collective work is presumed to have acquired only the privilege of reproducing and distributing the contribution as part of that collective work, any revision of that collective work, and any later collective work in the same series." In other words, unless you agree to something different, a magazine acquires only one-time rights when it publishes a story or article.

HOW YOU DO IT

To secure copyright for a published, non-dramatic, literary work, here is what you must do:

First: Publish the work *with the copyright notice.* The law requires that a copyright notice in a specified form "shall be placed on all publicly distributed copies" of the work, on the title page, or (more commonly) on the back side of the title page, or as part of the colophon in a magazine. Use of the copyright notice consists of three elements: (1) the symbol "©", or the word "Copyright," or the abbreviation "Copr."; (2) the year of the first publication; and (3) the name of the copyright owner. For example: "Copyright 1979 Charles Brashers."

Unlike the old law, the new law provides procedures for correcting errors in the copyright notice, and even for curing the omission of the notice altogether. However, failure to comply with the requirement for copyright notice correctly may result in loss of some areas of valuable copyright protection. If not corrected within five years, you can blow your entire copyright.

Second: Fill out the proper application forms. For a non-dramatic literary work, the proper form would be Form TX. Write the Copyright Office for the blanks, then fill them out carefully, using a typewriter or dark ink, after reading the instructions.

Third: Send the required fee, the required copies, and the completed application to "The Register of Copyrights, Library of Congress, Washington, D.C. 20559." The fee for a

212

first copyright of a book is now $10, which must be paid by check or money order made payable to "The Register of Copyrights." You are required to deposit two copies of the published work with the Library of Congress (one copy of unpublished works and one copy of contributions to collective works). These are the copies that become evidence in infringement litigation. Send the fee, the copies, and the application together.

When the Registrar of Copyrights has processed your application and filed the copies, you will receive an official certificate of copyright, bearing the official seal of the Copyright Office. That certificate is your evidence of ownership.

Surprising as it may seem, many self-publishers never bother to copyright their work. This is often the case with publishers of small booklets, reports, etc. Sometimes small publishers worry too much about someone "stealing" their precious literary creations. Years ago I wrote advertising literature that sold over 20,000 copies of an import-export booklet. I was surprised when the author revealed that he had never bothered to copyright this excellent mail order seller. "Why worry," he explained. "Soon after you have a winner going, you'll have competition. They may not knock you off word for word, but they will use some of your general concepts if they are good." I guess he is right about that. Especially in non-fiction writing, we all take a little from here and a little from there. Still, copyrighting makes a lot of sense. It's inexpensive and very obtainable.

SPEAK OUT FOR PROFITS

Writers and self-publishers can greatly increase personal income through workshops, seminars and public speaking engagements. This requires some skill in the area of speaking before a group. This skill can be acquired. Joining a local Toastmasters group (clubs are available in most cities across the United States and Canada) can be a big step in developing poise, power and self-confidence, while speaking on your feet. This supportive organization can help you overcome your fears and teach you how to become a better communicator. Dues are very reasonable, less than $50.00 per year.

I also strongly recommend you get in touch with my friend, the dynamic Dottie Walters. She is a marvelous woman who is one of the world's best and most inspiring public speakers. Her rise from unskilled housewife to prominent business tycoon (she is president of her company, Hospitality Hostess Services, and heads a staff of over 200 hostesses serving the southern California counties of Los Angeles, Orange, San Diego, San Bernardino, and Riverside. Her task force of women welcome a staggering 5,000 new families to Southern California on behalf of 3,000 clients monthly! In addition, she is nationally recognized as a leading rally speaker, active in the National Speakers Association, and publisher of a speakers' newsletter, *Sharing Ideas Among Speakers,* as well as author/publisher of several books on speaking, sales, and motivation.

Dottie has shared the platform with Dr. Norman Vincent Peale, Dr. Robert Schuller, and many other famous speakers, often as the only woman on the program. Dottie is President of four corporations, as well as being a well known author and speaker. Her book, *"Never Underestimate the Selling Power of a Woman"* is a best-selling classic on that subject. (Published by Frederick Fell Company, New York, NY)

A one year subscription to Dottie's very helpful newsletter, "Sharing Ideas Among Professional Speakers and Their Friends" costs only $36.00. If you would like to see a sample copy first, send only $3.00. Order from: Royal CBS Publishing, 600 West Foothill Blvd., Glendora, CA91740.

WHAT'S IT WORTH?

Although most conventional publishers of books, magazines, or journals spell out clearly the fees they will render to their writers, dozens and dozens of other kinds of free lance jobs have no set fees. Each writer must determine his or her own worth.

Listed here are a collection of jobs requiring free lance imput and rough fee guidelines for same. I realize many of my *Words for Wealth* will demand higher pay for their writing skills, while others may choose to render their service for less money. That's each writer's own personal decision. Perhaps based on one's current work load, time availability, or a desire to eat regularly. The following jobs and rates will serve as a helpful guide.

Advertising. Very subjective, depending on type of work. My examples: Full page ad in national magazine, $400; ½ page ad, $225.00; 1 col. inch, $40.00. In local publications, full page ad, $250.00; ½ page ad, $150.00; 1 col. inch, $25.00.

Associations, writing for, on miscellaneous projects: $10 to $25 per hour or on a project basis.

As-told-to books. Author gets full advance and 50% royalties; subject gets 50% royalties.

Audio cassette scripts. $1,000 to $1,500 advance against 5 to 10 % royalties for 5 to 10 script/visual units.

Biography, writing for a sponsor. $500 up to $3,000 plus expenses over a 4-year period.

Book manuscript copy editing. $4 to $6 per hour.

Book manuscript rewriting. $1,000 and up; $400 per day and up.

Booklets, writing and editing. $500 to $1,000.

Business films. 10% of production cost on films up to $30,000. $150 per day. $20 per hour where % of cost not applicable.

Comedy writing, for night club circuit entertainers. Gags only, $7 to $10. Routines, $100 to $300 a minute. Some new comics try to get 5-minute routines for $100 to $150, but top comics may pay $1,500 for a 5-minute bit from a top writer with credits.

Commercial reports, for business, insurance companies, credit agencies, market research firms. $1.85 to $5 per report.

Company newsletters, "house organs." $50.00 per page.

Consultation fees. $75 to $100 per hour.

Conventions, public relations for. $500 to $5,000.

Correspondent, magazine, regional. $5 to $15 per hour, plus expenses.

Criticism, art, music, drama, local. Free tickets plus $5 to $15.

Editing, freelance book. $7 per hour and up.

Educational film strips. $1,200.

Educational films, writing. $200 for one reeler (11 minutes of film); $1,000 to $1,500 for 30 minutes.

Educational grant proposals, writing. $50 to $125 per day, plus expenses.

Family histories, writing. $400 and up.

Fiction rewriting. $150 for 10-page short story to $10,000 for complete novel rewrite, under special circumstances.

Folders, announcement writing. $25 to $350.

Gallup Poll interviewing. $6 per hour.

Genealogical research, local. $3 to $5 per hour.

Ghostwriting full-length books. Same rate as "As told to books (See above).

Government, local, public information officer. $10 per hour, to $50 to $100 per day.

History, local, lectures. $25 to $100.

House organs, writing and editing. $50 to $350, 2 to 4 pp.

Industrial and business brochures, consultation, research, and writing. $3,500.

Industrial films. $500 to $1,200 10-minute reel; 5 to 12% of the production cost of films that run $750 to $1,000 pe· release minute.

Industrial promotion. $10.00 to $60.00 per hour.

Industrial slide films. 14% of gross production cost.

Journalism, high school teaching, part-time. % of regular teacher's salary.

Library, public relations. $5 to $25 per hour.

Magazine stringing, rates recommended by American Society of Journalists and Authors, Inc. 20¢ to $1 per word, based on circulation. Daily rate: $200 plus expenses. Weekly rate: $750 plus expenses.

New product releases or news releases. $200 and up.

Paperback cover copy. $50 and up.

Pharmacy newsletters. $125 to $300.

Photo-brochures. $700 to $15,000.

Political campaign writing. $200 to $250 per week; $35 per page piecework jobs.

Programmed instruction materials, writing $1,000 to $3,000 per hour of programmed training provided. Consulting/editorial fees: $25 per hour; $200 per day, plus expenses, minimum.

Public relations. $150 to $200 per day plus expenses.

Publicity writing. $30 per hour; $100 per day.

Radio copywriting. $60 and up per spot.

Record album cover copy. $100 to $200.

Retail business newsletters. $200 for 4 pages. $350 for 8 pp.

Retainer for fund-raising writing for a foundation. $500 per month.

Retainer for publicity and PR work for an adoption agency: $200 per month.

Retainer for writing for business, campaign funds. Usually a flat fee, but the equivalent of $10 to $20 per hour.

Reviews, art, drama, music, for national magazines. $25 to $50; $10 to $20 per column for newspapers.

School public relations. $3.50 to $10 per hour.

Shopping mall promotion. 15% of promotion budget for the mall.

Slide film, single image photo. $75.

Slide presentation for an educational institution. $1,000.

Speeches by writers who become specialists in certain fields. $100 to $1,000 plus expenses.

Sports information director, college. $700 to $2,000 per month. Professional: $1,200 to $3,000 per month.

Syndicated newspaper column, self-promoted. $5.00 weeklies; $5 to $25 per week for dailies, based on circulation.

Teaching creative writing, part-time. $15 to $50 per hour of instruction.

Teaching high school journalism, part-time. % of regular teacher's salary.

Teaching home-bound students. $10 to $15 per hour.

Technical typing. 50¢ to $1 per page.

Technical typing masters for reproduction. $3 per hour for rough setup then $2 to $4 per page or $5 to $6 per hour.

Technical writing. $10 to $20 per hour.

Textbook and Tradebook copy editing. $5 to $8 per hour. Occasionally 75¢ per page.

Translation, literary. $25 to $50 per thousand words minimum.

Travel folder. $100 and up.

TV filmed news and features. $15 per film clip.

TV news film still photo. $5 to $10.

TV news story. $25 to $50.

This list gives you a general idea what to charge for your valuable writing services. Now let your own good judgment and availability make the final decision on "What's It Worth?"

WRITING AND THE LAW

Although you don't have to be an attorney at law to be a writer, some knowledge of legal matters can be very helpful. Common sense will usually keep you out of a bind, but here is a crash course in legal matters with which writers often come face-to-face.

How About the Copyright? Be certain you know that the publications for which you intend to write articles or stories are copyrighted before you submit. Always look for the legal copyright notice (©), which usually appears on the title page or at the bottom of the table of contents. If you plan to submit your work to an uncopyrighted publication, you may wish to obtain a copyright yourself. To do this, you produce copies (a few xeroxed copies stapled together of your typewritten copy will do) with the official copyright notice (© 1980 by Russ Von Hoelscher, for example), and then register your work with the Copyright office. Request application forms from: Registrar of Copyrights, Library of Congress, Washington, D.C. 20559. After filling out the simple form, you return it, plus two (2) copies of your work and the $10.00 fee. Uncopyrighted work falls into the *public domain*. In which case, anyone can use it without infringing on the original author's rights.

Rights. You may be able to sell your manuscript many times, depending on what rights you retain or surrender when you make the first sale. Here is a brief description of these "Rights."

1. *First North American Serial Rights.* This allows a periodical to publish your work for the first time in America and

Canada. Most publications will realize that you are simply offering them "First time rights" only—the opportunity to publish your work one time only! However, don't take any chances of a misunderstanding. State in writing that you offer *First Rights* only!

2. *Reprint Rights* (or, Second Serial Rights). This allows a publication to reprint your work that has already been published elsewhere. It also allows a periodical to publish part of an already-published book (self-publishers take notice!).

3. *Simultaneous Rights*. Some publications want the whole hog, including TV, movie rights, etc. Be careful here because when you grant "All Rights" you lose all control of your own writing.

Russ Von Hoelscher's advice: Keep as many rights as you can. The more rights you hold the better your position regarding future sales.

WHEN THEY WON'T PAY

When you push pencil or tap typewriter keys for cash and recognition, you must realize most editors are incompetent...out to test your level of patience. You've gotta' hang in there and maintain your equilibrium. However, *when the push comes to the shove*, and your work has been published, but you haven't gotten paid, it's time to get after your just due. Send off two letters—ten days apart. In letter No. 1 remind the editor of his obligation and request immediate action (his check by return mail); in letter No. 2 (make sure this one is sent by registered mail), again ask—make that "demand" payment or suggest you intend to pursue legal action. If no answer comes within ten days, take action! Consult with your attorney and/or file a small claims court suit. Write detailed letters stating your case to the Chamber of Commerce and Better Business Bureau in the publication's home town, and also to the District Attorney in the town of the publication. Most writer's who get the shaft limp away licking their wounds, shedding their tears in their own stale beer. This is stupid! The course of action I have outlined may not always bring satisfying results, but it at least gives you a fighting chance to get what you were promised. You strike a blow for yourself and all your brother and sister free-lancers when you stand up for your rights! Now don't go off *half cocked*. Use good judgment. Most editors are overworked and underpaid. As a group they are honest people. You must not confuse delays with fraud. Give the publication the benefit of the doubt, but do go after them hammer and tong once it is evident they plan to stiff you.

PARA PUBLICATIONS is definitely the leading publication in the fast-growing self-publishing movement.

In addition to important magazines and our newsletter, we highly recommend the following manuals and books.

THE SELF-PUBLISHING MANUAL by Dan Poynter. "The Cadillac of the do-it-yourself publishing trend." The S-P Manual is "must reading" for all writers who intend to publish their own works. Mr. Poynter runs America's largest one-man self-publishing company. He is a marketing self-made pro who is highly qualified to teach you the skills and techniques of result-getting writing, publishing, promoting and profitable book distributing. The author of twelve books with sales approaching Two Million Dollars, Dan is a leading practitioner of exactly what he preaches. This book is the perfect companion to the book you are now reading. Order your copy for only $9.95 postpaid from Para Publications, Box 4232, Santa Barbara, CA 93103.

THE LAZY MAN'S WAY TO RICHES BY Joe Karbo. This is probably the No. 1 best-selling mail order book of all time. Joe has taken in millions selling this classic at ten dollars per! Von Hoelscher says: "This book is very important reading for all self-publishers who intend to sell their books by mail." Karbo is a mail selling genius. He also will make you hungry for success. A real inspirational mover, shaker and money-maker! You know the price. $10.00 postpaid! Order from the man, himself: Joe Karbo, 17105 South Pacific, Sunset Beach, CA 90742.

ONE BOOK/FIVE WAYS, published by William Kaufmann, Inc. This is a book that every self-publisher will value. *One Book/Five Ways:* The Publishing Procedures of Five University Presses. This grew out of a project of simulating the publication of a gardening book, with all the reader reports, financial projections and marketing plans for five different publishers reproduced in facsimile. (Incidentally, a sixth publisher decided the project was so good that it published the book, entitled *No Time For Houseplants*, commercially.)

This marvelous source-book is available from the publisher, William Kaufmann, Inc., One First Street, Los Altos, CA 94022 for $18.75 hardcover and $9.75 paperback. I don't know of any other source that has so many examples of editing, typographical design, layout and marketing information.

Bill Kaufmann, a small publisher who has won national recognition for the quality of his titles, has also issued *Into Print:* A Practical Guide to Writing, Illustrating and Publishing by Mary Hill and Wendell Cochran ($6.95). It is especially valuable if you have a self-help or general textbook to self-publish or to market to other publishers, and you need to understand how to handle charts, graphs, photographs and other illustrations.

PUBLISHING SHORT-RUN BOOKS
By Dan Poynter

Mr. Self-Publishing himself, author of the great bestseller, *The Self-Publishing Manual*, is also the auther of this winner.

Publishing Short-Run Books describes the new techniques and machinery available for producing professional quality softcover or hardcover books in small, yet economical quantities.

Describing typesetting, pasteup, printing, and binding, Dan Poynter's book is designed to be sold in instant print centers and copy shops. The book will provide printers with another product while demonstrating the capacity of their shop. Printers who have to answer the same customer questions day after day will find the book to be a great time saver.

This is a classic case of finding a need and filling it. While selling his very successful publishing book, *The Self Publishing Manual* through instant print centers, Poynter discovered that these shops do not offer instruction in how to paste up material for reproduction. In developing the manuscript, the author found new techniques and technology which could be combined to produce books quickly and economically in the short run.

This is an ideal do-it-yourself system for educators needing just a few copies of a special book for a class, business executives who need professional-looking material for presentations, poets who desire a small private printing, publishers who wish to test the market before investing in a large press run, authors who are trying to get the attention of a publisher (it is easier to sell a book than a manuscript), printers who want to make a dummy of a book, and anyone who is in a hurry to break into print.

Dan Poynter is the author of twelve books, four of which have been translated into other languages. As the name of his publishing company (Para Publications) would imply, Poynter began with popular books on skydiving and technical books on the parachute. He penned the first book on hang gliding which has been through the press nine times for 125,000 in print. He is also the producer of a unique circular format book on the Frisbee. Last year he wrote *The Self-Publishing Manual*, a book which immediately became well known in the publishing industry for its marketing advice. Poynter has served on the board of COSMEP, the international association of independent publishers. His firm, Para Publications, is located in Santa Barbara, the home of more than 85 book publishers and 30 magazines.

Publishing Short-Run Books, How to Pasteup and Reproduce Books Instantly Using Your Copy Shop is available in instant print centers, bookstores, and direct from the publisher at $6.95 postpaid from Para Publications, P.O. Box 4232, Santa Barbara, CA 93102.

FINDING FACTS FAST
By Alden Todd

This book is tailor-made for every writer in the land. Here is a book that could save you hundreds of hours while you slave away doing factual research. A real gold mine of information, sources, and most important of all, *powerful research techniques* that produce fast results! Today, there is just too much information and an overabundance of factual data for any person not to develop your fact-finding tactics and techniques. The heart of this great workbook is the unique blend of methods of thought, planning, and skillful research tools it teaches. After reading this book cover-to-cover, there will be virtually no information you want to know that you cannot find. And that makes *Finding Facts Fast* worth many times the low price of $3.95 plus $1.00 postage/handling for this handsome trade paperbound edition. Order from: Ten Speed Press, P.O. Box 7123, Berkeley, CA 94707.

TOWERS CLUB USA
NEWSLETTER

For many years Jerry Buchanan has been publishing this excellent newsletter to benefit all self-publishers and free-lance writers. It is filled with solid "meat and potatoes" on getting a book into print and then successfully selling your book or report once it rolls off the press. Write to Mr. Buchanan for a sample copy and full details on other outstanding books and reports he offers by mail. Towers Club, P.O. Box 2038, Vancouver, WA 98668.

BOOKS

Most of the reference books may be found in your local library. In addition, there are many good books on writing, publishing, printing, marketing, distribution, etc. A few are listed here. Check the card file in your library and visit a nearby bookstore. Write to the publishers for latest price and delivery information.

Brochures on books of interest to writers and publishers are available from:

The Writer, Inc.
8 Arlington Street
Boston, MA 02116

R.R. Bowker Co.
P.O. Box 1897
Ann Arbor, MI 48106

Writer's Digest Books
99333 Alliance Road
Cincinatti, OH 45242

Para Publishing
P.O. Box 4232
Santa Barbara, CA 93103

REFERENCE BOOKS AND DIRECTORIES

AB Bookman's Yearbook
P.O. Box AB
Clifton, NJ 07015

AD Guide—An Advertiser's Guide to Scholarly Periodicals
American University Press
Services
One Park Avenue
NYC, NY 10016
Lists editors of specialized journals.

American Book Trade Directory
R.R. Bowker Co.
P.O. Box 1807
Ann Arbor, MI 48106
Lists booksellers, book clubs, etc.

American Library Association
Membership Directory
50 East Huron Street
Chicago, IL 60611
Lists the names and addresses of 31,000 members.

American Library Directory
R.R. Bowker Co.
P.O. Box 1807
Ann Arbor, MI 48106
Lists 33,000 U.S. and Canadian libraries.

Ayer Directory of Publications
West Washington, PA 19106
Publication circulation, rates, etc.

Book Buyers Handbook
American Booksellers Assn.
122 East 42nd St.
NYC, NY 10017

Book Publishers of the United States and Canada
Gale Research Co.
Book Tower
Detroit, MI 48226

Books in Print
R.R. Bowker Co.
P.O. Box 1807
Ann Arbor, MI 48106
Lists all books currently available by title and author.
Annual.

Subject Guide to Books in Print
R.R. Bowker Co.
P.O. Box 1807
Ann Arbor, MI 48106
Lists all books currently available by subject.
Annual. Non-fiction.

Subject Guide to Forthcoming Books
R.R. Bowker Co.
P.O. Box 67
Whitinsville, MA 01588
A preview. Bimonthly. Non-fiction.

Paperbound Books in Print
R.R. Bowker Co.
P.O. Box 1807
Ann Arbor, MI 48106

Lists all soft cover books currently available by subject,
title and author as well as addresses of publishers.

Broadcasting Yearbook
1735 DeSales St., N.W.
Washington, DC 20036

Contemporary Authors
Gale Research Co.
Book Tower
Detroit, MI 48226
Lists biographical information on authors.

The Dewey Decimal Classification and Relative Index
Forest Press, Inc.
85 Watervliet Avenue
Albany, NY 12206

Directory of College stores
B. Klein Publications
P.O. Box 8503
Coral Springs, FL 33065

Directory of Mailing List Houses
B. Klein Publications
P.O. Box 8503
Coral Springs, FL 33065

Directory of Private Presses and Letterpress Printers
    and Publishers
Press of Arden Park
861 Los Molinos Way
Sacramento, CA 95825

Directory of Small Magazine/Press Editors and Publishers
Dustbooks
P.O. Box 100
Paradise, CA 95969

Directory of Syndicated Features
Editor and Publisher
575 Lexington Ave.
NYC, NY 10022

Educational Directory
One Park Avenue
NYC, NY 10016

Encyclopedia of Associations
Gale Research Co.
Book Tower
Detroit, MI 48226
Lists over 13,000 national organizations

Exhibits Directory
Association of America
Publishers
One Park Avenue
NYC, NY 10016
Lists book fairs and exhibits.

The Foundation Directory
Columbia University Press
562 West 113th St.
NYC, NY 10025

The Foundation Grants Index
Columbia University Press
562 West 113th St.
NYC, NY 10025

Guide to American Directories
B. Klein Publications
P.O. Box 8503
Coral Springs, FL 33065
When you run out of leads, use this list of all the other
directories.

International Book Trade
Directory
R.R. Bowker Co.
P.O. Box 1807
Ann Arbor, MI 48106
Lists 30,000 booksellers in 170 countries which handle
U.S. publications.

International Directory of Little Magazines and
  Small Presses
P.O. Box 100
Paradise, CA 95969
A comprehensive listing of small publishers.

International Literary Market Place
R.R. Bowker Co.
P.O. Box 1807
Ann Arbor, MI 48106
Lists publishers, agents, suppliers, etc., in 160 countries
outside the U.S. and Canada.

International Yearbook
Editor and Publisher
575 Lexington Ave.
NYC, NY 10022
Lists newspaper personnel, ad agencies, etc.

Literary Market Place
R.R. Bowker Co.
P.O. Box 1807
Ann Arbor, MI 48106
Very important. Lists agents, artists, associations, book
clubs, reviewers, exporters, magazines, newspapers, news
services, radio & TV, and many other services. Annual.

Magazines for Libraries
R.R. Bowker Co.
P.O. Box 1807
Ann Arbor, MI 48106
Lists 6,500 magazines of interest from over 60,000 available.

Mail Order Business Directory
B. Klein Publications
P.O. Box 8503
Coral Springs, FL 33065
Lists 5,900 mail order and catalogue houses.

Market Guide
Editor & Publisher
575 Lexington Ave.
NYC, NY 10022

National Trade and Professional Associations of the
    U.S. and Canada

Columbia Books, Inc.
734 15th St., N.W. #601
Washington, DC 20005
A directory of organizations.

National Union Catalogue
Library of Congress
(Available in your local library)

Publishers' Trade List Annual
R.R. Bowker Co.
P.O. Box 1807
Ann Arbor, MI 48106
A compilation of publishers' catalogues.

Small Press Record Of Books In Print
Dustbooks
P.O. Box 100
Paradise, CA 95969

Standard Rate & Data Service
5201 Old Orchard Road
Skokie, IL 60076
A series of directories covering all types of advertising
media and mailing lists.

Ulrich's International Periodicals Directory
R.R. Bowker Co.
P.O. Box 1807
Ann Arbor, MI 48106
61,000 Periodicals listed.

Vinebrook Documents
P.O. Box UP
Bedford, MA 01730
Huenefeld's forms for publisher planning, control, etc.

Working Press of the Nation
National Research Bureau
424 North Third Street.
Burlington, IA 52601

Lists newspapers, magazines, TV/radio, feature writers
and internal publications. Includes (old) Gebbie House
Magazine Directory.

Writer's Handbook
The Writer, Inc.
8 Arlington Street
Boston, MA 01226
Lists over 2,000 places to sell manuscripts, etc. Annual.

Writer's Market
Writer's Digest
9933 Alliance Road
Cincinnati, OH 45242
Lists over 5,000 paying markets for writing, etc.
   Writer's Digest also publishes market directories for
photographers, artists, song writers and craft workers.

Writer's Yearbook
Writer's Digest
9933 Alliance Road
Cincinnati, OH 45242
Information on writing, markets, etc.

MAGAZINES FOR AUTHOR-PUBLISHERS

Write for a sample copy and current subscription rates.

AB Bookman's Weekly
P.O. Box AB
Clifton, NY 07015

Abraxas Magazine
2322 Rugby Row
Madison, WI 53705

Advertising Age
740 Rush Street
Chicago, IL 60611

American Book Publishing Record
R.R. Bowker Co.
P.O. Box 67
Whitinsville, MA 01588

The American Book Review
P.O. Box 188
New York City, NY 10003

American Bookseller
122 East 42nd Street
New York City, NY 10017

American Libraries
50 East Huron Street
Chicago, IL 60611

Azimuth
P.O. Box 842
Iowa City, IA 52240

Book Production Industry
P.O. Box 429
Westport, CT 06880

Booklist
50 East Huron Street
Chicago, IL 60611

Bookswest Magazine
3757 Wilshire Blvd. #100
Los Angeles, CA 90010

Broadcasting Magazine
1735 DeSales Street, NW
Washington, DC 20036

Canadian Author & Bookman
P.O. Box 120
Niagara-On-The-Lake, Ont.
Canada

The College Store Journal
528 East Lorain Street
Oberlin, OH 44074

Direct Marketing Magazine
Hoke Communications, INc.
224 Seventh Street
Garden City, NY 11530

Directions Magazine
Baker & Taylor
1515 Broadway
New York City, NY 10036

Editor & Publisher
575 Lexington Avenue
New York City, NY 10022

Forecast Magazine
Baker & Taylor
1515 Broadway
New York City, NY 10036

Graphic Arts Monthly
222 South Riverside Place
Chicago, IL 60606

The Horn Book Magazine
Park Square Bldg.
31 St. James Street
Boston, MA 02116
Books for children and young adults.

Incentive Marketing
Hartman Communications, Inc.
633 Third Avenue
New York City, NY 10017

The Independent
156 Pleasant Street
Arlington, MA 02174

Introduction to Mail Order
1008 Dawn Street
Bakersfield, CA 93307

Kirkus Reviews
200 Park Avenue South
New York City, NY 10003

Learning Today
P.O. Box 956
Norman, OK 73070

Library-College Omnibus
P.O. Box 956
Norman, OK 73070

Library Journal
R.R. Bowker Co.
P.O. Box 67
Whitinsville, MA 01588

The Library Scene
88 Needham Street
Newton Highlands, MA 02161

NewsArt
Attn: Harry Smith
5 Beekman Street
New York City, NY 10038

Potentials In Marketing   A Lakewood Publication
731 Hennepin Avenue
Minneapolis, MN 55403

Printing Impressions
401 North Broad Street
Philadelphia, PA 19108

Public Library Quarterly
Haworth Press
149 Fifth Avenue
New York City, NY 10010

Publishers Weekly
R.R. Bowker Co.
P.O. Box 67
Whitinsville, MA 01588
Western Correspondent: Patricia Holt
2566 Washington Street #1, San Francisco, CA 94115
This is the magazine of the publishing industry.

San Francisco Review of Books
2140 Vallejo Street
San Francisco, CA 94123

School Library Journal
R.R. Bowker Co.
P.O. Box 67
Whitinsville, MA 01588

Select Press Review
Bridge Street
Milford, NH 03055

Small Press Review
P.O. Box 100
Paradise, CA 95969

Len Fulton's magazine for authors and small publishers. Highly recommended!

Stony Hills
P.O. Box 715
Newburyport, MA 01950

Weekly Record
R.R. Bowker Co.
P.O. Box 67
Whitinsville, MA 01588

West Coast Review of Books
Rapport Publishing Co.
9420-D Activity Road
San Diego, CA 92126

West Coast Writer's Conspiracy
P.O. Box 3041
Seal Beach, CA 90740

The Writer
8 Arlington Street
Boston, MA 02116

Writer's Digest
9933 Alliance Road
Cincinnati, OH 45242
Inspiration reading for writers.

Zip
North American Bldg.
401 North Broad St.
Philadelphia, PA 19108

NEWSLETTERS FOR AUTHORS AND PUBLISHERS

Write for a sample copy and current subscription rates.

BP Report On The Business Of Book Publishing
Knowledge Industry Publications
2 Corporate Park Drive
White Plains, NY 10604

Classified Ad Letter
Joseph A. Zodl
303 Main Street
Little Ferry, NJ 07643

Graphic Communications World
P.O. Box 12000
Lake Park, FL 33403

The Huenefeld Report
P.O. Box UP
Bedford, MA 01730

Key Classified Ad Newsletter/Mail Order Counselor
Voice Publications
Bernard Lyons
Goreville, IL 62939

LCAN Newsletter
Attn: Gary Lagier
P.O. Box 2056
Sunnyvale, CA 94087

LJ-SLJ Hotline
R.R. Bowker Co.
P.O. Box 67
Whitinsville, MA 01588

P.E.N. American Center Newsletter
47 Fifth Avenue
New York City, NY 10003

Self-Publishing for Profit Newsletter
Jim Wildman
3328 Indian Mesa Drive
Thousand Oaks, CA 91360

Towers Club USA Newsletter
Jerry Buchanan
P.O. Box 2038
Vancouver, WA 98661

Writer's Newsletter
Books West
3757 Wilshire Blvd. #100
Los Angeles, CA 90010

Writer's Newsletter
110 Morgan Hall
Indiana University
Bloomington, IN 47401

PAMPHLETS OF INTEREST
TO AUTHORS AND PUBLISHERS

Federal Trade Commission
Washington, DC 20580
1. Shopping By Mail? You're Protected!
2. FTC Buyer's Guide No. 2
3. Consumer Alert—The Vanity Press News release
   dated 19 July 1959
4. Vanity Press Findings. Dockets 7005 and 7489

Popular Mechanics
224 West 57th Street
New York City, NY 10019
1. Profits From Classified Ads. $1.00

Superintendent Of Documents
U.S. Government Printing Office
Washington, DC 20402
1. Instructions For Mailers, Domestic
2. Postal Bulletin
3. International Mail
4. U.S. Government Purchasing and Sales Directory,
   $4.00
5. Selling to the Military, $1.80

Memo To Mailers
P.O. Box 1600
LaPlata, MD 20646 (free)

P.E.N. American Center
47 Fifth Avenue
New York City, NY 10003

1. Grants and Awards Available to American Writers. $2.25

Literature Program
National Endowment for the Arts
2401 E. Street NW
Washington, DC 20506
1. Assistance, fellowships and residencies for writers

Poets & Writers, Inc.
201 West 54th Street
New York City, NY 10019
1. Awards List. $2.50
2. The Sponsors List. 75¢
3. Literary Agents: A Complete Guide, $2.50

Departments of the Army and Air Force
Hqs. Army and Air Force Exchange Service
Dallas, TX 75222
1. Contract Terms and Conditions (AAFES Form 4200-13/19)

Bank of America
Small Business Reporter, "Mail Order Enterprises"
P.O. Box 37000, Dept. 3120
San Francisco, CA 94137
$1.00

Chicago Advertising Agency
Ad Guide
28 East Jackson Blvd.
Chicago, IL 60604
$1.00

The Copyright Office
Office of Public Affairs
Library of Congress
Washington, DC 20559
1. General Guide to the Copyright Act of 1976

PROFESSIONAL ORGANIZATIONS

Write for an application and inquire about benefits and
dues. Many associations publish a magazine or newsletter.

American Booksellers Association
122 East 42nd Street
New York City, NY 10017

American Library Association
50 East Huron Street
Chicago, IL 60611

The Association of American Publishers, Inc.
One Park Avenue
New York City, NY 10016

The Association of American University Presses
One Park Avenue
New York City, NY 10016

The Authors Guild
234 West 44th Street
New York City, NY 10036

Aviation & Space Writers Association
Cliffwood Road
Chester, NJ 07930

Book Publicists Of Southern California
6565 Sunset Blvd. #515
Hollywood, CA 90028

The Christian Booksellers Assn.
P.O. Box 200
Colorado Springs, CO 80901

COSMEP (Committee of Small Magazine Editors and
    Publishers)
P.O. Box 703
San Francisco, CA 94101
This is the national organization for small publishers.

COSMEP East
Robert Kalenchosky
255 Humphrey Street
Marblehead, MA 01945

COSMEP South
P.O. Box 19332
Washington, DC 20036

International Book Printers Assn.
1730 North Lynn Street
Arlington, VA 22209

The National Assn. of College Stores
528 East Lorain Street
Oberlin, OH 44074

The National Writers Club
1450 South Havana #620
Aurora, CO 80012

New England Small Press Assn.
45 Hillcrest Place
Amherst, MA 01002

P.E.N.
156 Fifth Avenue
New York City, NY 10010

Poets & Writers, Inc.
201 West 54th Street
New York City, NY 10019

Western Book Publishers Assn.
P.O. Box 558
Corte Madera, CA 94925

Western Independent Publishers
P.O. Box 31249
San Francisco, CA 94131

Women Writers West
2067 Linda Flora Drive
Los Angeles, CA 90024

The Woman's Salon
Attn: Sallie Finch Reynolds
24 Bay Avenue
Sea Cliff, NY 11579

The World Guild
119 North Auburn Street
Cambridge, MA 02138

CHAIN BOOKSTORES

For a complete list, see *Literary Market Place* and *The American Book Trade Directory* in your local public library. Direct your letter to the "small press buyer." Here are America's two largest chains:

B. Dalton/Pickwick
Attn: Jerry Rogart, Small Press Buyer
9340 James Avenue
Minneapolis, MN 55431

Walden Book Co.
Attn: Tom Simon
179 Ludlow Street
Stamford, CT 06904

U.S. GOVERNMENT PROCUREMENT OFFICES

The Adjutant General Department of the Army
Attn: DAAG-REL
Washington, DC 20314

Acquisitions Librarian
Chief of Naval Education and Training Support
General Library Service Branch N32
Pensacola, FL 32509

Acquisitions Librarian
Air Force Libraries Section
AFPMPPB-3
USAF Military Personal Center
Randolph Air Force Base, TX 78148

Veteran's Administrtion Library
810 Vermont Ave., NW
Room 976
Washington, DC 20420

International Communications Agency
Attn: Acquisitions Librarian
1750 Pennsylvania Avenue
Washington, DC 20547
  or:
Paul Steere
ECA/FL
International Communications Agency
1717 H Street #756
Washington, DC 20006

Army and Air Force Exchange
Procurement Office
Attn: Acquisitions Librarian
The Pentagon, Room 5E479
Washington, DC 20310

Co. Comm., Navy Resale Systems Office
Third & 29th Streets
Brooklyn, NY 11232

U.S. Coast Guard
Code G, FER-1/72
Washington, DC 20590

U.S. Marine Corps
Headquarters. Marine Corps
LFE
Washington, DC 20380

For the addresses of other government offices, call the local office of your congressperson. Look up the name in your telephone directory.

EXPORTERS

ADCO Int'l Co.
80-00 Cooper Ave. #3
Glendale, NY 11227

Feffer & Simon, Inc.
100 Park Avenue
New York City, NY 10016

Kaiman & Polon Inc.
456 Sylvan Avenue
Englewood Cliffs, NJ 07632

Worldwide Media Service, Inc.
386 Park Avenue South
New York City, NY 10016

For a complete list, see *Literary Market Place* in your local public library.

BOOK PRINTERS

Compare local prices in your area and then compare these with specialized book printing firms found in the Literary Market Place.

Section Three—

Home Mailorder Opportunities

MAIL ORDER — A VERY
EXCITING AND PROFITABLE
WAY TO DO BUSINESS

Almost everyone loves to receive mail—personal mail and business mail. It is fun to open letters from far-off places and check out the contents. Now imagine opening a huge stack of letters filled with cash, checks and money orders and you will understand one main attraction of the mail order business. Another big attraction is that you can launch a home-based mail sale business with only limited cash to invest. Many of today's successful mail order tycoons made a successful start with less than one thousand dollars to invest.

HOW MUCH CAPITAL
DO YOU NEED

Many of today's profitable mail order dealers and companies started with very limited capital. Even today, many ads still claim:

"Get started in mail order for less than $100,"
or
"Start your own mail selling business without cash."

Horse feathers! Inflation being what it is in the 1980's, you need some capital to launch any kind of business, even a part-time, small, home-based mail order operation. I would recommend not less than $500 as a bare minimum, and $1,000 to $2,000 would be far more adequate. $5,000 plus would be ideal.

GETTING STARTED FROM SCRATCH

A home-based mail order business can literally be started from the kitchen table. Many operators started in just that way, before proceeding to "more businesslike quarters" in the home or an outside office.

When the kitchen table offers the only necessary space, use it. However, if at all possible, search out other areas of your house or apartment that offer more privacy. Your own home office or a spare bedroom that can be converted to office space is ideal. Even open space in a garage may serve your initial startup needs.

BASIC SUPPLIES AND EQUIPMENT

(1) a desk and chair
(2) file cabinet
(3) envelopes and letterheads
(4) typewriter
(5) storage area/folding table
(6) miscellaneous office supplies (rubber bands, paper clips, envelope openers, glue, typewriter correction liquid, etc.
(7) a large wastebasket
(8) proper lighting
(9) postage stamps
(10) checking account
(11) a bookkeeping system

You may, of course, improvise. Any table, including the kitchen table, may serve as your desk during your initial start. However, do get yourself a desk, even if it is a used one from the Goodwill or Salvation Army, as soon as you can. Your own desk will give you a more positive feeling of "being in business for yourself." Likewise, you could use a spare closet or your own bookshelves in place of a file cabinet at first, but again, purchase a sturdy four-drawer file cabinet as soon as possible.

It is almost impossible to do business without using a typewriter. You can either buy one second-hand or rent a nice model by the month at reasonable rates. If you can't even "two-finger type," a typing course at a local adult education school should have you pecking away in good order, and these classes usually charge very low tuition. If you are married or live with someone with office skills, they can be of real help to you.

You need storage space to keep the items you intend to sell by mail. And the other items on my list (envelopes, stamps, office supplies, etc.) are essential to any kind of mail order business.

Don't under-estimate the importance of adequate lighting. Also, purchase a large comprehensive journal at an office supply store and get started right by keeping good business records. Your recordkeeping is vital. It will tell you in which direction your business is heading. A separate checking account for your mail order business is important. Make notations as to what every check went for (supplies, advertising, rentals, etc.) and this will assist you in keeping good records.

You also need a phone on or near your desk or work area. It may be called the mail order business, yet you will still find yourself using the telephone often to order supplies, obtain information, etc. You may or may not wish to use your own phone number in your ads, catalogs and circulars going to your customers. Some mail order companies do, with satisfactory results; others prefer that all business be done by mail.

WHO IS QUALIFIED?

Almost anyone of average intelligence with true success desire is more than qualified to begin a mail order business.

BUSINESSMEN—Any businessman or woman will already possess most of the basic knowledge and skills to operate a mail order venture.

SALES PEOPLE—Many men and women active in sales, either to business or consumers, have launched successful mail order selling careers, either part-time or fulltime. Their knowledge of what makes people "buy" can greatly aid them in mail order selling.

HOUSEWIVES—A part-time mail order business can liberate the housewife who is bored and has extra unproductive hours on her hands. In years past, mail order was a "man's business," but the 1970's saw many hundreds of women get involved in mail selling. You can expect to see this trend continue and grow.

RETIRED PEOPLE—It has been estimated that over 25% of the one-person or one couple mail order firms are run by retired folks. A home-based mail selling second career can have a rejuvenating effect on senior citizens who find themselves with too much leisure time. By becoming active in mail order, many seniors earn needed extra income and may even extend their life span by building their self-esteem through business activity.

THE WHOLE FAMILY—The Donovans of Milwaukee, Wisconsin, launched a mail order business a few years ago that involved the whole family. Since 1979, Mr. and Mrs. Donovan and their two teenage girls and one pre-teenage boy have manufactured and sold homemade kites by mail. Joe Donovan says that the home mail order business brought the family closer together than anything else ever had. Good enough reason for others to consider total family involvement in a home-oriented business.

HOW TO GET STARTED

Most successful mail order operators started with a single product. The mighty retail sales giant, Sears, started their vast empire with only one product. Many recent entrepreneurs have done likewise. Joe Sugarman launched his very lucrative JS&A sales company with a single product (a pocket calculator) and now handles dozens of fast-selling electronic products, gadgets and gift items.

If you're making a shoestring mail order start, I strongly recommend you get your new enterprise off the ground with a product or service that you have some control over. If you page through the display and classified mail order advertising pages of various magazines and newspapers, you will no doubt notice many mail selling firms that want to put you in business selling their products—using their ads, sales literature, catalogs, etc.—as the basis of your entering a mail trade business. My advice: Don't go into mail order on this premise. The vast majority of folks who enter mail order exclusively handling someone else's wares lose their shirts! They usually are "out of business" within six months! It is ok to sell books, gifts, novelties and other products controlled by others, but only in addition to the products you have some direct control over.

For example: If you make and sell jewelry by mail, it may be a very good idea to offer similar items furnished by other suppliers. Why not rake in extra profits? However, your own products should be highlighted and the basis of your mail sale efforts.

Don't try to make your start only selling someone else's products. Rarely have I ever seen a beginner make money in mail order only offering some other firm's wares. Among the most heavily advertised mail order setups are those pushed by various gift catalog dealers. These firms offer attractive catalogs (for a price!) with your name printed as dealer. The orders come to you. You then subtract your commission (usually 40% or 50%) and then send the order to the prime source to fill. I have never heard of an independent mail order dealer prospering from this approach. Recently a young woman in El Cajon, California, told me she bought 1,000 gift assortment catalogs. She mailed them to a list (purchased from the very same catalog dealership). Her reward? Only two orders that brought in $28. She kept half of that amount for her effort—$14 income from a total of $325 in expenditures (the total amount she spent for catalogs and names plus postage and mailing costs). You can't get rich with that kind of negative cash flow! Start right—with your own service or product!!

FIND A MARKET FIRST

Too often, mail order beginners prepare a product or service first and then go shopping for a market. Even mail trade veterans are often guilty of this dangerous mistake. I don't care how great your product or service is or how "in love with it" you and your friends are, sound marketing techniques demand that you target your potential market prior to preparing your products or services.

Ben Suarez is one of the most innovative and dynamic mail order promoters/copywriters in the world. He has sold many millions of dollars worth of books, manuals and other "paper products" by mail. Yet, his first mail order venture was a total flop. He prepared and published a book that, through a plastic wheel on the cover and computerized tables inside, could add, subtract, multiply and divide. Ben thought he had a big winner, only to discover he did not have a tailor-made market and was unable to "reach" a market.

Later he realized the importance of finding a ready-made market before going into production. This proven marketing strategy, combined with his great flair for copy and promotion, brought him huge success marketing books on astrology, health, mail order, etc. His "7 Steps to Freedom" is one of the better mail order marketing manuals ever published (see "Recommended Reading" section in the back of this report).

WHAT'S IN A NAME?

Don't choose your new company name in a haphazard fashion. The name you hang on your new fledgling firm could be a liability or an asset. It can help entice orders or turn potential customers off.

Many new mail order dealers simply use their own name. If it is your name, it need not be registered, which is required by most states when fictitious names are used. Although this practice works for some, often it is wiser to use a company name that is either catchy or gives a better description of the products you sell.

The late mail order genius, Joe Karbo, earned millions using his own name to sell his famous classic "The Lazy Man's Way to Riches." Using his own name fit perfectly with the kick-back "Lazy Joe" image his ad copy was conveying. Ben Suarez took just the opposite approach in his road to fortune. Selling books from his own home, he gave his new company a grand name—The Publishing Corporation of America! And when he was selling over a million of his "Life-Luck Horoscopes," he created the perfect name to market the horoscopes—The International Astrological Association. Now, think about it! Wouldn't you feel better about ordering astrology items from The International Astrological Association than in placing your order to just a person's name? Keep this in mind when you pick a name to do business with. In some cases, your own name may do fine; in others, you can give yourself a powerful image by selecting a name that fits well with the product or service you sell.

Be careful not to limit yourself. I heard of a company in St. Paul, Minnesota, that called itself the A&B Yo Yo Company that manufactured and sold yo-yos, by mail as well as to stores, for some years but then branched out into other areas —gifts, toys and books—when yo-yo sales fell. Soon they found it necessary to change their name. If you label yourself

264

as a yo-yo company, as an astrological association or a fruit-cake mail order baker, you may have an image problem if you expand into other areas, especially unrelated areas.

HOW ABOUT A LOGO?

While I place real importance on choosing a name to do business under, many logos are little more than an ego trip for their owners. A strong logo design can help national products and can even be a plus for a small mail order dealer if it is catchy or fits well with the company name. However, a logo for logo's sake, especially the new designs that leave you wondering "What does it mean?", will not aid the mail order operator. If you use a logo, make sure it "fits" your company name and the image you wish to project.

OFFER TRUE VALUE

There is an old mail order axiom that goes something like this: "Put most of your money into advertising and only a little into your product!" The theory is not without foundation. In many cases, mail customers have only your advertising as a criteria for placing their orders. Often they don't really know what to expect when their mailman delivers your package. This fact of mail selling has led many dealers to "promise the moon but only deliver a few specks of moon dust."

While I agree that much of your money must go into your sales vehicle (ads, circulars, brochures, catalogs or whatever), nevertheless, I urge you only to sell products you would be willing to order at prices you would be willing to pay. The real ripoff artists who promise a lot and deliver very little usually don't last long. Repeat business is a major factor in

265

reaching mail order success, and nobody ever reorders from someone whom they feel cheated them. Then too, a guarantee of satisfaction is usually required to sell anything by mail. And if you guarantee satisfaction, you must refund returned merchandise or face trouble from the Post Office.

You will earn more money in the long run, and sleep better nights, by offering your mail order clients products and services you're proud to ship. Honesty may not always be the best policy, but it seems to be the only one that works!

BUILD AN IMPRESSIVE IMAGE

Don't make the mistake of announcing to the world "I'm a mail order beginner!" Honesty and modesty are admirable traits, but don't mistake a poor business attitude and image for openness.

Your customers are being asked to order products they know very little about from a company they know nothing about. That's a tall order, and you can't blame them for being more than a little skeptical.

One professional method to help build confidence is to produce professional-appearing advertising and sales material. Also, quality letterheads and envelopes are a must! Do all you can to convey an impressive businesslike image. Quality printed matter and well-designed ads cost only slightly more than sloppy promotional material and sales literature. Too often the money you save on slipshod printing and advertising is lost many times over on lost sales.

I'm not telling you to run out and purchase materials from

the most expensive printer and artwork illustrator in town. By all means, shop around. Price is a consideration. Just make sure your printed materials project a professional image. By requesting samples and quotes from many sources, you'll probably benefit both ways; (a) quality work and (b) reasonable rates.

Another important point in your relationship to a printer: Find one who not only offers decent quality but also one who comes close to meeting his deadlines. I say "comes close" because, frankly, most printers, even the good ones, run a day or two or more "late." It just seems to be standard in the profession. Keep this fact in mind. Plan far enough ahead and allow a little extra time for "unforeseen delays."

CHOOSING THE RIGHT PRODUCTS

It is my belief that my chances to succeed are greatly enhanced when I am handling products and services that I truly enjoy offering to my customers. That's a good premise to begin with. However, the many cold, hard facts of mail order selling must be compatible with the product I wish to sell.

HOW MUCH INVESTMENT WILL IT TAKE: Before making a start, you should make an estimate of the time, energy and capital you will have to invest to develop your product or service. You must decide if the money and effort is worth the potential reward.

RESEARCHING YOUR TARGET MARKET: As mentioned before, this may be factor number one in determining your overall mail order success. You start with a concept of what you will sell. For the sake of an example, let's say your hobby is hand-decorating Christmas cards for friends and relatives. Now you have a bright idea that you can use your art talent in designing cards to make money in mail order. Time to do market research. A good place to start would be your local library. Since women buy over 90% of greeting cards and personal stationery items, it would be wise to copy down the names and addresses of every publication that has a high female readership in the big Standard Rate and Data directory at the library. Among the leading publications in this category would be magazines like "House Beautiful," "McCall's," "Needlepoint," etc., but you would, no doubt, find listings for over two hundred different publications that reach the women's market and accept mail order advertising. Now, your research might strongly indicate a potential large market for your hand-painted cards. This being the case, you may decide to place a few small ads in various magazines to test your market. You do not expect to "strike it rich" with this small investment. You simply want to test the market you have discovered. You would have to price your greeting cards as reasonably as possible. In order to pull orders from small space ads or classified ads, you probably will have to price your hand art cards at prices under $5—maybe 1 card for $2 or 3 for $4 would do for our hypothetical example. Let's assume that 25¢ in supplies (card stock and water colors) is needed to produce each card. That would give you a respectable cost to sell markup. Let's now assume it takes you 10 minutes to hand-color each card. This would mean you can only produce 6 cards per hour. Selling them at $2 or less each wouldn't make a person rich, especially when you consider advertising cost, postage, handling and general operating expenses. Nevertheless, it may be a good idea to run such ad tests. You could consider the project strictly for market evaluation. If the test proves fruitful, then you can go into mass production. In place of hand-painted cards, you can have your artwork lithographed by a quality printer and turn them out by the thousands at a tiny fraction of the time, effort and money needed to do them by hand.

The above is meant only as a brief, simplified description of a marketing strategy. It should, however, give you some insight into the process of how to test and develop a marketing strategy. This particular example is not so far-fetched. The Current Company in Colorado Springs, Colorado, had its start in the basement of its founder's home, designing and selling cards and personalized stationery and gifts. Today, Current does 65 million dollars per year and mails over 30 million pieces of direct mail. They own their own huge office and warehouse and employ 1,250 people in Colorado Springs.

All great success stories began with one good idea. What's yours?

HOW LONG WILL IT TAKE
TO SHOW A PROFIT?

This is a very subjective question. Each product and service needs an individual marketing plan. Some items can be sold at a profit on "direct response" space advertising or a direct mail plan. Others need the two-step approach (ads and/or sales literature produce "inquiries" and follow-up materials are sent to convert them into sales). Another approach is to sell a product on a break-even or even slight loss basis, hoping to earn nice profits by offering backend (follow-up offers) items.

Although there is just no way to make any blanket assertion regarding potential profits, I would have to say that you should expect very small, if any, real profits during the first several months of your mail selling career. Like many other types of business, it does take time to establish a profitable mail order business. Over 90% of the people who launch a mail order operation throw in the towel within the first six to nine months. This is unfortunate since this business takes a lot of "git and grit" and the ability to bounce-back when things look bleak (as they often will!). Also, keep in mind that many of mail order's top pros (Joe Sugarman, Ben Suarez, Brainerd L. Mellinger, etc.) agree that one super success will erase several failures in mail order.

> If you hit one big winner out of every five to ten attempts, you can overcome all the other setbacks and still earn substantial profits.

The mail order business is not for people who can't cope with problems. It is for those men and women who are willing to accept problems as challenges to be overcome. Only the imaginative and resourceful-type person will rise to the top of this wild and wacky, upside-down business that offers such huge potential. The plodder (a person with one basic marketing plan that works) can earn a nice living in mail order, but unlimited, million-dollar success goes to the creative doer—the person with bright ideas and the determination to put them into practice.

KEEP IT EASY TO MAIL. The name of the game is "mail order," and with today's ever-increasing postage costs, I strongly recommend that you search for products that are easy to package and mail and as lightweight as possible. Also, beware of items that can easily be broken. For many years the Post Office has had a high rate of damaged articles (if you ever watched how packages are handled on the back area of Post Office loading docks, you would not wonder why), and recently, even United Parcel Service (UPS) has had an increasing breakage and damage problem. Try to go with products that can take a little punishment and still survive.

Also, since shipping costs are a big consideration, the lighter the overall weight, the better.

Almost anything, including bathtubs, can be and has been sold by mail order. However, I prefer to stick to paper products, gifts, novelties, jewelry, and other merchandise that is relatively lightweight.

HOW BIG A MARKUP?

Another subjective question. It really depends on how well your ads or sales literature pull. As a general yardstick, I recommend at least a 4 to 1 markup on any prime offer that you sell for under $100. And I consider a 4 to 1 the bare minimum. I'm talking about your mainline offer. On backups, catalogs and package inserts, you can do fine with much smaller markups. It is your main stay offer that should be 4 to 1 or even better! Don't let huge markups make you think you're overcharging. Many mail order publishers work with markups in the 5 to 1 to 15 to 1 range. It would be nice if these markups accurately reflected the overall profit picture. They do not. Ad costs, printing, postage, etc. will always take the largest slice of the pie.

TEST! TEST!! TEST!!!

Testing is the magic key that opens one of the main doors leading to mail order success. Don't tie up large amounts of cash in products before you fully test the market you have found. Recent laws require that you must have a developed product prior to placing ads or making direct mailings. In the past, the sharp operators placed their ads before they ever developed the product. If the ad pulled well, they rushed into production. If the ad flopped, they refunded any orders that did come in and went back to their drawing boards for new ads on other possible products. It was a sweet little racket that sure increased their chances of big success. One big hit could wipe out a half dozen or so misses plus make a profit to boot. Then all they needed to do was gear up for a big rollout, using direct mail, or start placing ads in all available space that met the demographics of their now validated hot offer.

OK. The rules have changed. You must have something to sell before you try to sell it. It does seem reasonable! Still, you must cut production costs to the bone. Produce as small an amount as possible to run your tests. Sure, 500 widgets will probably cost you twice as much—per unit— as 5,000. So what? Who wants to stuck with 5,000 widgets that aren't selling?

In the case of books, manuals and reports, I suggest you type (rather than typeset) the first edition. Have your local printer run off 100 or 200 copies and staple it together. If it becomes a "hit," you can go back and improve the type, the printing and the binding. Why go into large press runs till your tests indicate you have a good seller worthy of promotion?

WHICH MEDIA TO TEST IN

If you choose a product that is in any way similar to other products on the market, your test grounds should probably be the same ones they are advertising in.

If you pick a product or service not currently being advertised, then it's wise to use the media in which related products are being advertised.

Although newspapers and magazines may be the most commonly used test vehicles, don't overlook direct mail. Direct mail is very personal, and through careful mailing list selection, you can often pinpoint your market.

Daily newspapers are great places to test items of general appeal. They offer almost "instant test results" as opposed to many weeks or months you may have to wait to test magazine or direct mail results. Use the dailies when you can, but for many offers they won't work because the readership is so broad and not at all selective.

BUYING FROM MANUFACTURERS
IMPORTERS, PUBLISHERS, ETC.

The quickest way to jump into the mail order business is to purchase items already manufactured, imported or published.

As mentioned before, the more control you have over what you sell, usually, the better your chances are to succeed. However, there are glaring exceptions to this rule.

We know of a mail order man in San Francisco who does very well selling special ski and aviator style sunglasses by mail. He got started a few years ago by purchasing several gross from another San Francisco importer. Today he does his own importing, ordering huge quantities from Taiwan and Japan. This mail dealer never had an "exclusive" on these sunglasses. They are sold by others through retail specialty shops, sporting goods stores, etc. However, he was the first to make a line of special, smart styles available by mail.

Another couple, also in the San Francisco Bay area, buys imported food delicacies from the Orient, France and Great Britain and makes them available to gourmet mail order buyers. Although similar items may be available in certain highbrow specialty stores and fine restaurants, their business has prospered.

Likewise, the would be mail order tycoon often will find items manufactured for gift shops, toy shops or other retail stores that also lend themselves (good markup, a market that can be defined, relatively light, sturdy, etc.) to mail order promotion.

A FORTUNE IN CLOSE-OUTS

Many mail order dealers have hit pay-dirt in the buying and selling of close-out merchandise.

A Seattle mail order firm purchased a set of cookbooks that had been "over-printed and under-promoted" to book-stores. By paying at only 10% of listed cover prices, they had

274

plenty of latitude to launch a successful ad campaign and reap substantial profits.

A St. Paul mail order entrepreneur purchased many thousands of miniature "cowboy and Indian toy sets" at less than 10¢ on the retail dollar and turned them into mail order winners by placing ads in several different comic books.

A San Diego mail order man bought a $25 business book at only one dollar per copy, in large quantities, and earns big profits via direct mail.

A Phoenix mail order lady bought 1,000 authentic southwestern landscape paintings from a department store close-out and earned over $25,000 in less than three months through mail sales.

The lesson I wish to instill in you is this: Run, don't walk, every time you learn of a big close-out in your area. Through imagination and good mail order promotion, you could earn a bundle on "unwanted merchandise." When you can get products at 5¢ or 10¢ on the dollar, you will have plenty left over for advertising/mailing costs.

Another point you must consider: Close-outs in small quantities won't work. Sometimes close-outs are offered in group lots. While such sales may be a boon to many retail shop owners, they usually will not benefit the mail order operator. A little of this, some of that and just a few of these does not lend itself to mail order selling, unless you come up with a great group sales idea. Also, if your close-out source offers to sell you four dozen widgets for your mail order test, you must be darn certain the other four thousand (or whatever) will be available a few months down the road if your tests give you a big green light.

Often, a close-out source will give you a "take it or leave it" proposition—you can buy cheap, but you must buy now! If this be the case, you must decide if the potential profit is worth the risk.

Close-outs can make you lots of greenbacks or they can dip you in red ink. You probably will have to have at least a little "riverboat gambler" in you to work this market. Nevertheles, it is a potentially lucrative field that you at least should consider.

One redeeming factor that can save a mail order entrepreneur from dipping deep into red ink, even if the mail order promotion does not get off the ground, is finding another buyer for the close-out merchandise you bought. If you bought dirt cheap, you should be able to sell the merchandise for what you paid for it. You might even be able to sell out for a profit.

REPEAT BUSINESS IS IMPORTANT

Whenever possible, seek those products that lend themselves to repeat business. While some dealers earn substantial money from "one shot" sales, most of the mail operators who build powerful mail order empires do so through repeat sales.

Repeat business does not mean that your customers will be buying the very same items from you over and over (although this is true of foodstuffs, disposable merchandise, etc.). It does mean your mail customers become multiple buyers. If you sell items that please your customers, your own customers become your best source of additional business.

When you offer quality merchandise (your own or merchandise obtained elsewhere), you build customer confidence. Happy, satisfied and confident customers are pleased to favor you with many repeat orders.

A common tactic to capitalize on happy, satisfied customers is to offer a "loss leader." Mail Order entrepreneurs learned this profitable technique from their retail sales brethren.

Here's how it works in mail order:

The mail order operator places small or large ads for a specific low-priced product. For the sake of an example, let's say this dealer sells herbs and other "natural" products by mail. In order to obtain a huge response, the entrepreneur advertises "12 packets of Ginseng herb tea" for only $1. Ginseng has been a popular herb for several years. Many Orientals believe it is a great health aid and also restores sexual energy. Word has now reached the West, and ginseng, in any form (tea, pills, powder) sells well.

Nowadays, it's impossible to make money in mail order with a dollar item. However, our sharp herb and natural products mail dealer is using his 12 packs of ginseng tea as a loss leader. After paying for his ads, mailing, handling, etc., he may find it has actually cost him $1.50 for each time he receives a dollar sale. A losing proposition on the front end. But now, let's suppose this dealer has prepared a nifty 24-page catalog—chock-full of natural products, herbs, creams, jells, vitamins, etc.—that is included in every $1 order that is mailed to his customers. If we carry this example one step further, we can say that most of the dollar herb tea buyers will be very pleased with his or her purchase. Since happy customers tend to reorder, a sizable pull on the "back end" can turn front end losses into big repeat order profits!

The loss leader tactic is not for everyone, but it does spell mail order success for some.

MAIL ORDER ADVERTISING

Once you have a good grasp of what you need to know to enter the world of mail order, have developed a product and know that a market does exist for what you plan to sell, you are ready to consider the best method to reach your potential mail order customers.

Will you use space advertising (classified or display) to sell direct from the ad or will you use the inquiry/follow-up (two-step) method?

...or would your product sell best through sales agents that you acquire through mail order ads to enlist direct sales people?

...or is your offer more suited for a direct mail campaign?

...or is the electronic media (radio and television) more suited to generate mail orders?

...or will you use all or a combination of the above selling methods?

Let's consider each various media method. The more you know about all available media, the easier it will be for you to make a decision on which advertising approach suits you and your chosen products.

Let's start with a step-by-step analysis and proven approach for operating a classified advertising mail order business.

CLASSIFIED ADVERTISING

Many mail order entrepreneurs make their mail order starts via classified advertising. Many operators have found success using this approach. Mail order beginners with limited advertising knowledge and/or limited cash are often best advised to "test the mail trade waters" in this medium.

A short (20 words or less), well-written classifed is often the lowest cost method of advertising with the best overall dollar-for-dollar return. They usually produce the highest "cost per inquiry" and "cost per sale."

PINPOINT THE MEDIA

As with display ads, you must be certain that your classified ads are in the correct media. Start by searching for all available media "likely" to fit your specific offer.

Write for several sample copies to "likely" magazines and newspapers listed by Standard Rate and Data. This great media directory is available at most public libraries. However, classified ad information is not always mentioned. When you find a magazine that appears tailormade for advertising your product, write for it. It may accept classified ads or at least small display ads, which can serve the same purpose.

Some magazines which do not have classifieds will accept small ½" display ads. Other publications without classifieds do not accept any ad under the 1" size. If you're unfamiliar with the magazine, request a sample copy and rate card to find out.

Your ad budget may not expand beyond a test ad in only half a dozen publications. Nevertheless, it is wise to select your classified ad media from as many publications as possible. Receiving free sample copies of hundreds of various newspapers and magazines is a bonus to operating your own mail sales business. There are a few publications which will only send you a rate card and no sample. Most will include a current or recent back issue in their media package. I, for one, would not advertise in any publications that I have never seen. I urge you to become familiar with any publication you use.

SALES AND INQUIRIES?

I have found that well over 90% of the successful classified ad dealers use "two-step" inquiry advertising. Making classifieds pay on the "order direct basis" is not very easy. Still, some dealers do make this method pay.

Information sellers of "how to plans," "sources of supply," "recipes," etc., often are able to get cash with order from a small classified ad.

Listed below are a few such ads that have been running for many months during the past year, leading me to believe they are working quite well for their operators.

105 WAYS TO MAKE BIG
MONEY FROM YOUR HOME.
NEW BOOKLET, ONLY $2.
NAME & ADDRESS.

100% NATURAL ROACH AND
WATERBUG REPELLANT.
ONLY $2. IT WORKS! NAME &
ADDRESS

COLLEGE WITHOUT CAMPUS
EARN YOUR DEGREE THE
EASY WAY, BY MAIL. INFOR-
MATION BOOK, ONLY $3.
NAME & ADDRESS.

SWEET POTATO PIE.
MOUTHWATERING GOOD 100
YEAR OLD RECIPE. ONLY $1.
NAME & ADDRESS.

The above sampling of classified ads should give you some insight into how some dealers are using a few words to ask for the order direct from the ad.

Direct orders from classified ads do not work for most offers. However, low priced offers (usually $3 or less) sometimes will click. Keep in mind...when you're selling items at only a dollar or two, you need a flock of orders before you can make money on the proposition.

For most dealers, it is the "inquiry ads" that produce best overall results.

Here is a sampling of inquiry-type classified advertising:

**PENNY STOCKS THAT YIELD
BIG PROFITS. FREE REPORT.
NAME & ADDRESS.**

**RAISE INVESTMENT
CAPITAL.
DETAILS, FREE. NAME &
ADDRESS.**

**SELL WORDS! EARN MONEY
AS WRITER/PUBLISHER. NO
EXPERIENCE. FREE DETAILS.
NAME & ADDRESS.**

**MAKE MORE MONEY SELLING
FABULOUS LINE OF SHELL
JEWELRY. FREE BOOKLET.
NAME & ADDRESS.**

You will notice... all of these inquiry ads have one thing in common—they all use the magic word FREE! If you use your advertising to generate inquiries, always use this motivating four-letter word.

Some dealers, especially newcomers, offer free literature but request the reader to enclose a Self-Addressed Stamped Envelope (SASE) or a loose stamp to cover postage. This tactic will help you cut your postage bill. It also will greatly reduce the number of replies you receive. Overall, when advertising "free details," it is more profitable to keep it simple and keep it easy to reply. If you offer free information, let it be free!

If you're offering a large catalog that is both expensive to print and mail, it may be advisable to ask for one dollar. In such cases, you may offer the sender a $1 refund with his first order.

Example:

**SAVE 80% ON POPULAR TOOLS. NAME BRANDS!
CATALOG $1 (REFUNDED WITH ORDER).
NAME & ADDRESS.**

Each mail dealer must decide which approach is best (order direct, inquiry or refundable fee), but for the vast majority of successful classified operators, the two-step inquiry technique works best.

GETTING THE MOST FOR THE LEAST
MONEY SPENT

Good classified ad writing is nothing less than good advertising copy in capsule format. While I would not suggest a beginner write his own large display ads, circulars, sales letters or catalogs, most alert mail dealers, even beginners, can learn how to write a good classifed ad of 20 words or less.

Since ad rates in national publications range anywhere from 75¢ to $7.50 per word for classified ads, you must use as few words as possible to convey your message.

But don't use this kind of a "few words that say little" approach:

MAKE MORE MONEY!
NAME & ADDRESS.

The above ad saves some money on advertising cost by using a very few words. It is also almost certainly doomed to failure, even if it pulls a large amount of inquiries. Since there are literally thousands of different ways to earn money, chances are remote that this "blind ad" will receive enough selective inquiries to make it pay off. When it comes to inquiry ads, it is how much net total income is earned from mailing your sales literature (after deducting all expenses) that determines whether you have a winner or not.

Now here is basically the same ad with just two more words added:

MAKE MONEY WRITING ARTICLES.
FREE DETAILS. NAME & ADDRESS.

This ad may generate a smaller response, but at least every inquiry will know you're offering information relating to writing. Thus, you will be mailing your offer to people who have some idea as to what they are responding to. This type of responder is far more qualified than someone who answered a blind ad and has absolutely no idea as to what type of mail business you operate. The more qualified the responder (up to a certain point!), the better your chances to get the order.

Don't misunderstand me, it is important that there be some

285

"mystery" in all your advertising. I believe in Elmo Wheeler's sales philosophy, "sell the sizzle, not the steak," and I also know mail order customers love to open letters and packages with some "surprise" in them. Thus, the sharp operator gives them a "taste" of what is offered but holds back enough to "whet their appetite." This should never be a problem with classified ads. Using only 20 words or less (the average classified ad is only 15 words), you can only offer a very brief description—"taste"—of what you're promoting.

The blind ad brings in the blind inquiry. Rarely will you see (pardon the pun!) profits from this approach. Use punchy words, including the word FREE, and tell them a little about your product or service.

HOW TO WRITE A CLASSIFIED AD

(STEP-BY-STEP)

(A) Look over dozens of publications' classified sections to get a "feel" for classified ads. Pay particular attention to competitor ads.

(B) Take a large piece of paper and write down everything of interest you would list about your service or product if you could use as many words as possible with no regard to space or expense.

(C) Determine and circle which words are the "key words," most likely to motivate the reader.

(D) Incorporate the five important elements of a good classified ad:

286

(1) Gain the reader's attention.
(2) Make your promise.
(3) Tell what it is.
(4) The price (or "free").
(5) Your abbreviated address with "key code."

Here is an actual successful classified ad that incorporates all five important elements:

MAKE $500 DAILY SELLING INFORMATION BY MAIL, FREE REPORT. PROFIT, 8361-C VICKERS, SAN DIEGO, CA 92111

The above 15 word ad, counting the zip code (some publications don't charge for the zip) employs all five elements. The "C" in 8361-C Vickers is the "key" for this particular ad. It is important to key all ads so you can determine which media works best for your offers.

Note: If you counted 16 words in the above ad, you have counted "San Diego" as two words. In fairness to advertisers in all cities—even a long one like San Juan Capistrano—publishers now count any city name as only one word. That's just about the only "break" they give advertisers. Zips used to be free in nearly all publications. Now most charge an additional word for your zip code.

TESTING

Once you have a product and a market for a classified ad campaign, it is time to test. Since time is important in mail selling, you should arrange for quick testing, if possible. It can take up to three months to place advertising in monthly media. A long wait time. You can cut this time in half or less by testing in weekly publications.

The supermarket tabloids (National Enquirer, Globe, The Star, Modern People) offer excellent media for many products and services. Grit offers good general (rural oriented) mail order media.

Even faster testing can be done in daily newspapers. Just keep in mind. dailies go to everyone and anyone. It is a "shotgun approach" that won't work for every type of offer.

Key point: No medium will work for every type of offer. You must seek out the media whose general editorial, overall content and advertising thrust is best suited to your own offers.

Don't overspend testing any one publication. Rather than place multiple runs in only a few publications, it is usually best to run "one time tests" in several potentially good media. Your key coding will then tell you which ones to reschedule in.

ORDER RESULTS—
NOT THE NUMBER OF INQUIRIES
—DETERMINE SUCCESS

If you're selling payment with order, the response to your ad will make or break your offer. However, in the case of inquiry advertising, the bottom line is followup sales.

Anyone who has been active in running classified inquiry ads for any time knows that some publications pull many inquiries, but few convert to orders, while others pull several orders on smaller amounts of inquiries. The bottom line tells the tale.

Your quest must always be to find those special (for you!) classified columns that will produce a ton of inquiries, followed by a high yield of actual orders.

While hunting for your rich mother lode advertising media, you should stick with any and all media that produce a profit, even a small profit. Nobody ever lost money in mail order making a profit.

As for how long to run classified ads in any media in which a test proves profitable, my standard advice is for as long as it shows a bottom line profit.

"Till forbid" is the term you can use to place ads in all media that tests indicate to be profitable. Placing individual insertion orders takes time, and you run the risk of missing publication deadlines. "Till forbid" simply means you are granting the publication the right to run your ad until such time as you forbid—cancel!

CLASSIFICATION IS IMPORTANT

In dealing with classified media, especially those with several pages of classifieds like the National Enquirer, it is important to be listed under the right "Classification."

Once you achieve some mail sales success, you may wish to test your ads under various classifications. Until then, play copycat! Place your ads under the same classifications as your competitors. If you have no real competitor, search out related products in choosing your heading to run under.

If your service or product is unique and has no competition and is not related to any other offers, you will have to use old fashioned common sense to pinpoint the heading. Some publications offer a "Miscellaneous" heading. Readership often falls off under this label. It is only a last resort for an ad that in no other way can be classified.

HOW TO PREDICT (QUICKLY)
AD RESPONSE

It helps the mail dealer to be able to predict advertising results quickly. This allows time to resubmit ads to all media that are "working."

Following is a predicting method that, while not 100% accurate, serves as a good barometer:

DAILY NEWSPAPERS: ½ of total response will be reached within 3 days of receiving your first order or inquiry.

WEEKLY NEWSPAPERS OR MAGAZINES: ½ of total response will be reached within 6 days of receiving your first order or inquiry.

MONTHLIES: ½ of your total response will be reached within 16 days of receiving your first order or inquiry.

BI-MONTHLIES: ½ of your total response will
be reached within 25 days of receiving your first
order or inquiry.

I have found this rule applies to either display or classified advertising.

The bottom line is always your chief concern. Even when using the two-step inquiry approach, it is how many orders that are ultimately generated that makes or breaks your overall advertising approach.

MAILINGS AND FOLLOW-UP

In using inquiry advertising, it is essential that you get your sales literature to your prospect while he or she is hot. Fast turn-around is most desirable. All inquiries should be processed quickly. If your two-step mail program is working smoothly, you will mail your offer to each prospect within 24 to 48 hours of receiving his inquiry.

How many times should you follow-up? This question can only be answered as it relates to your own singular proposition. You mail and remail as long as it is profitable to do so.

Only by testing will you be able to determine this. However, at least two follow-ups to your original mailing (spaced 10 to 15 days apart) should be made.

A company in Missouri that offers a home study correspondence course has found it profitable to make nine consecutive mailings (the original plus 8 follow-ups, spaced two weeks apart) to every single inquiry they receive. This is far more than the number used by most mail dealers. It does illustrate my point. Your own testing and records will tell you how many mailings you can afford to make to every inquiry you receive.

Four mailings (the original and 3 follow-ups) is average for most offers.

DISPLAY ADVERTISING

Much of what has already been said concerning classified advertising (defining a market that can be reached, selecting products to reach your market that are conducive to mail sales, testing, etc.) also applies to display advertising.

Preparing copy for display ads is usually best left to professional copywriters. It is not impossible for you to learn how to write result-getting space advertising, but it is certainly no job for the inexperienced. The money you save in not paying a good copywriter could be only a small part of the money wasted on advertising that falls flat.

Some dealers make the very same type of mailing each time. Others try a variety of sales literature to sell the same product or service at the same price. Still others change the offer somewhat or even offer discounts in their follow-up program.

RECORDS TELL YOU WHERE YOU'RE AT. Since the bottom line is all important, you must keep accurate records.

ALL ABOUT CIRCULATION

Your ad cost per 1,000 readers is an important consideration. Next to selecting the "right" publications for your ads, you want the most cost-effective advertising.

Example: If you're paying $1,200 for a full-page ad in a magazine that has a circulation of 100,000, you are paying $12 per 1,000 circulation.

If you pay $2,100 to reach a 300,000 circulation, you are paying only $7 per 1,000 circulation. A substantial difference.

Always learn a publication's true circulation. Don't be misled by "readership" claims. Publishers tend to greatly inflate their possible "readership."

"Moneysworth" often makes claims of "five million readers," yet official circulation audit figures put "Moneysworth's" actual circulation at about 800,000. Now "Moneysworth" has a proven record as an excellent place for many types (especially business opportunities) of mail advertising. It's just that they want you to believe five or six different people, on the average, read every issue that they print and mail. Methinks Publisher Ginzburg may be a bit optimistic!

Many publishers inflate their readership by three to six times actual circulation. It's a common practice, but one that, in my opinion, over-estimates their correct circulation and readership.

The type of circulation a publication has can also help you

293

in making your advertising decisions.

The more copies a publication sends out by mail (subscriptions and samples), the more responsive it is likely to be for your mail order advertising. Newsstand buyers, as a whole, are not nearly as likely to be mail order buyers as folks who receive their publications by mail.

Reviewing a copy of Standard Rate and Data will help you select suitable publications for your ad budget. This directory will also give your vital readership demographics, circulation figures and other hard facts (not inflated ad claims) that will help you in your advertising media selection process.

After everything is said and done, it is the bottom line (Did your ad pull enough response to earn a profit?) that will separate the "right and wrong" media for you. However, you should have your eyes wide open from the start. You can only benefit by getting a "feel" from looking through a sample copy of every publication you are considering as an advertising vehicle. You should also have updated and actual circulation figures to help you make an advertising decision.

Your publication is being considered as
an advertising medium for our new, 420
page manual, "How to Start Making Money
in a Business of Your Own".

Please forward your media package to
include an ABC statement of circulation,
your readership demographics, a recent
sample copy and an advertising rate
card. Would you like us to send you a
review copy of this new hardcover book?

Please place us on file to be notified
of future rate or policy changes.
Thank you.

Sincerely,

Russ von Hoelscher
Marketing Director

8361 Vickers,
Suite 304
San Diego,
CA 92111

Profit Idea$

295

FIRST TIME ADS USUALLY PULL BEST

Since the same ad repeated in various publications generally will not pull as well as the first insertion, I strongly recommend you place your ads on a "one time basis" in all untested media.

This is almost always true when you are advertising for "direct order response" (some types of inquiry ads will produce steady results over many insertions.)

The falloff for cash-up-front direct orders from the larger display ad is usually at least 10% and sometimes as high as 50% on every consecutive repeat.

The falloff is always higher from publications which have a majority of readers as subscribers than those which have a high sample copy (as is the case with newsstand publications) readership.

Mail dealers advertising specialized courses, soliciting salesmen, etc., often run their ads for several months or years, issue-after-issue, in various media, while operators selling a specific book, gift item or other type consumer product seldom can make the proposition pay beyond two or three consecutive insertions, and the first insertion is almost always the best puller.

If your ad pulls well in an April issue and is marginally profitable in the May issue of the publication, it would probably be wise to drop out of that medium, at least until October or November, at which time you may wish to retest.

Joe Karbo found that even in the best media for his "Lazy Man's Way to Riches" ads, he had to stagger his advertising to keep profits up.

The only media he dared use more than three or four times in one year was a select group of daily newspapers. The Sunday Los Angeles Times pulled so well for his book offer that he ran large space ads one Sunday out of each month for long periods of time.

FREE PUBLICITY

There is no better kind of advertising than FREE publicity! And if your product is in any way unique, you may be able to arrange for some great free editorials in appropriate media.

Free editorials are mostly offered by consumer publications with "shopping sections." The editors of these publications are willing to offer timely write-ups on products that they feel will be a genuine interest to their readers. Whenever possible, these publications prefer to offer these free editorials to their own established advertisers. However, if your product is really unique, it is a candidate, even if you have never placed an ad in their publication.

Editorial mentions are only one kind of free publicity that may be available to your service or product. It is established procedure for business and trade publications to offer free write-ups for any new service or product that pertains to their industry. Don't overlook these journals when considering sources of free publicity.

BOOK REVIEWS

If you're selling books, booklets, manuals or courses, the "book review" is an excellent source of unpaid advertising. This is the most effective and least expensive means of promoting your literary efforts.

Using Standard Rate and Data again as a source of potential media (and literally thousands of publications review books), you should easily find at least 200 or more publications as potential sources for your book reviews. If only 20% of these respond with a printed review, results could be very gratifying. Since editors are a busy lot, I strongly recommend you include your own "sample review." You may be surprised at how many will print it just as you submit it, especially if it is well-written and at least somewhat objective.

FREE EDITORIAL MENTION

You solicit editorial mentions by sending a news release plus a sample of your product with a clear 3x4 or 4x5 photograph of your product (if the product is quite expensive, you may wish to send only the photo and release).

The news release should be in letter format. It should give a brief description of your product and its benefits (for editorial purposes, editors want factual information, no glowing ad copy hype).

One good way to learn how to give your product or service a factual write-up is to study recent issues of the "shelter" magazines (House Beautiful, Better Homes & Gardens, etc.).

298

Since free write-ups can be an excellent source of thousands of dollars of free advertising and publicity, you may wish to consider having a professional copywriter prepare your releases. The stakes here are high. A few positive mentions in national publications can generate a harvest of orders.

It is vital that you do not waste your time, effort and samples to the wrong media. If your product is aimed at hunting enthusiasts, don't bother requesting editorial mention in publications aimed at women. Editors offer write-ups to unique services and products that they think will interest a large section of their readership.

ELECTRONIC MEDIA ADVERTISING

The booming cable TV market has opened new fertile grounds for mail order advertising. More and more entrepreneurs are testing this medium. The expanding cable TV industry has created a vast, often cost effective, marketplace.

TV advertising on the major three networks is far too expensive for most small businessmen, but the bustling local and national cable TV industry is now within reach of many mail dealers. Ad rates are competitively low, especially on local channels. If you have products or services that have mass-market appeal, you should investigate this growing marketplace.

For either radio or TV, evening hours, in particular "late evening" (after 10 p.m. and into the "wee hours" of the morning), have proven to be profitable for several mail order entrepreneurs.

Ad rates are lowest during the late evening and early morning hours. Also, most people are at home or in a place where they can reach for pen and paper to respond to your pitch.

Recording 30 to 60 second radio ads is quite reasonable. Far more expense is involved in preparing a 30 or 60 second video taping of your ad. Some direction is required—good staging—and unless you are an articulate and interesting speaker, you probably will have to hire an announcer. Models also could be required. It will all cost you money. Nevertheless, for the right mass-appeal products, television advertising can produce spectacular results.

PER-INQUIRY OR
PER-ORDER ARRANGEMENTS

Per-inquiry (P.I.) and per-order (P.O.) advertising is a vehicle for mail orders with a proven product!

As soon as the mail beginner hears about P.I. or P.O. advertising, he or she is usually very anxious to "jump on this bandwagon." Sorry, my friend. It doesn't work that way. Publications, radio stations and television stations which do handle this form of advertising (and hundreds do, nation-wide) are generally only interested in offers that have a proven profitable track record.

A standard P.I. or P.O. deal has the publication or TV or radio station obtain inquiries or orders at their own address. They then "sell" the inquiries or orders to the mail order company they made an arrangement with.

Per-order (P.O.) deals are usually the most profitable for

both the ad medium and the mail dealer. The station or publication generally demands that the dealer furnish the advertising (camera-ready or cassette tape or video tape). They then run it (in their publication or "on the air") whenever they have unsold advertising space or time, for as long as it generates a favorable response. The publication or TV or radio station usually expects about ½ (50%) of the total price of most products they promote for a mail order company. On "high ticket items," they often will accept a smaller percentage.

This form of ad arrangement can be a super bonanza for any mail order firm. If you have a proven product (and by "proven" I'm talking about one that has earned you a nice profit by advertising it in a conventional manner), by all means, consider making a P.I. or P.O. deal.

To know which channels are currently offering P.I. or P.O. deals, start flipping your radio or TV dial late in the evening. When you hear and see various music offers such as "101 country music hits for only $9.95" or an ad for a "miracle set of carving and chopping knives," you probably have discovered a station that accepts special advertising arrangements.

The publications that accept these deals will be found to have several pages of different ads running over a single name and address. Sometimes the publisher uses the magazine's address, other times an independent company address is set up by the publisher to run these special offers.

In publications, full page ad space is usually desirable. The publisher inserts his name where yours would normally appear.

REMNANT SPACE ADVERTISING

Most magazines today are offset printed (from camera-ready copy) in press signatures of four or eight pages. If a magazine is working with a printer who uses, for example, eight page signatures, he must conform by submitting 80 pages, 88 pages, etc. 81 to 87 won't work.

Although magazines are pasted-up well in advance of their "on sale date," a publisher who comes up with an "odd number of pages" needs filler quickly.

Using the above example, let's say Mr. Publisher finds himself with 84 ready-to-print pages. That's four too many or four too few for the combination of eight page signatures his printer requires. (Of course, the amount could be 76, or 92 or any amount that did not include even multiples of 8 pages.) Since he is not about to cut back the number of pages by 4 (unless he had 4 pages of editorial fillers or public service notices he felt were expendable), he will go after 4 more pages—quickly. An extra article or many fillers and announcements could do the trick. However, they won't produce revenue.

A desire for more ad revenue to fill blank pages may lead our publisher to offer some ad space at substantial discounts.

Most of the "heavy hitters" in mail order advertising buy a large portion of their space ads at discounts far below the prices quoted on the publishers' various rate cards. They obtain discounts by contracting to buy a large amount of ad space months or even years in advance or by letting certain publishers know they have both camera-ready ads (usually

302

full-page ads are required) and cash money on hand to cover a "fast insertion" in the publisher's magazine.

Remnant ad space is not seeking the rank beginner. However, once you begin to build a solid mail order operation and have enough cash on hand to handle, and suitable copy to quickly accept, cut-rate advertising offers (discounts run from 20% to 50%), you can begin to contact various publishers. Obviously, you should only contact media that is suited for your offer.

I do not wish to lead you to think that all publishers make remnant deals. Some do and some don't! However, you'll be surprised how many do, under certain conditions, when they know you have ad copy and cash money and are ready to take quick action.

Whom should you approach once you're in a position to go after these special ad deals? Why not every single publication you can afford? There is no charge for asking, and the worst they can say is "no." Just make sure you're ready and able to keep your end of the bargain when some say "yes!"

This is "hush-hush" information you won't find in most books about mail order selling. While many publishers will make remnant arrangements, they don't want to advertise the fact and have their regular rate card clients clammoring for special deals. Also, they don't want to be solicited by rank beginners who have small ads and little money and who still want special consideration.

These deals go to large ads (almost always full-page ads) from mail order pros.

If you are fully ready and able to use this dynamic information, by all means, go for it! If you're not yet ready, keep this budget advertising ploy in mind for future reference. Perhaps a year or two down the pike it will be something you wish to actively pursue.

Remnant space can be a valuable, big discount source of advertising. Use it when you can.

(4) Submit all of your future advertising to the media by using the "Insertion Order" form, deducting 15% from their rate cards. Most publishers also allow agencies an extra 1% or 2% for sending cash with order.

Discounts of 15% to 17% can amount to a tidy sum over a year of advertising. Money saved is money earned! Isn't it time you established your own advertising agency? Who knows, in addition to saving plenty of money on your own advertising, from time to time others may request that you place orders for them. It won't cost them a penny more, and you then could pocket up to 17% just for handling the transactions.

My own advertising agency was started just to save me money on my own spare advertising, but over the years I have earned extra profits by placing ads for various copywriting clients. It is an added bonus to setting up your own ad agency to save money on your own ads.

HOW TO ESTABLISH
YOUR OWN ADVERTISING AGENCY

The next best thing to remnant space discount advertising is taking an agency discount of 15% to 17% off regular rates on all advertising you place.

How do you do it? Simple! Establish your own advertising agency!!

It really is quite simple to set up your own ad agency, and if you use a fair amount of space, savings will be considerable.

Here's the easy, step-by-step procedure:

(1) Use a name different than your regular mail order company name. If you're simply using your own name to sell by mail, use some variation for your agency name. Example; John Miller Sales could start an agency as J.M. Advertising. If your company name is Mid-America Seed Company, perhaps Mid-West Advertising could serve as your "agency name."

(2) Register and license your ad agency name if your state requires this.

(3) Have a local printer run off a couple hundred "Insertion Order" sheets (You may copy the form reprinted here. Type in your new agency name under "Agency").

(4) Submit all of your future advertising to the media by using the "Insertion Order" form, deducting 15% from their

rate cards. Most publishers also allow agencies an extra 1% or 2% for sending cash with order.

Discounts of 15% to 17% can amount to a tidy sum over a year of advertising. Money saved is money earned! Isn't it time you established your own advertising agency? Who knows, in addition to saving plenty of money on your own advertising, from time to time others may request that you place orders for them. It won't cost them a penny more, and you then could pocket up to 17% just for handling the transactions.

My own advertising agency was started just to save me money on my own space advertising, but over the years I have earned extra profits by placing ads for various copywriting clients. It is an added bonus to setting up your own ad agency to save money on your own ads.

DIRECT MAIL

Direct mail/marketing is a $100 billion dollar per year business. It's big and getting bigger!

While most mail trade beginners usually plunge into space advertising (classifieds or display) when they start a mail order venture, the majority of established mail order pros use direct mail for part or all of their selling activities.

MAILING LISTS

At the center of any direct mail effort is the mailing list you use. Powerful copywriting, expert printing, good graphics,

INSERTION ORDER

AGENCY: TO:

PRODUCT: DATE:

ADVERTISER:

dates of insertion	number of times	caption to read	key or code	space ordered

COPY TO READ:

SPECIAL INSTRUCTIONS & REQUESTS:

RATE:

_____times at $_____   Less____% frequency discount $_____

= $_____   Less____% agency commission $_____

Check #_____   Less ____% cash discount $_____

By:_____   Net amount of this order $_____

307

etc. are very important, but mailing lists are the heart of any direct mail effort.

Mailing lists fall under three categories:

(1) In-House Lists
(2) Mail Response Lists
(3) Compiled Lists

A dealer's own in-house list is by far the firm's most precious commodity. These are the people who have ordered or inquired at least once. Within the in-house list, at the very core, are the company's "family jewels" - the multiple buyers - the best of all the house names.

The mail response lists are names who have responded to another company's offer. There are several thousands of such lists, in all fields and classifications, available on the mailing list rental market. Standard Rate & Data Services, Inc., 5201 Old Orchard Road, Skokie, IL 60077, publishes the "mailing list bibles" for both business lists and consumer lists in the "Direct Mail Lists, Rates and Data Directories." In thumbing through their huge directories, you will find many thousands of both response and compiled lists in almost any classification you could possibly think of, as well as many that probably never entered your mind.

Compiled lists are generally not as "responsive" as lists generated from actual orders and inquiries. However, excellent results can be had using a recently compiled list. Then too, compiled lists are often the only available means to reach a specific market. Compiled lists can be as broad as listings of millions of home owners to as selective a list as names and ad-

308

dresses of people who own homes valued at one million dollars or more. Thousands of compiled lists are available, and new classifications are constantly appearing.

One big factor concerning all types of mailing lists (yours, theirs or compiled) is recency. You should mail to your own house list at least three times or more per year. When possible, mail to rented response lists that are new on the list market or which have recently been cleaned. Clean names (with most undeliverables—called nixies"—removed) are also vitally important.

DIRECT MAIL VS SPACE?

Direct mail is a very personal form of advertising. It outpulls space advertising when "more copy" is needed to induce the order. Display ads, even large ones, usually are under 500 or 600 words, and that could be using small type. Using direct mail, you can easily use several thousand words to put your message across. (However, one should never use more words than are needed to state your offer and your proposition clearly.)

It also can be the most cost-effective method to reach the exact type of reader you wish to communicate with.

If you sell new wine-making kits by mail, space ads in several of the "shelter" publications may produce favorable results. However, the vast majority of readers of these magazines will be uninterested in your kit. On the other hand, if you rent a mailing list of 10,000 members of the National Wine and Cheese Society, you know you will be reaching individuals who are very interested in wine and who should be interested (if you have a good product at a fair price - and good "copy" to promote it) in your new wine-making kit.

Direct mail lists allow you to zero in on a potential market as no other advertising vehicle can.

Your own mailing lists can also be a chief source of additional revenue. The main purpose of your in-house list -customers or inquiries - is to generate follow-up business. A profitable secondary use of these lists is income obtained from renting your names to other mail order dealers. Profits from renting your names to other companies can be very substantial. A list renting for $50 per thousand will yield $40 to you, after paying the normal 20% brokerage fee. With some mail order operations, capital received from renting their own customer lists represent the difference between overall profit and loss.

Trading your customer list with another mail order company can also be an excellent way to achieve more direct mail business. In trading with a competitor, be certain you are trading like-for-like. If you are furnishing 5,000 recent buyers, you want 5,000 of their recent buyers in exchange, not a list of two year old buyers or a list of inquiries only.

Since there is a degree of "flim-flam" in the mailing list business, it is often wise to do all of your buy, sell and trade list business through a reputable broker.

DIRECT MAIL ADVERTISING COPY

Next in importance to the right mailing lists for your offer is the copy you send. The right list, married to dynamic copywriting, is an exciting combination that will produce very favorable results! Good copywriting is not the art of using words - it is the art of selling!

TEN COMMANDMENTS
OF EFFECTIVE COPYWRITING

(1) Does the writer know his product inside out? Has he or she looked at it from all sides and discovered every possible benefit?

(2) Does the writer know how to sell the target market? Is the copy in the "language" that will motivate this selective audience?

(3) Does the writer make promises and guarantees and indicate that the promise will be kept and the guarantee honored?

(4) Does the headline "grab" the reader's attention and make him or her anxious to read on?

(5) Is the copy believable? Will the prospect trust what the writer is saying?

(6) Is the copy clear and concise? Are all the words used (regardless of how many or how few) aimed at making a strong but reasonable presentation in order to sell the prospect?

(7) Is the copy exciting? Can the reader "feel" the writer's great enthusiasm?

(8) Is the copy complete? Is it easy for the prospect to

understand all key points? Have all likely doubts and questions been anticipated and answered?

(9) Is the main selling vehicle (sales letter, brochure, etc.) backed up by the right cast of supporting material (publisher's letter, order blank, reply envelope, etc.)?

(10) Is the complete direct mail piece designed to sell? Has it been made easy for the reader to place his or her order?

ADVANCE PLANNING — CRUCIAL TO DIRECT MAIL SUCCESS

Hopefully, one plans every business effort. It makes good sense to do so. In direct mail it is vital.

Here are some guidelines to preparing a direct mail effort:

(1) No less than 75 to 90 days prior to "mail day," conceptional planning starts. One has a product and sets plans in motion for a mailing. Resources, including anticipating a total budget, are of primary importance.

(2) With at least seven or eight weeks lead time, a decision is made on the direct mail format (a "standard format" could include a two to four page letter or brochure, an advertising circular, order form and return envelope).

(3) As soon as a format is chosen, work on the "rough advertising copy" is begun by you or your staff or an outside professional.

(4) At the same time that copy is being prepared, make ar-

312

rangements to cover all printing needs. Envelope printers often require up to a month to fill orders, especially large orders. (Unless you have a proven low-cost, quality printer that you enjoy working with, you should request competitive bids on the envelopes, circulars and sales letters you will need.)

(5) At least four to five weeks prior to your mail date, you should make your final mailing list selections, ordering any outside lists you may need.

(6) Four weeks prior to "mail day" you should give the ok on the copy you will use and make arrangements to have it composed (typesetting, art work, etc.).

(7) Three weeks prior to mailing, your "camera ready copy" should be at your printer. Since most printers are notorious for missing deadlines, you should allow "extra time" for delays.

(8) Two to three weeks before "mail day," make arrangements for the actual mailing. If you're doing it "in-house," arrange for extra help if needed. If a mailing house company is going to do it for you, you should have had a preliminary discussion already and now you would be going over final details.

(9) Four to five days before going into the mail, mailing lists and printed sales literature and envelopes should be printed and in the hands of whoever will be doing the mechanics of sorting, stuffing, etc. At this time also, the local Post Office should be informed (they appreciate this courtesy on all mailings over 10,000) of your intentions. If you or your

mailing house is not affixing postage, this would be the time to place appropriate money at the Post Office to cover the mailing.

(10) Mail Day! Good planning has led to a smooth mailing. Now, you only have to fight your anxiety as you anticipate results.

PREDICTING DIRECT MAIL RESULTS

In looking over many fourth class bulk mail records for Profit Ideas and both first and fourth class results for Publishers Media, I have developed the following method of predicting direct mail results.

First Class Mail: ½ of all orders that you will receive will be reached within 6 days of the first day you receive orders.

Fourth Class Bulk: ½ of all orders that you will receive will be reached within 20 days of the first day you receive orders.

Although orders from first class mail will trickle in over many months and fourth class mail results can drag on for a year or more, I have found the above time table to be 98% accurate. Don't confuse the first day you receive orders with the day you mail. For example, you may receive your first orders on a first class direct mailing six days after the day you mail. This would mean 12 days total would pass before you reached ½ of your total response of this mailing.

314

THE DIRECT MAIL FORMAT

Letters:

(A) First in importance in the direct format is the letter (remember: direct mail is suppose to be one-to-one, personal advertising). The letter can be one page or many pages. The key is to use as many words as needed to sell your offer, but no more than necessary.

(B) The most popular and proven mailing piece consists of an outside envelope, letter, circular, order card and reply envelope.

(C) All important sentences should be highlighted by bold type, caps, italics or underlining.

(D) A two or three page letter usually has more pulling power than a one page letter.

(E) A neatly typed "personal style" letter usually is more effective than a professional-looking, typeset letter.

Circulars:

(A) A professional-looking circular (typeset with photos and/or art work) is usually the best way to support a personalized letter that contains no photos or art work.

(B) The more expensive your offer is, the more professional-looking your circular (but not your letter) should be.

Outside envelopes:

(A) While a combination of larger or smaller sizes of envelopes have proven to be effective for various offers, the standard size No. 10 works best for most.

(B) Teaser copy that relates to the copy inside usually increases response.

Reply Envelopes:

(A) Any reply envelope generally increases results.

(B) Postage-free reply envelopes usually outpull those that require your customer to affix a stamp.

Order Card of Form:

(A) A separate order form will usually outpull one that is printed on your circular that needs to be cut out.

(B) An order form with an "official" looking guarantee will usually outpull one that simply states a guarantee.

Postage:

(A) Postage-metered or stamped envelopes sometimes will outpull a pre-printed permit.

(B) There is little difference in pull between first class or bulk rate. However, if you use first class, always use a big bold type to let the receiver know he is receiving a FIRST CLASS mailing.

INCOMING MAIL

The morning mail should be picked up early if you receive it from a rented Post Office box. If you have it delivered to your home or office address, you are at the mercy of your mail carrier. In either case, here is a method that you, your spouse or someone who works for you can use to handle the day's mail.

(1) Open all mail.

(2) Sort mail into piles of (A) orders, (B) inquiries, (C) bills, (D) advertising and (E) "white mail."

Let me digress to make sure you understand the five categories. Orders and/or standard inquiries would be response from direct mailings or space ads. Bills would be invoices to you from suppliers, equipment rental firms, utility companies, etc. Advertising is offers sent you from other mail order dealers. "White mail" is letters from buyers or inquiries that require personal attention and a specific answer not found in your regular sales literature.

(3) Type labels from orders and/or inquiries. Use multiple carbon sheets and "key" each label so that you know exactly what was ordered and the date.

Example:

07581-MOESG
Robert Miller
100 Ocean Avenue
San Diego, CA 92138

This would tell us that on July 5, 1981 (07581), Robert Miller ordered this book - "Mail Order Entrepreneur Success Guide" (MOESG). There are simpler and more complex ways to code, but this example should suffice.

(4) Place labels and postage on orders and inquiry envelopes. To "stay ahead" of your incoming mail, it is wise to pre-package orders and inquiry mail. In this way it is ready for postage and labeling and fast turnaround.

(5) Place the extra carbon copies of the labels on index cards and file (in the case of a two-step inquiry ad program, you may wish to set up a follow-up system). Let's say your program required three follow-ups after the original mailing, spaced 14 days apart. Using two file folders to cover a two month span can accomplish this. If an inquiry is received, let's say, July 14, then we would include a July 28 label in our July folder and two labels (8/11 and 8/25) in the August folder.

(6) Take care of your "white mail" by answering questions, settling complaints, etc.

(7) Go through the advertising you received. Handle and release everything in one of three ways: (A) place an order for something you want or need that will help your business, (B) file for future reference (supply catalogs, etc.), or (C) throw it away.

Anyone in mail order selling for any length of time knows it is all too easy to get bogged down with stacks of mail. This can create a real problem. To avoid getting behind on your business mail, take care of your mail handling responsibilities daily.

You can lose valuable repeat business by taking too long to fill orders or inquiries (a 48 hour or less turnaround is good business practice), and you can even get yourself into hot water with the Post Office and other consumer agencies if you're extremely tardy filling orders. The law now requires that all orders be filled within 30 days or the customer be sent an explanation as to when it will be filled, along with the option for the customer to get a full refund if he or she does not want to wait any longer.

ADDRESSING SYSTEMS

If you plan to stay in contact with your customers with regular follow-up mailings, as most established dealers do, or wish to rent your mailing lists, you need an addressing system. Here are your options:

Computer Controlled System. Your mailing list is key punched on computer card stock and entered into a computer retrieval system. Your computer company can then give you a printout by states or sectional center breakdown on paper, cheshire labels, gummed labels or magnetic tape. This system is probably the best way to go when you have a large mailing list.

Scriptomatic Systems. This system places a coating of special carbon on card stock. Each time the card is used, a little amount of the carbon is applied to an envelope. The carbon addressing part of the card is on the top of each card and there is plenty of room below for you to log orders or inquiries in pencil or pen. Thus, this system serves a dual purpose - (A) it is a rapid mailing vehicle and (B) it is a recordkeeping system.

319

Addressograph System. Here metal plates are used that require machine cutting. The advantage here is that, although more costly, these plates will last indefinitely, whereas the Scriptomatic System and other "paper plate" type systems must be replaced every few years.

SHIPPING ORDERS

It is very important that all orders be quickly processed and shipped. Every day an order is delayed, the probability of complaints, cancellations and returns increases. It is often wise to send a postcard the day the order comes in, telling the customer that the order has been received and that it is being sent by parcel post or UPS.

If you're shipping something that is quite heavy and bulky, UPS is often a better choice than the Post Office.

STAY FRIENDLY
WITH YOUR LOCAL POST OFFICE

It will pay you real dividends to have an amicable relationship with everyone who works at your local Post Office.

Although postal workers are supposed to treat everyone impartially, I have seen "preferred service" given to customers well-liked by postal employees.

POST OFFICE BOX
OR STREET ADDRESS?

"Nobody can live in a little post office box and customers

know this. They prefer dealing with folks who use a regular street address.''

The above gospel has been preached by many mail order pros for a long, long time. While I won't call it bad advice, I do believe the times and attitudes have changed a lot in recent years. A postal box gives you the best service. Mail will usually reach a P.O. Box one day sooner than a residence or office. Also, inside a post office you can handle all your mailing and postage needs.

If you do use a P.O. Box exclusively, it's often a good idea to list your phone number in your ads or on your sales letters. This tells customers you are very reachable. Mail order customers like to believe they are dealing with "real live people" who will be responsive to their orders or requests for more information, etc. The "closer" they feel to you, the more apt they are to favor you with their business.

USE A MONEY-BACK GUARANTEE

Mail order customers expect you to offer a guarantee. For most dealers, overall returned merchandise is quite low. Nevertheless, a Money Back Guarantee is of real importance. It instills confidence in the potential buyer. It tells him or her that you aim to please and that you won't take the money and run. A 30 day return guarantee is most often used by mail order dealers, but even a short 10 day guarantee is far better than no guarantee.

In recent years, several large mail dealers have begun to employ a very special guarantee whereby the customer's check or money order is held uncashed for 30 days. Joe Karbo, a very innovative bookseller, originated this unique guarantee enroute to earning millions on a very popular book titled "The Lazy Man's Way To Riches." In recent years dozens of others have copied this approach. Joe was a real pro and a true genius in selling books by mail. Still, I do not recommend this approach for the just-getting-started-in-mail-order entrepreneur. In the early stages of mail selling, your cash flow is going to be vital and you'll probably need to bank every dollar the same day it arrives at your home, office or post office box.

MAKE IT EASY TO ORDER

While the personal or business check is still the most popular vehicle of ordering, the sharp entrepreneur makes it easy to order. Profit Ideas accept checks, money orders, Visa, Master Card or cash. I suggest you do likewise.

TELEPHONE ORDERS

Between 20% and 40% of all orders received by many mail order firms are obtained by using a toll-free 800 number. Once you have your business moving, even if only a parttime start, you owe it to yourself to at least consider renting an 800 service from a telephone marketing company. At the very least, you should use your own telephone number on your ads, letters and circulars, especially if you have back-up offers that will benefit from personalized explanation.

Several of the leading mail order book, newsletter and magazine publishers (Chase Revel, Howard J. Ruff, etc.) have set up elaborate telephone systems to assist their subscribers and buyers with various business opportunities, investment information, etc. Many sharp dealers offer this service "free." As an exciting and profitable result of their "free services," they often sell the caller additional plans, books and subscriptions. They enjoy the best of two worlds - (A) they provide a much-appreciated service and (B) they often turn public service into personal profit.

SELL THROUGH OTHER DEALERS

If you have a service or product that is under your control (you're either the "prime source" or have some kind of mail order exclusive), you may wish to consider selling wholesale to other mail order dealers. True, you will have to sell at a much lower price per unit than direct to customers; nevertheless, ad costs are usually greatly reduced also. Many established firms earn either (A) their chief revenue or (B) substantial additional revenues in selling products to other dealers, inside or outside the mail trade.

DROP SHIP SELLING

In addition to, or in place of selling your products or services to other agents and dealers for their resale, you may want to consider drop ship mail order selling.

You may wish to use drop ship selling on both ends - (A) making your products available to others via drop shipping or (B) offering similar items to what you're now selling that can be drop shipped for you by other sources of supply.

The beauty of drop shipping is, with the exception of sales literature or ads, no money is tied up in merchandise. Drop ship items are placed in ads or in direct mailings. When orders arrive, the dealer subtracts his "commission" (usually ½ the money received) and then sends the order on with a completed shipping label for the prime source to fill and ship.

While I never recommend drop shipping as a main source of your mail order income (you will recall what I had to say earlier about "ready-made" mail order setups and catalog imprint deals, all forms of drop shipping), I do think it is wise to either order and sell or sell via drop shipping, products and services that compliment your main offer. For example, some dealers ship orders to customers without any sales literature enclosed. I strongly recommend including several circulars, etc. as package inserts on all orders you fill. These backup offers can be for items that other dealers will drop ship for you. They can produce many easy "bounceback" orders that cost you very little to obtain.

Offering your services or merchandise to other dealers to sell through drop shipping can also reap you many cost-effective orders. You ought to have a high enough markup built into your offers that by accepting ½ off retail prices you still greatly prosper.

DO EVERYTHING
TO PLEASE YOUR CUSTOMERS

To win success in mail order you must do everything possible to please your mail customers.

I have already mentioned the importance of handling orders, inquiries and "white mail" as quickly as possible. Most mail order entrepreneurs do a reasonably good job at processing and mailing orders and inquiries. It is the special request letters, some of which are long and tedious, and various complaints or misunderstandings that too often pile up unanswered. While I strongly urge you to send off orders or inquiries in 48 hours or less, you may take a little longer to respond to your unclassified mail, which I call "white mail."

Some mail dealers have found it works well to set aside a specific time each week (it could be Monday afternoons or Friday afternoons) to get completely caught up with all white mail received the previous week. However you decide to handle your white mail, just make certain you take care of it on a regular basis. Nothing less than at least once a week will do, and in case of urgent requests for personalized information or a very irate complaint, it should be taken care of without any delay.

Satisfied customers are the rockbed foundation on which mail order fortunes are built. Keep them happy and they will keep sending in their orders.

HOW TO BUY OR SELL
A MAIL ORDER BUSINESS

99% of all mail order ventures start from scratch. Of those which survive and thrive (and unfortunately the majority fail in less than one year), their operators often continue to operate them for many, many years.

In the past, the buying and selling of small mail order businesses has been sparse, with only infrequent transactions. Recently, interest in acquiring profitable mail order companies has dramatically increased. Often, larger mail order companies actively seek to buy smaller firms which operate in the same field. (The large gift house often buys out small gift and novelty setups. Also, recently, many large publishers have expressed strong interest in buying out small, independent publishers.)

HOW TO BUY
A MAIL ORDER BUSINESS

Many of the same guidelines that one would use to buy any kind of business apply to buying a mail-operated business. Mail selling in actuality is a method of doing business and not a business per se.

Finding profitable, established mail order setups that are for sale is far more difficult than locating gas stations, food stores or toy shops that are for sale.

326

WHERE TO LOOK

The "Business Opportunity" classified sections in leading newspapers, such as the New York Times, Chicago Tribune and Los Angeles Times, are a good place to look for mail order businesses that are for sale. Business brokers are another possible source of this selective information. You can check out those in your area and/or in the closest major city. Trade magazines like "Direct Marketing" or "Zip" may help you in your quest.

HOW MUCH SHOULD YOU PAY?

The true value of any business is (A) how much does the business earn today and (B) how much is it likely to earn, run by you?

The key to present earnings is the bottom line. The "potential" of the business must be considered, as must be "gross sales." However, "net earnings" or "salary plus earnings" if the business pays the owner a regular salary should be the most important determinant.

While there are no buying guidelines etched in granite, here are my thoughts on the subject:

• Tax returns are usually the best set of books for you to examine concerning net profit.

• If tax returns reflect small or non-existent profit, and you are still told "this mail order operation is earning a bundle" using tax loopholes, etc., and if you're still interested, you and/or your accountant should demand to see all cancelled

327

checks and deposits and bank statements for at least the last twelve months. A set of books means nothing; as the old adage tells us, "Figures don't lie, but liars can figure." Cancelled checks, deposits and bank statements are not infallible proof of a business's profitability but they sure beat just examining someone's "books."

• Demand to see information on all advertising/direct marketing for the past year. Some slick operators have been known to cancel advertising or direct mail campaigns several months prior to putting a mail order business on the market. The "drag" from past mailings or ads helps to show a less than accurate cash flow. It may appear a good deal of money is being generated from a very modest advertising/mailing budget. However, within a few weeks or months of obtaining such a firm, the new owner could be in for a sober awakening.

• Determine the cost of establishing each new customer against the average amount of money obtained from an order.

• Determine the actual amount being spent on rent, utilities, rentals and general "doing business" expenses. Will you likely spend as much? Less? More?

•On "for sale" mail order businesses that gross less than a quarter of a million dollars annually, don't offer to pay more than five times net. If the business for sale nets to the owner (salary and/or earnings) $35,000 yearly on gross business of $175,000 (a respectable 20% net return), I would not consider a selling price over $175,000 (which, in this example, would be equal to one year's gross).

Any business doing less than a quarter million dollars gross per year has probably captured only a very limited part of its potential market. You're going to have to use a great deal of your own skill and ability to maintain or increase upon current profitability.

HOW TO SELL A MAIL ORDER BUSINESS

To find a buyer for a mail order business that you own, simply reverse the steps found in my "how to buy" advice. Also, offer your business for sale through a third party (a business broker is often best). Make certain that any information you will be disclosing is confidential and will only be released to serious persons of means and real desire to buy an active mail order business.

To guard against nosey competitors or those individuals who only want to know how you are making nice profits with thoughts of starting their own business using your success methods, it is often wise to instruct your selling agent not to disclose your name or the name of your firm during the early stages of negotiations.

Above all, when offering a mail order business for sale, tell the truth about your business and at the same time, also make a long list of every current and potential benefit a buyer could receive if he or she pays your price and takes over the venture.

RECOMMENDED BOOKS
ABOUT MAIL ORDER

SUCCESSFUL DIRECT MARKETING
by Bob Stone

This is a new, updated second edition of the "Direct Selling Bible." If you want the most factual guidebook on direct marketing ever published...If you want the facts on direct mail from A to Z, you need this great book! The first edition of this book has been given credit as the work that helped send the direct marketing boom into orbit. This new, revised, second edition is even better! No one in mail order/direct marketing can afford to be without a copy. Loaded with useful information and selling techniques that pull orders! $25.95 is the price, which includes postage and handling. Hoke Communications, 224 - 7th Street, Garden City, NY 11530.

HOW TO START AND OPERATE A MAIL
ORDER BUSINESS by Julian L. Simon

Another "must reading" book for anyone who plans to be active in mail selling. This updated version of Mr. Simon's classic is loaded with step-by-step mail order success guidelines: how to start fulltime or parttime, the opportunities mail order offers you, why people buy by mail, the future of mail order and direct mail, mail order marketing techniques, successful advertising methods, how to find profitable products, choosing the best ad medium, recordkeeping and much, much more.

This book will help educate the mail order beginner or re-educate the mail sales veteran. The price is $22.95, postpaid, from Hoke Communications, 224 -7th Street, Garden City, NY 11530.

7 STEPS TO FREEDOM by Benjamin Suarez
Mr. Suarez is one of the world's best mail order copywriters
and promoters. In this blockbuster, Ben gives his own proven, step-by-step guides on how to assemble a workable and
highly profitable advertising plan and system. The book is
both very practical in nature (loaded with some of the best
advertising and promotional information ever offered) as
well as very interesting (Mr. Suarez presents an in-depth
business and personal autobiography).

Everything is here in this big oversized manual to show you
how one man went from deep in debt to smashing, million-
dollar mail order success and how you can learn from his early mistakes and greatly profit from his more recent super-
successes! Order your copy for only $20, postpaid, from The
Publishing Corporation of America, 4626 Cleveland Avenue,
N.W., Canton, OH 44709

**HOW MAIL ORDER FORTUNES ARE
MADE** by Alfred Stern
Here is another valuable mail order manual written by one of
the industry's pioneers and real pros. In addition to his sage
advice on how to get started, advertising advice, how to obtain free publicity, the best method to fill orders, etc., he has
also included many success stories on how others made their
fortunes in the wild and wacky mail selling business. A copy
is yours for $9.95, postpaid, from Premier Distributing,
16254 Wedgwood, Ft. Worth, TX 76133.

HOW TO SELL BOOKS BY MAIL plus
**"DIRECTORY OF WHOLESALE BOOK
SOURCES**
Another great manual plus source directory for anyone in-

terested in selling information by mail. Selling books, booklets and reports can be one of the most lucrative and hassle-free mail order businesses. Order both "**HOW TO SELL BOOKS BY MAIL**" and "**THE DIRECTORY OF WHOLESALE BOOK SOURCES**" for only $6.95, postpaid, from Profit Ideas, 8361 Vickers St., No. 304, San Diego, CA 92111.

THE LAZY MAN'S WAY TO RICHES
by Joe Karbo

Joe passed away late in 1980, but this bestseller (possibly the all-time best-selling mail order book) will, no doubt, continue to sell briskly for many years to come. An "instant success" since Joe self-published it early in the 1970's, it remains important reading for all mail order operators. Mr. Karbo was a mail order advertising and promotion genius. As a tribute to his genius and success, his space ad approach to selling this book is among the most imitated in mail order circles. You may order a copy for $10 from the Karbo family. Karbo, 17105 South Pacific, Sunset Beach, CA 90742

PASSPORT TO RICHES
by Dan Anderson

An outstanding book on making big bux in the mail order business, written by a real pro. It's all here; how to get started right, how to develop winning ideas, how to select a winner, how to test, zeroing in on your market, plus much, much more. This is a remarkable book that you should own. Only $12.95 postpaid from Dan Anderson, 15012 Redhill Ave., Suite A, Tustin, CA 92680.

REFERENCE DIRECTORIES

AMERICAN PUBLISHERS DIRECTORY
K. G. Saur Publishing
175 Fifth Avenue
New York, NY 10010

BOOK PUBLISHERS OF THE USA
Gale Research Co.
Book Tower
Detroit, MI 48226

DIRECT MARKETING MARKET PLACE
R. R. Bowker Co.
P. O. Box 1807
Ann Arbor, MI 48106

DIRECTORY OF SMALL MAGAZINES
Dustbooks
P. O. Box 100
Paradise, CA 95969

DIRECTORY OF SYNDICATED FEATURES
Editor & Publisher
575 Lexington Avenue
New York, NY 10022

INFORMATION MARKETPLACE
R. R. Bowker Co.
P. O. Box 1807
Ann Arbor, MI 48106

AYERS DIRECTORY OF PUBLICATIONS
210 W. Washington Square
Philadelphia, PA 19106
Circulations, ad rates, etc.

BROADCASTING YEARBOOK
1735 DeSales Street, N.W.
Washington, DC 20036

DIRECTORY OF MAILING LIST HOUSE
B. Klein Publications
P. O. Box 8503
Coral Springs, FL 33065

EDUCATIONAL DIRECTORY
One Park Avenue
New York, NY 10016

EXHIBIT'S DIRECTORY
American Publishers
One Park Avenue
New York, NY 10016

DIRECTORY OF BOOKSELLERS
K. G. Saur Publishing
175 Fifth Avenue
New York, NY 10010

MAIL ORDER BUSINESS DIRECTORY
B. Klein Publications
P. O. Box 8503
Coral Springs, FL 33065

BOOK TRADE DIRECTORY
R. R. Bowker Co.
P. O. Box 1807
Ann Arbor, MI 48106

STANDARD RATE & DATA SERVICE
5201 Old Orchard Road
Skokie, IL 60076
Both publication, circulation,
rates, etc., and mailing list
directories.

WRITER'S HANDBOOK
The Writer, Inc.
8 Arlington Street
Boston, MA 02116

ULRICH'S INTERNATIONAL
Periodicals Directory
R. R. Bowker Co.
P. O. Box 1807
Ann Arbor, MI 48106

WRITER'S MARKET
Writer's Digest
9933 Alliance Road
Cincinnati, OH 45242

BOOK PRINTERS

CHAMPION PRINTING
P. O. Box 148
Ross, OH 45061

DINNER & KLEIN
600 S. Spokane Street
Seattle, WA 98124

KINGSPORT PRESS, INC.
P. O. Box 191
Kingsport, TN 37662

SPEEDY PRINTERS
23800 Aurora Road
Cleveland, OH 44146

BOOK CRAFTERS, INC.
P. O. Box 892
Fredricksburg, VA 22401

OFFICE SUPPLIES

DRAWING BOARD
P. O. Box 505
Dallas, TX 75221
a complete line

BUSINESS ENVELOPES
900 Grand Blvd.
Deerpark, NY 11729
envelopes

GRAYARC
822 Third Avenue
Brooklyn, NY 11232
a complete line

BEACON WHOLESALE PRINTING
P. O. Box 1750
Seattle, WA 98111
envelopes & letterheads

GRAPHICS AND ART SUPPLIES

IMPACT MARKETING, INC.
Box 35305
Edina, MN 55435
ad art/creative services

GRAPHIC MASTER
P. O. Box 46086
Los Angeles, CA 90046
graphics kit

THE PRINTERS SHOPPER
111 Press Lane
Chula Vista, CA 92010
clip art & supplies

VOLK CORPORATION
1401 N. Main Street
Pleasantville, NY 08232
clip art

BINDERS, BINDING & STAPLING PRODUCTS

A & M MAILING
10-64 Jackson Avenue
Long Island City, NY 11101

CHESHIRE DIVISION
Xerox Company
404 Washington Blvd.
Mundelein, IL 60060

FULFILLMENT SERVICES

Companies that will handle mail order inquiries or orders:

AM LETTER SERVICE, INC.
11419 Someset Avenue
Beltsville, MD 20705

SOUTHERN MAILING SERVICE
Box 16867
Memphis, TN 38116

FRIEDMAN RESEARCH, INC.
P. O. Box 2052
Canoga Park, CA 91306

W. A. STORING COMPANY
3730 Lockbourne Road
Columbus, OH 43207

INK-JET PRINTING

RESPONSE GRAPHICS
1480 Renaissance Drive
Park Ridge, IL 60058

INSERTING & MAILING

WESTERN GRAPHICS
7614 Lemon Avenue
Lemon Grove, CA 92045

CREATIVE MAILINGS, INC.
20850 Leapwoods
Carson, CA 90746

GLOBE MAIL AGENCY
125 W. 24th Street
New York, NY 10011

DATA-MAIL, INC.
510 New Park Avenue
West Hartford, CT 06110

UNITED MAILING, INC.
8711 Lyndale Avenue, So.
Minneapolis, MN 55420

ACE PARKER, INC.
3850 NW 30th Avenue
Miami, FL 33142

KEY PUNCH SERVICES

INPUT DATA CO.
600 Lincoln Blvd.
Middlesex, NJ 08846

METRO NATIONAL
401-03 Church Lane
Yeadon, PA 19050

LASER PRINTING

COMMUNICATION CORPORATION OF AMERICA
One Direct Marketing Plaza
Boston, VA 22701

K-PRINT, INC.
4455 LBJ Freeway
Dallas, TX 75234

MAILING LISTS

All of the below listed firms will send brochures, catalogs or data cards at your request. Lists available include responsive mail order buyers, opportunity seekers, compiled lists, etc.

GEORGE STERNE AGENCY
8361 Vickers St., No. 304
San Diego, CA 92111

INNOVATIVE COMPUTER TECHNOLOGY
1245 Logan Avenue
Costa Mesa, CA 92626

PRENTICE-HALL, INC.
Englewood Cliffs, NJ 07632

EDITH ROMAN, INC.
875 Avenue of the Americas
New York, NY 10001

DEPENDABLE LISTS
257 Park Avenue, So.
New York, NY 10010

MARKET DATA RETRIEVAL
Ketchum Place
Westport, CT 06880

ENTERPRISE LISTS
725 Market Street
Wilmington, DE 19801

HANK MARSHALL CO.
P. O. Box 2729
Laguna Hills, CA 92653

MAILING EQUIPMENT

SPECTRUM MAIL SYSTEMS, INC.
681 Main Street
Belleville, NJ 07109

RAYMOND ENGINEERING, INC.
704 Vandalia
St. Paul, MN 55114

TOLL FREE (800) TELEPHONE SERVICES

ANSWER AMERICA, INC.
One WUI Plaza
New York, NY 10004
800-221-2145

RING AMERICA
6220 N. California Avenue
Chicago, IL 60659
800-621-5800

AUTOMATED PHONE EXCHANGE
1849 Temple
Salt Lake City, UT 84116
800-453-4000

NATIONAL COMMUNICATIONS CENTER
3939 Cambridge Road, No. 104
Shingle Springs, CA 95682
800-852-7777

WHOLESALE OR DROPSHIP SOURCES

PROFIT IDEAS
8361 Vickers St., No. 304
San Diego, CA 92111
books & manuals

PREMIER DISTRIBUTING
16254 Wedgwood
Ft. Worth, TX 76133
book catalogs

INSIDERS
P. O. Box 879
New Hyde Park, NY 11040
closeouts, gifts, novelties,
etc.

PROGRESS PUBLISHERS
Box 1355
Sioux Falls, SD 57101
books, newsletter

ROBINSON
Box 415
New Hartford, NY 13413
wholesale rubber stamps

ECONOMY PRODUCTS
2064 N. Damen Avenue
Chicago, IL 60647
many wholesale items

MAIL ORDER
NEWSLETTERS

MAIL ORDER CONNECTION. Edited and published by Galen Stilson. Emphasis put on the important subject of mail-order advertising. Consulting editors include Luther Brock ("The Letter Doctor"), Paul Alexander, Joe Shivy, Craig Huey and the talented Rene Gram. MOC is an extremely helpful newsletter for the beginner or seasoned PRO. Write for current sample copy/subscription information to Stilson & Stilson, P.O. Box 2505, Bonita Springs, FL 33923.

DIRECT RESPONSE. This is Craig A. Huey's direct marketing newsletter. More sophisticated in its approach than MOC, it is a letter for mail order professionals, not rank beginners. A digest of vital information. For details write Infomat Inc., 25550 Hawthorne Blvd., Suite 304, Torrance, CA 90505.

CASH NEWSLETTER. A very interesting, very important newsletter that covers all sorts of moneymaking and money-saving topics. With special emphasis given to editor Doug Hafely's insights into operating a mail-order business. For more information, write Cash News, P.O. Box 1999, Brookville, FL 33512.